THE BLUES REVIEW
1996

FORWARD

Published by Sports Projects Ltd

ACKNOWLEDGEMENTS

The Blues Review 1996
First published in Great Britain in July 1996
by Sports Projects Limited

© 1996 Sports Projects Limited
188 Lightwoods Hill, Smethwick, Warley,
West Midlands B67 5EH.

ISBN 0 946866 34 1

Printed and bound in Great Britain

Editor: Brian Marshall

Statistics: Tony Matthews

Photographs: Roy Smiljanic and Empics

Design, layout and graphics: Vic Millward,
Nadine Goldingay and Phil Lees

KEY

❏	Player booked
■	Player sent off
32	Figure in goals column indicates time of goal
†56	First substitute and time of substitution
†	First player substituted
‡56	Second substitute and time of substitution
‡	Second player substituted

● *In friendly games, where several substitutes may have appeared, additional symbols are used in the following order: #, §, ††, ‡‡, ##, §§, ≠.*

Also available in this series:

The Blues Review 1995
ISBN 0 946866 24 4   Price: £8.95

A season of highs and lows ends with hope for the future

Birmingham City dropped a bombshell when they sacked Barry Fry two days after the end of the season – a decision which could have far reaching effects.

The restless Fry was always seeking the elusive and it sadly back-fired on him in the closing weeks of the season when the team took on a tired and often exhausted appearance.

As a result, Birmingham City tasted the bitter fruit of disappointment in a season which often promised great things, but in the end produced a barren trophy cupboard until they won the Birmingham Senior Cup 15 hours before Fry's sudden departure.

After the double success of the previous season, everyone had such ambitious dreams that the band-wagon would continue to roll on its merry way.

There was the high profile pre-season games with Birmingham giving themselves a taste of what to expect if they were to reach the premier division with matches against the likes of Manchester United and Chelsea

Fry quipped before his departure: "We were top of the pre-season league after 11 games!" But it did raise the question of whether the club had in fact taken on too much.

In our match by match analysis, the facts unfold and reveal a graphic picture of Blues' uneasy season.

Joint club-owner, David Sullivan, is hoping that they can learn from the experiences of the season. He did not think Barry Fry could have taken them into the Premier League and was not prepared to wait another twelve months to find out.

Fry himself will reflect on a season when they were involved in those exhausting Anglo-Italian Cup and Coca-Cola Cup ties which obviously sapped the strength of everyone in a season when the First Division should have been the one and only target.

This priority was apparently over-looked for long periods and when people realised that it was slipping from their grasp, heads began to roll.

But Birmingham is now becoming a very high profile club and its ever-growing number of fans are keen to taste something of the high life in the Premiership.

Everyone is hoping that the last few months of the season were just a hiccup and that Blues will get back onto the glory train and travel the rails to fresh successes.

This second volume of *The Blues Review* gives an insight into the hopes, ambitions and pitfalls of the owners, players and manager of Birmingham City.

Meanwhile, Trevor Francis arrived less than a week after Fry's departure, expressing thoughts that he would derive great pleasure from taking his old club into the Premier League. He faces a tough task as he will experience before the end of the 1996-97 season.

Brian Marshall
May 1996

CONTENTS

CONTENTS

Saturday 12th August 1995 • St. Andrew's • 3.00pm

BIRMINGHAM CITY 3 IPSWICH TOWN 1

Half time 0-0 • *Attendance* 18,910

Referee: David ALLISON (Lancaster)

Linesmen W.G. GOWERS and T. JONES

• IPSWICH •

Blue Shirts, White Shorts		Goals	Claret and Green Shirts, Claret Shorts		Goals
1	Ian BENNETT		1	Craig FORREST	
2	Gary POOLE		2	Mick STOCKWELL	
3	John FRAIN		3	Neil THOMPSON †	
4	Mark WARD		4	Tony VAUGHAN ❑	
5	Andy EDWARDS		5	John WARK #	
6	Liam DAISH		6	Steve SEDGLEY	
7	Jonathan HUNT ‡		7	Gus UHLENBEEK	
8	Steve CLARIDGE		8	Geraint WILLIAMS	
9	Ian MUIR †		9	Alex MATHIE	
10	Richard FORSYTH #		10	Ian MARSHALL	47
11	Paul TAIT	64	11	Claus THOMSEN	
	Substitutes			*Substitutes*	
12	Ricky OTTO ‡55	73	12	Lee CHAPMAN #82	
13	Louie DONOWA †45		13	Simon MILTON ‡76	
14	Jason BOWEN #55	85	14	Frank YALLOP †14 ‡	

BEFORE	P	W	D	L	F	A	pts		AFTER		P	W	D	L	F	A	pts
Blues	0	0	0	0	0	0	0		4	Blues	1	1	0	0	3	1	3
Ipswich	0	0	0	0	0	0	0		21	Ipswich	1	0	0	1	1	3	0

FACTFILE

Only four of Birmingham's close season signings, Andy Edwards, Ian Muir, Richard Forsyth and Jason Bowen, are on view... Interestingly only two players, Ian Bennett and Steve Claridge, were in the side from that which began the previous campaign... The crowd of 18,910 is the best of the day.

Subs come on to turn game

Barry Fry, resplendent in the new and very fashionable all red change strip, was his usual bubbling self as he sets the pre-match tone and the hopes of everyone of another exciting season.

The first bit of good news is that Liam Daish passed a fitness test after being injured against Manchester United, but there is some concern that Kenny Dalglish is in the crowd to run the rule over the Republic of Ireland defender.

In the sizzling heat Birmingham, as usual, kept their fans on tenter-hooks as their all out attacking policy failed to produce the goods in the opening 45 minutes.

Ipswich operated under the cloud of suffering relegation the previous season and there was very little real threat to the Birmingham Blues as they dominated the entire first half with some positive attacking play.

First impressions, however, were that Birmingham were in for a much harder season than when they won the Second Division title. There will be few easy games, although Ipswich faded badly as they seemingly lacked the heart to take on the vibrant Midlanders.

The only time they took the intiative was late in the first half and early in the second period. Ian Marshall should have put them ahead just before the break when he broke clear only to be foiled by Ian Bennett.

Two minutes into the second period Marshall made no mistake when put in possession by Steve Sedgeley and the former Everton man toepunted the ball past Bennett.

The turning point of the game occurred in the 55th minute when Fry sent on both Ricky Otto and Jason Bowen, a £325,000 signing from Swansea. At the break Louie Donowa had replaced Ian Muir and the inclusion of these three players completely destroyed Ipswich.

All of a sudden there was more width to Birmingham's play and Ipswich obviously did not know how to handle the situation. It was a new ball game and both Donowa and Otto exploited the extra space with embarrassing ease.

Paul Tait, Birmingham's goalscoring Auto Windscreens Shield final hero, who in the close season had been fined by the Football Association and warned to his future conduct for his anti-Aston Villa T-shirt display at Wembley, popped up for the equaliser after goalkeeper Craig Forrest had pushed out an effort from Bowen.

The best goal came from Otto, who had been left out of the side because of his inconsistency. In his programme notes manager Barry Fry had appealed to the fans to give the former Southend winger some encouragement and Otto responded with a cracking left footed cross-shot following a perfectly placed pass from Mark Ward.

At this stage it was exciting stuff and the final goal came from debut boy Bowen, who afterwards admitted that he was still far from fit. He scored with a neat shot after another defence splitting pass from Donowa.

In the glow of victory the quiet Welshman was pleased with both the prospects of himself and Birmingham. "On this performance we have the basis of a very good side which could enjoy considerable success," he said.

Fry emerged from the dressing room and said: "We are now a better team than last season, we are a better squad and a better club. We are more stable and with the fans I think we can all go forward and with a bit of luck, I think we can go up. It is a realistic shout but we have got to keep our feet on the floor.

"We are not frightened of any team and when Kevin Francis, Dave Barnett and Peter Shearer come back it is going to be a tremendous time for me. It will be like spending two or three million pounds."

Tuesday 15th August 1995 • St. Andrew's • 7.45pm

BIRMINGHAM CITY 1 PLYMOUTH ARGYLE 0

Half time 1-0 • *Attendance* 7,964

Referee John LLOYD (Wrexham)

Linesmen D.P. MORRISON and P.M. ROBERTS

Black and Silver Striped Shirts, Blue Shorts		Goals	Green and White Shirts, Black Shorts		Goals
1	Ian BENNETT		1	Nick HAMMOND	
2	Gary POOLE		2	Mark PATTERSON	
3	Gary COOPER ❏	44	3	Paul WILLIAMS	
4	Mark WARD †		4	Wayne BURNETT	
5	Andy EDWARDS		5	Micky HEATHCOTE	
6	Chris WHYTE		6	Keith HILL	
7	Louie DONOWA		7	Chris BILLY	
8	Steve CLARIDGE #		8	Ronnie MAUGE ❏	
9	Jason BOWEN		9	Adrian LITTLEJOHN	
10	Ricky OTTO		10	Kevin NUGENT	
11	Paul TAIT ‡		11	Gary CLAYTON	
	Substitutes			*Substitutes*	
12	Ian MUIR #77		12	Chris TWIDDY	
13	Richard FORSYTH †45		13	Micky EVANS	
14	Jonathan HUNT ‡45		14	Doug HODSON	

FACTFILE

Gary Cooper returns following a suspension imposed after he was sent off against Brighton last season – to score the winner... Liam Daish is rested and replaced by Chris Whyte, who is the centre of attention from Coventry City boss, Ron Atkinson... Super show from Pilgrims' 'keeper.

Goalscorer – Gary Cooper.

Cooper cracker separates sides

The first surprise occurred when the Birmingham Blues ran out in their new gear of dark blue and silver stripes – a colour scheme which was to match the mood of the game.

The strip was later to get the St. Andrew's club in hot water with the Football League, who pointed out that they can only wear the first choice gear in home games but are able to sport any colours they like away from home.

Not surprisingly the new look Plymouth side, under the managership of Neil Warnock, quickly made known their intention to nullify the home side and the key was to stifle the midfield engine room of Mark Ward.

But this was no excuse as Barry Fry's men still had enough of the game to have swamped the Pilgrims. Nicky Hammond, however, was in an inspired mood on the night as he demonstrated on several occasions keeping out some reasonable goal attempts from Ricky Otto and Steve Claridge.

Surprisingly Otto was not so positive as against Ipswich and slipped back into some of his old frustrating tactics.

Perhaps it was the small crowd following a glut of home games. As it was, Otto failed to turn on the skill which had destroyed Ipswich in such devastating fashion in the previous match.

The game was drifting and Plymouth were obviously content with the situation and appeared quite happy with the stalemate. Boosted by their ability to weather Birmingham's attack they even gained in confidence to stage some break-away attacks and could have taken a surprise lead but for the agility of Ian Bennett.

Chris Billy took full advantage of a struggling Gary Poole and cut inside to set up Kevin Nugent who then conspired to bungle his shot from inside the six yard area straight at Bennett.

The pace of Adrian Littlejohn was also of some concern to Birmingham's defence and he slipped through after collecting a careless pass from Cooper and fired in a shot on the run which forced Bennett to make a flying save to keep out the ball going into the top left hand corner of the net.

Typically, Birmingham pulled the game out of the fire in a situation which has become associated with their style of play.

Cooper gathered a pass from Paul Tait and went on a solo run into the heart of Plymouth's defence. Like many one footed players he found great difficulty in changing direction and when he did decide to shoot he had to resort to hitting the ball with the outside of his left boot.

Barry Fry later agreed that the first half was not very good. To a question he answered: "You are entitled to your opinion, and I absolutely agree with you.

"It took us a long time to get going and Gary Poole in particular was struggling. When I took off Steve Claridge and asked him to take off the captain's armband he didn't have the strength!

"The result was just what Plymouth wanted. A 5-0 win for us would have killed off the second leg. Now Plymouth are still in with a shout and will have double the crowd they would have expected if we had scored a big win."

Ricky Otto waits for a slip-up.

Saturday 19th August 1995 • The Valley • 3.00pm

CHARLTON ATHLETIC 3 BIRMINGHAM CITY 1

Half time 0-0 • Attendance 9,692

Referee Eddie LOMAS (Manchester)

Linsemen P.R. SHARP and M. TINGEY

Red Shirts, White Shorts		Goals	Blue Shirts, Blue Shorts		Goals
1	Mike SALMON		1	Ian BENNETT	
2	John HUMPHREY		2	Gary POOLE	
3	Paul STURGESS †		3	John FRAIN †	
4	Keith JONES		4	Mark WARD ❑ ‡	
5	Richard RUFUS		5	Andy EDWARDS	
6	Stuart BALMER		6	Liam DAISH	
7	Mark ROBSON		7	Jonathan HUNT	
8	Garry NELSON ‡	67	8	Steve CLARIDGE #	
9	John ROBINSON		9	Jason BOWEN ❑	54
10	David WHYTE #		10	Gary COOPER	
11	Lee BOWYER	69	11	Paul TAIT	
	Substitutes			*Substitutes*	
12	Kim GRANT †67	88	12	Louie DONOWA †45	
13	Colin WALSH ‡79		13	Ricky OTTO ‡45	
14	Phil CHAPPLE #89		14	Richard FORSYTH #45	

BEFORE		P	W	D	L	F	A	pts		AFTER		P	W	D	L	F	A	pts
4	Blues	1	1	0	0	3	1	3		10	Blues	2	1	0	1	4	4	3
23	Charlton	1	0	0	1	0	1	0		13	Charlton	2	1	0	1	3	2	3

FACTFILE

Blues first defeat of the season... Jason Bowen made his first start and marked the occasion with a goal to put Blues in the lead... but Blues suffer only their second league defeat in 17 games... all three subs used at half-time... Barry Fry is scathing of his players after a disastrous last half hour's play.

Half-time changes backfire

After playing so many games at St. Andrew's the trip down to the Valley at Charlton must have been a shock to the system.

An away day in the capital was seen as the opening salvo for the Birmingham Blues to maintain their challenging position in the top five. But all the best laid plans can come asunder and when Birmingham drop a brick it smashes into smithereens and no one escapes the fall-out.

There was little in the goalless first half to indicate the shocks in store after the break. Barry Fry, however, was not happy and his decision to make three half time substitutions was an indication of how he read the below par performance in the opening 45 minutes.

Player-coach Mark Ward was again one of the players hauled off to be replaced by the former England non-league international, Richard Forsyth, while John Frain made way for Ricky Otto and Steve Claridge was side-lined by the inclusion of Louie Donowa.

Usually, these kind of changes have a dramatic effect upon the Blues, but for some unknown reason the whole exercise back-fired with the same consequences of someone blocking off the exhaust pipe of a car.

Birmingham's defence, not unknown to open the floodgates a few months ago, allowed Charlton the freedom of the Valley. Birmingham's players must have been star-gazing or, to be more precise, plane spotting as the Spitfires and Lancaster bombers made their way above the ground following the Thames to the city of London for the VJ celebrations.

But there was nothing for Birmingham to celebrate, with the exception of Jason Bowen's goal nine minutes into the second half when the Welshman scored with a great shot.

This lead gave Blues false optimism and Charlton hit the Midlanders with two goals in two minutes to equalise and go ahead.

Garry Nelson had an easy tap-in for the equaliser and then Lee Bowyer turned and scored. The saddest sight of the game was skipper Liam Daish, who had not shown his best form, being given the run-around by substitute Kim Grant before the striker scored Charlton's third two minutes from the end.

As usual, no one escaped the whip-lash of Barry Fry's tongue in the after-math. He stated that the three changes had been made because he had never before seen John Frain "roasted so badly".

The Birmingham boss added that Ward had a shocking first half and Claridge was described as "hopeless" by Fry.

He also stated that he had not seen his goalkeeper Ian Bennett have to make a save – only pick the ball out of the back of the net on three occasions.

Even Daish, Fry's top rated defender, did not escape the wrath of the Birmingham boss. He added: "Our central defenders never picked up anyone and in the end we got we deserved. Let's hope that we can learn something from the defeat."

Jason Bowen celebrates his goal.

Tuesday 23rd August 1995 • Home Park • 7.45pm

PLYMOUTH ARGYLE 1 BIRMINGHAM CITY 2

Birmingham win 3-1 on aggregate
Half time 1-0 • *Attendance* 6,529
Referee Clive WILKES (Gloucester)
Linesmen M. NORTH and W. TOMS

Green and White Shirts, Black Shorts		Goals	Black and Silver Striped Shirts, Blue Shorts		Goals
1	Nick HAMMOND		1	Ian BENNETT	
2	Chris TWIDDY		2	Gary POOLE ❏	
3	Paul WILLIAMS		3	Gary COOPER	
4	Wayne BURNETT #		4	Mark WARD ❏ †	
5	Micky HEATHCOTE	44	5	Andy EDWARDS ❏	52
6	Keith HILL		6	Chris WHYTE	
7	Chris BILLY		7	Jonathan HUNT ‡	43
8	Ronnie MAUGE		8	Steve CLARIDGE	
9	Adrian LITTLEJOHN		9	Jason BOWEN	
10	Kevin NUGENT ‡		10	Scott HILEY #	
11	Gary CLAYTON †		11	Steve CASTLE	
	Substitutes			*Substitutes*	
12	Mark SAUNDERS †57		12	Richard FORSYTH ‡81	
13	Danny O'HAGAN ‡77		13	Neil DOHERTY #89	
14	Mickey EVANS #85		14	Louie DONOWA †45	

FACTFILE

Former Plymouth players, Scott Hiley and Steve Castle, make their first full senior appearances of the season... Ricky Otto omitted from side after being detained by police in London on an alleged drugs offence... Hunt scores the winner direct from a corner-kick.

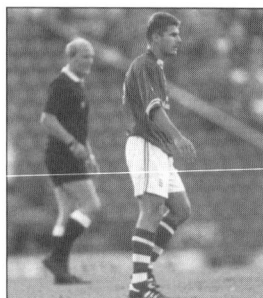

Steve Castle –
back home at
Home Park.

Edwards opens his account

Even before Birmingham left St. Andrew's for the long trip to the South-West there was disquietening news that Chris Whyte was not happy with his position at the club.

In a face-to-face confrontation with manager Barry Fry the utility defender requested a free transfer. This blow-up occurred only a few days after it had been disclosed that Coventry City's boss, Ron Atkinson, had been interested in acquiring his former defender.

Fry's immediate reaction was typical. He said: "I told Chris that he could not have a free transfer. We want £200,000 with £100,000 as a down payment if he was to be transferred.

"But we don't want to lose the fellow. He has given us good service and can slot into a number of positions. "After I told him what we were prepared to do I made him captain for the Plymouth game!"

Whyte, who scored in the previous game at Home Park in a vital win which took Birmingham to the top of the division and ultimately to the championship and was then dropped for the next match at Wembley, took over from skipper Liam Daish.

Daish had not fully recovered from the injury sustained against Manchester United in a preseason game.

Another absentee was Ricky Otto who had been cautioned by the police on a drug offence on his week-end stay in London following the Charlton game.

Fry said it was not right to include Otto in the game. He added: "What with all the fuss he isn't in the right frame of mind for the game. It has absolutely bowled him over."

In the circumstances Fry took the opportunity to draft in the two former Plymouth players, Scott Hiley and Steve Castle. Only hours before Hiley had agreed a new contract after signing a week to week deal after failing to agree on new terms during the summer.

There was an air of apprehension about Birmingham's prospects in view of the changes.

Hardly surprising in the circumstances Birmingham failed to get away to a good start and their indifferent showing was compounded a few seconds before the break when Plymouth's skipper, Mike Heathcote, who had earlier missed an open goal, headed in a cross at the far post from a Keith Hill cross.

Fry's response was to again call off player-coach Mark Ward, who struggled to produce his best form. Louie Donowa was drafted in and to say the change was dramatic is an understatement as within a two minute spell Birmingham not only equalised but took the lead.

Andy Edwards, who had threatend to score on several occasions, moved up for a Jonathan Hunt corner which was pushed back for Donowa to cross to the far post where the Birmingham defender was on hand to notch his first goal.

This goal put Birmingham in front again on aggregate and the Blues produced the perfect counter-punch to knock out Plymouth with Hunt scoring direct from a corner following a mistake by a couple of Plymouth defenders.

Everything then worked out on the night but sailing so close to the wind leaves little space in which to manoeuvre in future and Fry might well chance his arm once too often in similar circumstances.

Andy Edwards scores the winner.

Saturday 26th August 1995 • St. Andrew's • 3.00pm

BIRMINGHAM CITY 3 NORWICH CITY 1

Half time 1-0 • *Attendance* 19,267

Referee Richard POULAIN (Huddersfield)

Linesmen R.A. ROBERTS and R.A. SMITH

Blue Shirts, Blue Shorts	Goals	Yellow Shirts, Green Shorts	Goals
1 Ian BENNETT		1 Bryan GUNN	
2 Gary POOLE		2 Danny MILLS	
3 Gary COOPER		3 Mark BOWEN	
4 Mark WARD †		4 Mike MILLIGAN †	
5 Chris WHYTE		5 Jon NEWSOME	
6 Andy EDWARDS		6 Spencer PRIOR	
7 Jonathan HUNT	22,47,71 pen	7 Neil ADAMS	
8 Steve CLARIDGE		8 Mike SHERON	86
9 Jason BOWEN		9 Ade AKINBIYI	
10 Louie DONOWA ‡		10 Andy JOHNSON ‡	
11 Scott HILEY		11 Darren EADIE	
Substitutes		*Substitutes*	
12 Ken CHARLERY		12 John POLSTON	
13 Richard FORSYTH †55		13 Daryl SUTCH †21	
14 Steve CASTLE ‡60		14 Jamie CURETON ‡64	

BEFORE	P	W	D	L	F	A	pts	AFTER	P	W	D	L	F	A	pts
5 Norwich	2	1	1	0	3	1	4	4 Blues	3	2	0	1	7	5	6
10 Blues	2	1	0	1	4	4	3	14 Norwich	3	1	1	1	4	4	4

FACTFILE

Jonathan Hunt's third hat-trick in 26 games since his move from Southend... First visit of Norwich City to St. Andrew's since 1983-84... Skipper Liam Daish again absent due to injury sustained against Manchester United, as is Ricky Otto due to an injury picked up during the week.

Hero Hunt grabs smart hat-trick

Norwich City, the second successive club to arrive at St. Andrew's following their relegation from the Premiership, are unbeaten in their first two games, but manager Martin O'Neill is fully aware that a tough game is in the offing on the strength of his own experience against the Blues last season.

Another big crowd is in the stadium and the over-flowing car-parks indicate that Birmingham are attracting a new clientele, as these fans begin to realise that the new era is gathering pace and not running out of steam.

Ricky Otto is again missing and this is due to an injury picked up in a private game against Sheffield Wednesday and had no connection with his police involvement a week earlier.

This results in Scott Hiley making his first full appearance of the season at St. Andrew's in a game which takes a long time to ignite.

The only action of the opening exchanges occurs when Jonathan Hunt is involved in an incident which leaves him with a bloody nose. Norwich in their rashness contemptuously ignore the injured lion at their peril.

Following a few dangerous sorties by Mike Sheron, Birmingham swiftly counter-attack and Jason Bowen proves to be more than a handful for Jon Newsome with one reverse header creating a good opening for Steve Claridge.

The writing was on the wall when Claridge sent Jonathan Hunt clear down the right hand channel with no opposition from any Norwich defender.

Hunt, showing great aplomb, chips the ball over the head of Bryan Gunn into the far corner of the net with the Norwich goalkeeper looking on powerless to take any action.

This goal visibly gave Birmingham immense confidence and Norwich were suddenly made aware of their task in what was turning out to be an extremely difficult game for the besieged Canaries.

Two minutes into the second half Gunn was again a spectator. Mark Ward put Hunt in possession on the left and the Birmingham player fired a cross shot which ricocheted off both posts before going over the line.

A whirlwind had hit Norwich and they could hardly believe the force of the Birmingham storm. Hunt, normally an unobstrusive player, hammered in another shot which Spencer Prior handled.

There was never any doubt who was going to take the penalty. Hunt grabbed the ball and advanced to the penalty spot to slot the ball past Gunn for his hat-trick

Norwich then hit back with a series of dangerous raids, but Birmingham were well worth their win with Hunt taking the plaudits, but also acknowledging the fine support roles of Jason Bowen and Richard Forsyth, who were also an important key to Birmingham's success.

Afterwards Fry was in his usual raptures. "There is no way we are going to release Jonathan Hunt," he claimed, "I will ban scouts of other clubs even coming to watch him!"

Fry was delighted with the class act and was complimented by Norwich manager, Martin O'Neill, who admitted: "This game proves to my players the size of their task if they want to be in the promotion hunt. Birmingham have spent a lot of money and will be difficult to beat if they can maintain this kind of form."

Hat-trick hero – Jonathan Hunt.

Wednesday 30th August 1995 • McAlpine Stadium • 7.45pm

HUDDERSFIELD TOWN 4 BIRMINGHAM CITY 2

Half time 1-1 • *Attendance* 12,305

Referee Neale BARRY (Scunthorpe)

Linesmen C.J. FOY and R.E. McGREGOR

Blue and White Striped Shirts, White Shorts	Goals	Red Shirts with Blue and White Trim, Red Shorts	Goals
1 Steve FRANCIS		1 Ian BENNETT	
2 John WHITNEY ❑		2 Gary POOLE	
3 Lee SINNOTT		3 Gary COOPER	
4 Pat SCULLY		4 Mark WARD	11, 72
5 Tom COWAN ❑ ■		5 Chris WHYTE ❑	
6 Sam COLLINS		6 Andy EDWARDS	
7 Richard LOGAN		7 Jonathan HUNT ‡	
8 Darren BULLOCK	70	8 Steve CLARIDGE	
9 Paul DALTON	7, 51	9 Jason BOWEN	
10 Andy BOOTH		10 Scott HILEY #	
11 Ronnie JEPSON	63	11 Louie DONOWA †	
Substitutes		*Substitutes*	
12 Iain DUNN		12 Richard FORSYTH ‡56	
13 Tony NORMAN (Gk)		13 Steve CASTLE #56	
14 Simon BALDRY		14 Neil DOHERTY †45	

BEFORE		P	W	D	L	F	A	pts	AFTER		P	W	D	L	F	A	pts
4	Blues	3	2	0	1	7	5	6	9	Blues	4	2	0	2	9	9	6
19	Huddersfield	3	1	0	2	2	6	3	11	Huddersfield	4	2	0	2	6	8	6

FACTFILE

Blues second successive away defeat... There is still no Daish, who is nursing his troublesome ankle injury sustained against Manchester United... It's Blues worst defeat since they crashed 5-2 at Watford in December 1993... Barry Fry starts the search for defensive cover, Notts County's Michael Johnson is the target.

Dire defence is Blues' downfall

It was a happy Birmingham City outfit which travelled to Yorkshire with memories still fresh in their minds of their 2-1 win over Huddersfield on the last day of the season which confirmed them as Second Division champions.

On the back of that impressive win over Norwich City, the bandwaggon was really starting to roll.

They were nestled comfortably in fourth place and poised to demonstrate their confident form against struggling Huddersfield.

Manager Barry Fry had little difficulty naming a team. He predictably went for the same side as that which beat Norwich, little realising what lay in store.

Fry was looking for another impressive performance at the smart Sir Alfred McAlpine stadium, but it quickly became apparent that Birmingham were at odds with themselves.

The writing was ominously on the wall as early as the seventh minute when Paul Dalton opened the scoring for Huddersfield after Ronnie Jepson had quickly exposed the uncertainty of Chris Whyte and Andy Edwards going for high crosses.

As the game progressed the more Jepson and his striking colleague Andy Booth became more and more confident and it was ultimately to prove the cornerstone of their handsome win.

Under pressure Mark Ward, who only the previous day had been warned to behave himself and not get involved in bookable offences, equalised in the eleventh minute with a tremendous shot from 25 yards.

Out of sorts Louie Donowa predicatably made way for Neil Doherty at half time, but it was Huddersfield who were firing on all cylinders when Booth set up another gift goal for Dalton six minutes into the second half.

This goal resulted in a double substitution with Richard Forsyth and Steve Castle taking over from Jonathan Hunt, who was never in the picture on this occasion, and Scott Hiley, but Birmingham again let themselves down badly as Huddersfield steamed further ahead with two more goals from Jepson and Darren Bullock.

It was then significant that even when Huddersfield found themselves reduced to only ten men, when Tom Cowan was sent off in the 71st minute for a second booking, Birmingham could not take full advantage of the situation in which they found themselves.

Ward, to his credit was a driving force in midfield but even he could not insure against the defensive mistakes which were to prove extremely costly on the night with Whyte and Edwards both having nightmares in the rearguard.

A thunderbolt free-kick from Ward in the 72nd minute was another blockbusting goal and despite showing a lot of effort in a late spell when a Castle header hit the crossbar, Birmingham were a well beaten team.

Manager Fry was typically forthright when he said: "We were a shambles in defence and gave them three goals. Huddersfield must have thought it was Christmas."

Two-goal Mark Ward.

Saturday 2nd September 1995 • Oakwell • 3.00pm

BARNSLEY 0 BIRMINGHAM CITY 5

Half time 0-0 • *Attendance* 11,129

Referee Terry HEILBRON (Newton Aycliffe)
Linesmen M.J. DOUGLAS and P.D. HARDING

Red Shirts, White Shorts		Goals
1	David WATSON ■	
2	Nick EADON	
3	Peter SHIRTLIFF	
4	Owen ARCHDEACON	
5	Adrian VIVEASH †	
6	Charlie BISHOP ■	
7	Martin BULLOCK	
8	Neil REDFERN	
9	Andy PAYTON	
10	Andy LIDDELL	
11	Darren SHERIDAN	
	Substitutes	
12	Gary FLEMING	
13	Lee BUTLER (Gk) †54	
14	Chris JACKSON	

Blue Shirts, White Shorts		Goals
1	Ian BENNETT	
2	Gary POOLE ❑	
3	Chris WHYTE	
4	Mark WARD	
5	Andy EDWARDS	
6	Michael JOHNSON	
7	Jonathan HUNT #	55 pen
8	Steve CLARIDGE	60
9	Jason BOWEN †	
10	Ken CHARLERY	73
11	Gary COOPER ❑ ‡	
	Substitutes	
12	Neil DOHERTY ‡80	86
13	Richard FORSYTH †68	76
14	Louie DONOWA #83	

BEFORE	P	W	D	L	F	A	pts
2 Barnsley	4	3	0	1	10	8	9
9 Blues	4	2	0	2	9	9	6

AFTER	P	W	D	L	F	A	pts
6 Blues	5	3	0	2	14	9	9
7 Barnsley	5	3	0	2	10	13	9

FACTFILE

Birmingham's biggest away win in 36 years and it was achieved over a team second in the table... New signing Michael Johnson from Notts County makes his first appearance in five goal second half blitz against Barnsley, who finish with only nine players... Ken Charley's first game for Birmingham.

On-form Blues set for the top

Following the disappointment of their previous trip to Yorkshire only a few days previously there were a few mixed feelings on the Birmingham coach which headed North.

Manager Barry Fry's reaction to the Huddersfield defeat was to sign the tenacious central defender Michael Johnson from Notts County and put him straight into the team to face Barnsley.

No one was really confident of the outcome but equally Birmingham are as unpredictable as the weather and change just as quickly.

Poor Barnsley suffered the back-lash, but enjoyed no small measure of luck, albeit in the first half when Birmingham completely dominated the exchanges and created numerous goal scoring chances and still went in without a goal to show for all their attacks.

Barnsley, however, could not survive this unrelenting pressure indefinitely and with Steve Claridge having easily his best game of the season there was never any real doubt about the outcome.

Claridge is often an enigma and even after all this time has still not seemingly fathomed out how to keep his stockings in a neat and tidy fashion.

But who cares when he can create havoc among the opposition defence as he demonstrated at Oakwell. It was hardly surpising that Claridge, with yet another new striking partner in Ken Charlery, a £400,000 close season buy from Peterborough, should be involved in the opening goal.

He made a long run after collecting a clearance from newcomer Johnson and was checked badly by goalkeeper David Watson who was given the red card for his trouble.

Barnsley sent on the former Aston Villa goalkeeper Lee Butler and his first touch of the ball was to retrieve it from the back of the net after Jonathan Hunt had converted the spot kick in the 54th minute to record his fifth goal in four games.

The Claridge-Charlery partnership worked well, with the former Posh striker shielding his partner well to create plenty of space in the Barnsley rearguard, which eventually enabled him to score his belated first goal of the season on the hour.

Ken Charlery deservedly got into the act with his first goal for the Blues with a powerful low drive after Steve Claridge had been involved in the build-up.

As usual, manager Fry drafted in all three of his substitutes and it was Forsyth who forced his way through for the fourth in the 76th minute when the former Kidderminster player took advantage of some earlier good work by Claridge and Charlery.

Neil Doherty grabbed Birmingham's fifth goal in the slaughter of Barnsley, who could not wait to get off the pitch as they were hit by one bombshell after another.

It could have been even worse, as Charlie Bishop was sent off in the last minute for handling a Forsyth shot and with Hunt substituted, Claridge, not for the first time, muffed the spot-kick.

Barnsley's manager Danny Wilson had to admit: "Credit to Birmingham, they gave us a right good stuffing."

Barry Fry was ecstatic. "It's the best we've played since I've been at the club.

"We should have had ten goals on the day, because we completely outplayed a very useful Barnsley side.

"I thought Claridge was brilliant, but with so many players missing because of injuries it was a tremendous display.

"I know there is a long way to go, but I believe we have the bottle to go on and win the Championship."

Tuesday 5th September 1995 • St Andrew's • 8.00pm

BIRMINGHAM CITY 2 GENOA 3

Half time 2-2 • Attendance 20,340

Referee Roberti BETTIN (Italy)

Linesmen A. de SANTIS and S. ZUCCOLINI

Blue Shirts, White Shorts		Goals	White Shirts, White Shorts		Goals
1	Ian BENNETT		1	Giampolo SPAGNULO	
2	Scott HILEY		2	Vincento TORRENTE	
3	Chris WHYTE		3	Gianluca FRANCESCONI ❏ #	
4	Mark WARD ❏		4	Danile Delli CARRI	
5	Andy EDWARDS		7	Marco NAPPI	32, 86
6	Michael JOHNSON		8	Mario BORTOLAZZI	19
7	Jonathan HUNT		9	Vincento MONTELLA	
8	Steve CASTLE †		11	John Vant SCHIP	
9	Jason BOWEN	7, 9	14	Alessando TURRONE	
10	Ken CHARLERY ‡		20	Gennaro RUOTOLA †	
11	GARY COOPER #		21	Roberto ONORATI ‡	
	Substitutes			*Substitutes*	
12	Jae MARTIN ‡57		12	Daniele SPINETTA	
13	Richard FORSYTH #65		16	Osca MAGONI †45	
14	NEIL DOHERTY †51		18	Massimiliano CORRADO ‡67	
15	Ian RICHARDSON		23	Fabio ROSSI #74	
16	Ian MUIR		25	Minico PAGUARINI	

BEFORE	P	W	D	L	F	A	pts	AFTER	P	W	D	L	F	A	pts
Blues (Eng Sec)	0	0	0	0	0	0	0	2 Blues	1	0	0	1	2	3	0
Genoa (Ital Sec)	0	0	0	0	0	0	0	2 Genoa	1	1	0	0	3	2	3

FACTFILE

Genoa, Italy's oldest club, attract a record crowd for an Anglo-Italian match outside a Wembley final... Michael Johnson makes his home debut... Only Birmingham's third home defeat in twelve months.

Bowen brace starts a classic

With ticket prices slashed to a fiver, plus the bonus of free beer, Birmingham City's selling power again worked wonders for the visit of the Italians. There was such a late rush of spectators that the kick-off had to be delayed for ten minutes, as there was obviously going to be another big attendance.

The fans were quickly treated to a sparkling start by Birmingham as the Italians seemingly under-estimated the opposition and appeared to be very sluggish at the start – tactics which were exposed by the ever-alert Jonathan Hunt who proved that he rarely misses an opportunity.

It was Hunt who put Jason Bowen in possession down the right channel and the former Swansea Town player turned quickly to fire in a low cross shot which Giampolo Spagnulo finger-tipped into the net just inside the post after only seven minutes.

Genoa, relegated at the end of last season from Serie A following a penalty shoot out, could hardly believe what had happened to them and two minutes later they were again in serious trouble. Hunt gathered the ball just outside the penalty area and released a quick pass which Bowen collected to advance and beat Spagnulo and there were thoughts of another Barnsley goalscoring spree. But Genoa are a much superior side to Barnsley, as was always evident once the game was in progress.

There was no doubt that scoring two goals in the opening ten minutes was a tremendous start for Birmingham, but the bubble was quickly pricked as the Italians picked up the pieces and gave a scintillating display of football to get off the hook. Mario Bortolazzi scored first directly from a free-kick that was taken so quickly that Birmingham were still shuffling into a defensive wall.

Vincento Montella, the new Italian sensation, then demonstrated why he is so highly rated when he skilfully put Marco Nappi in possession to equalise.

At this stage it was a fast, entertaining encounter with Mark Ward twice hitting tremendous shots from outside the area only to see Spagnulo make equally spectacular saves.

Ward himself became a little agitated and obviously had forgotten manager Barry Fry's warning to watch his temper. He became unnecessarily involved in a couple of incidents and finally tried the patience of Italian referee Roberti Bettin once too often and was shown the yellow card.

The skill of Genoa was most evident and both Nappi and Montella were class performers.

Birmingham managed to keep in the game, but there were ominous signs of a breakthrough by Genoa and really it was no great surprise when Nappi grabbed the 86th minute winner after an astute pass from Montella.

Manager Fry was philosophical afterwards, fully aware that Birmingham had been beaten by a very good team.

He said: "We obviously missed Steve Claridge with a slight groin strain but we thought it was advisable to give him a rest in preparation for the tough game against Crystal Palace at the weekend. Having said that, Ken Charlery, who was so good at Barnsley, never had a look in against Genoa. They gave us a good footballing lesson and I hope that the players learn something from this defeat."

Jason Bowen.

Saturday 9th September 1995 • St. Andrew's • 3.00pm

BIRMINGHAM CITY 0 CRYSTAL PALACE 0

Half time 0-0 • *Attendance* 19,403

Referee Mike BAILEY (Cambridge)

Linesmen B.P. ELLIOTT and N.E. GREEN

Blue Shirts, White Shorts	Goals	Red and Blue Shirts, Red Shorts	Goals
1 Ian BENNETT		1 Nigel MARTYN	
2 Gary POOLE		2 Mark EDWORTHY	
3 Michael JOHNSON		3 Jamie VINCENT	
4 Mark WARD †		4 David HOPKIN	
5 Andy EDWARDS		5 Chris COLEMAN	
6 Liam DAISH		6 Richard SHAW ❑	
7 Jonathan HUNT		7 Darren PITCHER	
8 Steve CLARIDGE		8 Ray HOUGHTON	
9 Jason BOWEN		9 Dougie FREEDMAN ‡	
10 Ken CHARLERY		10 Bruce DYER	
11 Gary COOPER		11 Damian MATTHEW †	
Substitutes		*Substitutes*	
12 Neil DOHERTY		12 Danny BOXALL	
13 Richard FORSYTH †70		14 George NDAH ‡75	
14 Steve CASTLE		15 Simon RODGER †66	

BEFORE	P	W	D	L	F	A	pts	AFTER	P	W	D	L	F	A	pts
6 Blues	5	3	0	2	14	9	9	5 Blues	6	3	1	2	14	9	10
11 Palace	4	2	1	1	8	7	7	14 Palace	5	2	2	1	8	7	8

FACTFILE

All the pre-match talk is of the increasing interest being shown by the 'Big Boys' in Jonathan Hunt... Crystal Palace had won their previous three games at St. Andrew's... First time that Birmingham fail to score in six games... Former Aston Villa mid-field star, Ray Houghton, is in the Palace side.

Strike force draws a blank

Top of the conversation list for Birmingham fans trooping to St. Andrew's for the visit of Crystal Palace was the growing interest being shown in Jonathan Hunt and whether he could mastermind another vital home win over the recently relegated London side.

Blackburn, Sheffield Wednesday and Spurs have all been represented at Birmingham's games with Hunt top of the shopping list and figures of £2m to £4m being suggested as the kind of money required to acquire his services.

But comments about Hunt's future quickly disappeared for the St. Andrew's faithful as they quickly realised that Palace were not going to become their third former Premiership victims.

Unlike Ipswich and Norwich, who were both hit three times by the Blues' goal machine, Palace displayed a resolution which plainly put Birmingham out of their stride.

They also ran up against a goalkeeper of top international quality in Nigel Martyn, who was to frustrate the Birmingham attack and in particular Ken Charlery.

Jason Bowen was tightly marked and as a result Birmingham's goal attempts began to come from long range efforts.

The little Welshman, however, attempted on one occasion to wriggle his way through, only to find himself effectively sandwiched between Jamie Vincent and Mark Edworthy. What was thought by many people to have been a certain penalty was not seen in the same light by the referee.

Birmingham also found Chris Coleman and Richard Shaw, two of the transfer seeking Palace defenders, in outstanding form and they slowly enforced their dominance on the game with Birmingham's usually high scoring attack unable to make much impression.

Martyn also continued to make some outstanding saves as he demonstrated in the second half when he once again thwarted Charlery.

The former Peterborough striker claimed: "I could hardly believe it when Martyn made those saves. I thought I had done enough to score."

As to be expected, manager Barry Fry was disappointed with the result and the performance. He later claimed: "We had eleven goalscorers in the squad but on the day not one could find the back of the net.

"To be honest, Palace looked the sharper side the longer the game went on and I could see them scoring.

"We didn't have the craft to break the deadlock and Palace, who are going to be in the promotion hunt, became stronger as the game progressed."

But such a performance is nothing new for Birmingham. They hit the high and low spots and that uncertainty is the big attraction for many fans.

On this occasion Birmingham were admittedly a little jaded and their two games a week programme, which has been going on since the middle of July, is obviously beginning to take its toll.

But there is no respite for Fry and his team and in the circumstances it is hardly surprising that the Birmingham manager is so intent on retaining the services of his young stars such as Hunt.

Steve Claridge awaits a long Ian Bennett clearance.

Tuesday 12th September 1995 • St. Andrew's • 7.45pm

BIRMINGHAM CITY 1 STOKE CITY 1

Half time 1-0 • *Attendance* 19,005

Referee Ian CRUIKSHANKS (Hartlepool)

Linesmen A. BLACK and K.R. BUTLER

S.C.F.C.

Blue Shirts, White Shorts	Goals	Red and White Striped Shirts, Red Shorts	Goals
1 Ian BENNETT		1 Carl MUGGLETON	
2 Gary POOLE		2 Ian CLARKSON	
3 Michael JOHNSON		3 Lee SANDFORD	
4 Mark WARD		4 Larus SIGURDSSON	
5 Andy EDWARDS		5 Vince OVERSON	
6 Liam DAISH		6 Graham POTTER	
7 Jonathan HUNT	29	7 Kevin KEEN #	
8 Steve CLARIDGE		8 Ray WALLACE	
9 Jason BOWEN		9 Paul PESCHISOLIDO	
10 Ken CHARLERY ‡		10 Keith SCOTT †	
11 Gary COOPER †		11 Nigel GLEGHORN ‡	
Substitutes		*Substitutes*	
12 Paul TAIT ‡68		12 David BRIGHTWELL ‡69	
14 Richard FORSYTH		14 Martin CARRUTHERS †49 51	
15 Ricky OTTO †60		15 Simon STURRIDGE #77	

BEFORE		P	W	D	L	F	A	pts	AFTER		P	W	D	L	F	A	pts
5	Blues	6	3	1	2	14	9	10	6	Blues	7	3	2	2	15	10	11
23	Stoke	6	1	1	4	5	12	4	20	Stoke	7	1	2	4	6	13	5

FACTFILE

Stoke include no less than six former Birmingham players in their squad at St. Andrew's... Birmingham's second successive home draw... Stoke's first point from five games... super-sub Carruthers strikes in double quick time... Muggleton in fine form to thwart Blues.

Hot-shot Hunt strikes again

Pre-match spice is never in short supply where Birmingham are concerned and on this occasion Stoke City were aggrieved that confidential transfer details regarding Paul Peschisolido had been revealed in the local press.

It transpires that Birmingham collect £10,000 for every goal over five scored in a 20 match block by the Canadian international.

As he was playing in his 57th game for the Potteries club there was an obvious added ingredient to the match as he took the field.

Peschisolido was very much at home as one of six former Birmingham players named by Lou Macari on the Stoke team sheet. It added a little extra interest and an incentive on the part of the players concerned to prove themselves in front of their old supporters.

Two of these players, Vince Overson and Graham Potter, were particularly conspicuous early on in the game, when the big central defender went forward to power his header just over the bar.

Overson, incidentally, was very impressed with the new-look Birmingham and stated: "I only wish this sort of development had taken place while I was at St. Andrew's. It would have made a tremendous amount of difference to the players at the time."

The central defender was a tower of strength for Stoke, but Birmingham had their problems inherited from the goalless draw four days previously against Crystal Palace.

Ken Charlery went close with an over-head kick which stretched Carl Muggleton to the limit as the Stoke goalkeeper continued to deny Birmingham's attack.

The turning point seemingly occurred in the 29th minute when Jonathan Hunt suddenly put Birmingham ahead with his sixth goal of the season with a low, left-footed, curling shot from the right which deceived everyone to wriggle into the far corner of the net.

Hunt, again under the scrutiny of several Premiership clubs including Spurs, Blackburn and Arsenal, displayed his craft but Birmingham still struggled to cash in on their superior attacking play. There always appeared to be a promise of more goals, but they never materialised with Muggleton in such sound form.

Not for the first time this season Birmingham fell to the sucker punch administered by Potter four minutes into the second period.

Only two minutes previously out of favour Martin Carruthers had been sent on by Macari and promptly dashed Birmingham's hopes of victory when the former Aston Villa striker latched onto Potter's free kick to score from close range.

Manager Barry Fry was quietly seething that his defence should concede such a goal. He later complained: "This is the fourth time this season that we have let the opposition score like this.

"We spend our time arguing instead of sorting out the defence to cut out the danger of the free kick. It's about time they were able to learn from their mistakes because they are now proving extremely costly.

"It's our second successive draw and at the end of the day I would have preferred to have lost one and drawn one. It would have given us an extra point."

Michael Johnson is stopped in full flow.

Sunday 17th September 1995 • The Hawthorns • 3.00pm

WEST BROMWICH ALBION 1 BIRMINGHAM CITY 0

Half time 1-0 • *Attendance* 18,875
Referee Kevin BREEN (Liverpool)
Linesmen C. JONES and J.D. WILSON

Blue and White Striped Shirts, White Shorts		Goals	Red Shirts with Blue and White Trim, Red Shorts		Goals
1	Stuart NAYLOR		1	Ian BENNETT	
2	Daryl BURGESS		2	Gary POOLE	
3	Paul EDWARDS		3	Michael JOHNSON †	
4	Stacy COLDICOTT ❑		4	Mark WARD	
5	Paul MARDON ❑		5	Andy EDWARDS ❑	
6	Paul RAVEN		6	Liam DAISH	
7	Kevin DONOVAN		7	Jonathan HUNT	
8	Dave GILBERT		8	Steve CLARIDGE	
9	Bob TAYLOR		9	Jason BOWEN	
10	Andy HUNT	29	10	Ricky OTTO ‡	
11	Ian HAMILTON		11	Paul TAIT #	
	Substitutes			*Substitutes*	
12	Tony REES		12	Gary COOPER †38 ❑	
14	Paul REECE (Gk)		13	Richard FORSYTH #71	
15	Lee ASHCROFT		14	Ken CHARLERY ‡45 ❑	

BEFORE		P	W	D	L	F	A	pts	AFTER		P	W	D	L	F	A	pts
5	Albion	7	3	3	1	10	7	12	3	Albion	8	4	3	1	11	7	15
6	Blues	7	3	2	2	15	10	11	11	Blues	8	3	2	3	15	11	11

FACTFILE

A mini Birmingham slump with only two points from three games during which time they have scored only one goal... their 38th defeat in 85 games between the two Midland clubs... Barry Fry not happy with attack that can't see its way to goal... changes will be made he promises.

Shot shy City draw a blank

Both club managers, Barry Fry and Alan Buckley, get involved in a colourful build-up for the televised local derby.

Fry claims: "I saw them play at Southend and their second half performance was the best I've seen from a First Division side this season. Alan tells me that they can play better than that on their day. It frightens me so much I'm wondering whether I should go to the match."

Fry had his life story serialised in the Evening Mail during the week, when he revealed that as a player his biggest regret was not making the grade at Manchester United due to the fact that he often devoted too much time to activities outside the game.

A regular horse racing fan, he admitted that he saw the folly of his ways and this now explains why everything associated with the game takes preference over almost everything in his life.

The passionate Birmingham manager acknowledges making mistakes and had reservations about including Ricky Otto in his side at the Hawthorns. But he has great faith in the winger and admits his own disappointment that the former Southend player has not lived up to expectations at St. Andrew's

Otto is given another opportunity to redeem himself. Unfortunately he fails to grasp his chance as illustarted as early as the fifth minute of the game when Mark Ward puts him clear but his weak, outside of the left foot, shot goes wide of the upright.

In retrospect it was this one incident which stained Birmingham's performance and ultimately led to their downfall.

Other players too had off-days. Liam Daish had a miserable match as did his fellow central defender, Andy Edwards.

Steve Claridge, following a poor start to the season, was completely out of touch and his general play explained why he had scored only one goal in ten games.

The bubbling Albion side always threatened danger with their neat build ups. Ironically, it was a long ball from Paul Edwards from inside his own half which led to Andy Hunt grabbing the only goal of the game.

Daish went in wildly on the slippery turf, lost his footing, and allowed Hunt to go through to grab his third goal in four games.

At half time Otto was replaced by Ken Charlery and there was a general improvement in the attacking play as Birmingham created numerous attacks, but to no avail as they usually foundered upon the defensive blockade of Paul Mardon, Daryl Burgess and Paul Raven.

Fry confirmed his misgivings about the performance when he later stated: "We were the leading scorers in the division but we never looked like scoring against Albion. In fact, I don't know where the next one is coming from.

"We played some good approach football but lacked a goalscorer and we didn't have a clue in the last third of the pitch. I'm running out of patience and unless there is a big improvement I will be looking to add to the squad.

"There are no excuses. We had more of the game than Albion, but they defended well and denied us any real chances."

Ricky Otto – missed opportunities.

Wednesday 20th September 1995 • St. Andrew's • 7.45pm

BIRMINGHAM CITY 3 GRIMSBY TOWN 1

Half time 2-1 • *Attendance 7,446*

Referee Scott MATHIESON (Stockport)

Linesmen B. BISHOP and A. MARTIN

Blue Shirts, White Shorts		Goals	Black and White Shirts, Black Shorts		Goals
1	Ian BENNETT		1	Paul CRICHTON	
2	Gary POOLE		2	Brian LAWS †	
3	Gary COOPER		3	Gary CROFT	
4	Steve CASTLE		4	Peter HANDYSIDE	
5	Andy EDWARDS		5	Ashley FICKLING	
6	Liam DAISH	75	6	Paul GROVES	
7	Jonathan HUNT	42	7	Tom WATSON	
8	Steve CLARIDGE	23	8	Jim DOBBIN	
9	Steve FINNAN †		9	Neil WOODS	34
10	Ken CHARLERY		10	Steve LIVINGSTONE	
11	Paul TAIT ‡		11	Nicky SOUTHALL	
	Substitutes			*Substitutes*	
12	Jason BOWEN †59		12	Jack LESTER †73	
13	Mark WARD		13	Jason PEARCEY	
14	Ricky OTTO ‡59		14	Joby GOWSHALL	

FACTFILE

Birmingham's lowest gate of the season... first win in four games... first cup meeting between the two clubs since 1966-67... a promising debut for the teenager Steve Finnan recruited in the close season from Welling... he is one of three changes from the team that lost to Albion on Sunday.

Ricky Otto – giving the Mariners a hard time.

Claridge ends goal drought

Lukewarm is the description for Birmingham's fans and their attitude to the early stages of the Coca-Cola Cup.

Three games without a win and only one goal could have been another explanation why so few of Birmingham's fans turned up to see their side claw their way back into the winners' frame.

The Mariners are never the most appealing of opposition, but they have a good Cup reputation in recent years as several clubs can verify not a great distance away from St. Andrew's.

The Humberside team arrives with player-manager Brian Laws forced to put out a much depleted team due to injuries and illness, with the result that they are quickly under a great deal of pressure from a Birmingham side that was not fully at ease.

There had been pre-match threats from manager Barry Fry to leave out the likes of skipper Liam Daish and Steve Claridge because of their indifferent form.

Fry relented in their cases, but did sideline player-coach Mark Ward, Jason Bowen and Ricky Otto, who is the centre of attention from Sheffield United.

It's admitted by Fry that he has been disappointed with Otto's overall contribution and would reluctantly agree to a transfer if the winger could command a £1m bid. He said: "I know Otto is a quality player but he cannot get on with the fans and the directors are not happy with his performances."

Fry, in turn, called for a more direct style of play instead of continually playing the ball square or backwards.

Steve Finnan was drafted into the team on the right and the immediate impression was that he was similar in style to Jonathan Hunt.

The 19-year-old, former Welling United player quickly slotted in and worked well with some good passes and crosses. Grimsby were under considerable pressure, but the lack of penetration continued to cause concern on the bench.

Claridge, with only one goal in his previous eleven games, worked hard and was rewarded in the 23rd minute when he bustled the ball into the net after goalkeeper Paul Crichton had failed to hold a header from Andy Edwards following a right wing corner by Finnan.

Just three minutes later Steve Claridge burst through again, and, not for the first time, appeared to hit the ball with his untidy bulging socks and the net result was a badly bungled shot from less than six yards with only Paul Crichton to beat.

The incident could explain a great deal about Claridge and his inconsistency. The blatant miss could also have proved costly as Grimsby, on the defensive for long periods, but dangerous on the break, equalised with an outstanding 35-yard cross-shot from the much travelled Neil Woods, who has had spells with the likes of Glasgow Rangers and Ipswich.

But not to be outdone in any shape or fashion, the much vaunted Jonathan Hunt then produced a 30-yard rocket which was always swerving away from Crichton to go into the top right hand corner of the net.

Persistent pressure failed to produce the goods for Birmingham until Daish went up to head in a Hunt corner in the 75th minute.

Then Ian Bennett earned his pay with a diving save from Steve Livingstone and from the cross the former Wolves striker headed against the bar.

Manager Fry afterwards expressed himself satisfied with the improved form and in particular the contribution of Finnan.

"He has outstanding talent and he could develop into a very good player indeed once he matures," said Fry.

Saturday 23rd September 1995 • Vicarage Road • 3.00pm

WATFORD 1 BIRMINGHAM CITY 1

Watford

Half time 1-1 • *Attendance* 9,422

Referee Andrew D'URSON (Billericay)

Linesmen C. BREAKSPEAR and J.J. WILKINSON

FORWARD

Yellow Shirts, Black Shorts		Goals	Blue Shirts, White Shorts		Goals
1	Kevin MILLER		1	Ian BENNETT	
2	Gerard LAVIN		2	Gary POOLE	
3	Richard JOHNSON		3	Gary COOPER	
4	Colin FOSTER		4	Mark WARD	
5	Keith MILLEN		5	Andy EDWARDS	
6	Craig RAMAGE		6	Liam DAISH ❑	
7	Darren BAZELEY		7	Jonathan HUNT	
8	Peter BEADLE † ❑		8	Steve CLARIDGE	
9	Tommy MOONEY		9	Steve FINNAN †	11
10	Gary PORTER		10	Ken CHARLERY ‡ ❑	
11	Jamie MORALEE ‡	7	11	Steve CASTLE	
	Substitutes			*Substitutes*	
12	David HOLDSWORTH ‡89		12	Jason BOWEN ‡84	
13	Steve CHERRY (Gk)		13	Ricky OTTO †67	
14	David CONNOLLY †56		14	Richard FORSYTH	

BEFORE		P	W	D	L	F	A	pts	AFTER		P	W	D	L	F	A	pts
11	Blues	8	3	2	3	15	11	11	13	Blues	9	3	3	3	16	12	12
19	Watford	8	2	2	4	10	11	8	20	Watford	9	2	3	4	11	12	9

FACTFILE

Paul Tait out with injury – Steve Castle comes in... Steve Finnan marks his league debut with a goal... Birmingham chalk up their third league draw in four games... The Blues are still leading scorers in the division but 11 of their 16 goals have come in just three matches.

Finnan strike salvages a point

A three goal burst against Grimsby gives an added boost to Birmingham's aspirations at lowly Watford, but the build up to the game has been strangely quiet.

It's an unusual situation for a Birmingham side that is normally banging the big drum. Even manager Barry Fry is subdued and that explains the situation as the Blues are desperate to improve their mid-table position.

There is no encouragement from the long term injuries, while club skipper John Frain admits that he is beginning to wonder if he has a future at St. Andrew's.

Left out of the side since the Charlton defeat, Frain has had words with Fry. The Birmingham stalwart said: "The manager has assured me that I am still in his plans, but if I am still out of the side by Christmas I will have to give serious thought to my future plans."

Meanwhile, Fry is forced to make a change with Paul Tait again on the injury list. Steve Castle is drafted into the side with manager Barry Fry hoping that his team can regain their goalscoring flair.

Any early hopes, however, are summarily dashed with Jamie Moralee giving Watford a dream start with a 7th minute headed goal that finished off a smart move.

To their credit Birmingham have enough belief in their ability to hit back at the opposition and this was patently obvious just four minutes after Watford's shock goal.

Birmingham won a close range free-kick and with both Mark Ward and Jonathan Hunt in attendance either could have been expected to test the Watford goalkeeper, Kevin Miller.

Instead teenager Steve Finnan stepped forward purposefully to blast home the equaliser past the former Birmingham 'keeper.

Back on level terms a vibrant Blues produced wave after wave of attacks, but they sadly lacked the finishing touch which is now becoming a major issue.

There is no doubt about the creative ability of the team, but they again lost sight of the objective of scoring.

Steve Claridge was a hard worker but has lost his shooting boots as the ball bobbles off in all sorts of directions.

There was no improvement either from Ken Charlery as the Birmingham attack became increasingly frustrated and dejected by their own shortcomings.

Young Finnan eventually makes way for the experience of Ricky Otto mid-way through the second half, but there is no real improvement in the finishing form of Birmingham's shot-shy attack.

Mark Ward controls the midfield but the domination tends to back-fire on Birmingham as they lack the space to take advantage of a defence-minded Watford side.

Chances go a begging throughout the second period and even in the final few minutes Birmingham could have grabbed maximum points. Unlike last season when they picked up several wins with a final surge for the line they have lost their way in the First Division.

Claridge had the best opportunity to atone but failed once again to beat Watford's hero, Miller, who took great delight in turning in a five start performance.

Barry Fry later bemoaned Birmingham's lack of goalscoring ability. "We desperately need someone to put away these chances," he said.

"I couldn't fault our effort but the finishing is abysmal."

Then it was revealed he was keen to try and persuade Gary Bull to have another spell at St. Andrew's.

"Frank Clark will let me have him for £50,000," said Fry, "but the problem is we cannot afford to match his present wages."

Saturday 30th September 1995 • St. Andrew's • 3.00pm

BIRMINGHAM CITY 0   OLDHAM ATHLETIC 0

Half time 0-0 • Attendance 17,269

Referee Roger FERNANDIZ (Doncaster)

Linesmen G.A. BEALE and M. CARRINGTON

Blue Shirts, White Shorts	Goals
1 Ian BENNETT	
2 Gary POOLE	
3 Gary COOPER	
4 Mark WARD	
5 Andy EDWARDS	
6 Liam DAISH	
7 Jonathan HUNT	
8 Steve CLARIDGE	
9 Steve FINNAN †	
10 Ken CHARLERY ‡	
11 Steve CASTLE #	
Substitutes	
12 Jason BOWEN ‡45	
13 Richard FORSYTH #67	
14 Ricky OTTO †45	

Orange Shirts, Black Shorts	Goals
1 Paul GERRARD	
2 Scott McNIVEN	
3 Chris MAKIN	
4 Nick HENRY	
5 Richard JOBSON	
6 Steve REDMOND	
7 Gunnar HALLE	
8 Richard GRAHAM	
9 Sean McCARTHY	
10 Nick BANGER †	
11 Mark BRENNAN	
Substitutes	
12 Ian SNODIN	
13 John HALLWORTH (Gk)	
14 David BERESFORD †12	

BEFORE	P	W	D	L	F	A	pts
9 Oldham	9	4	2	3	14	10	14
13 Blues	9	3	3	3	16	12	12

AFTER	P	W	D	L	F	A	pts
8 Oldham	10	4	3	3	14	10	15
17 Blues	10	3	4	3	16	12	13

FACTFILE

Fry enquires about availability of Paul Peschisolido at Stoke, but is told there's a £1.5m price tag on his head... Birmingham's fifth game without a league win... Blues have scored only two goals in this period and collected four points... Oldham extend their unbeaten run at St. Andrew's to five games.

Fry frustrated by lack of goals

Suddenly there are alarm bells beginning to ring around St. Andrew's and it is not to do with the security of the ground.

Barry Fry's team suddenly discover that scoring goals is beginning to be very hard labour and the easy 5-0 win at Barnsley has done no one any favours.

In fact, Birmingham's reputation has gone ahead of them and this has resulted in the opposition employing ultra-defensive tactics to contain Fry's high fliers.

Fry stays with the same squad as that which collected a 1-1 draw at Watford after dominating almost the entire game. Fry's belief is that the barren goals spell must end sometime and that the players in the side are capable of a goalscoring spree.

Oldham, however, have other ideas on this occasion and the strength of their defence and in particular their long serving central defender Richard Jobson is a feature of the early play.

Teenager Steve Finnan could have put a different complexion on the game if his superb left footed drive in only the second minute had found its way past Paul Gerrard in the Oldham goal.

The England under-21 international produced a top class save which was to serve as his bench-mark for the rest of the game.

Birmingham's lack of mid-field authority further imperilled their prospects. Mark Ward sprayed the ball around, but it was of little impact on a Jobson inspired Oldham defence.

As a result, Oldham appeared quite content to put up a defensive blockade and rely on snappy breakaways – to the consternation of Birmingham.

The virtue of this policy was seen when Liam Daish was beaten to the ball by Gunnar Halle

and Oldham's substitute Dave Beresford somehow managed to screw the ball wide.

Birmingham's only real chance in the second half occurred when Jobson, who had previously not put a foot wrong in the game, slipped and the ball ran through to Jason Bowen, only for the Welshman to see his shot smothered by the ever-elert Gerrard.

In the end Birmingham had Ian Bennett to thank for their point when Sean McCarthy had a shot blocked and from the rebound Mark Brennan saw his effort turned away by Blues' highly rated goalkeeper who had been offered a new five year contract just a few days prior to the game.

Afterwards, a downcast Barry Fry said: "In terms of play and possession we have been better than most teams we have played this season.

"But at the moment we do not have a natural goalscorer and I haven't any more money for new signings."

A worried Mark Ward afterwards expressed his concern about losing the support of the fans.

He said: "They were unbelievable last season and we can't let them down. But if there is any chance of going up we must win our home games against the likes of Oldham.

"Right at the moment, however, we do lack that bit of quality around the penalty box to produce the killer touch."

Steve Finnan – came close to giving Blues an early lead.

Tuesday 3rd October 1995 • Blundell Park • 7.45pm

GRIMSBY TOWN 1 BIRMINGHAM CITY 1

Birmingham win 4-2 on aggregate

Half time 0-0 • Attendance 3,280

Referee Kevin LYNCH (Knaresborough)

Linesmen P.A. ELWICK and R.R. RUSSON

Black and White Shirts, Black Shorts		Goals	Blue Shirts, White Shorts		Goals
1	Paul CRICHTON		1	Ian BENNETT	
2	Brian LAWS		2	Gary POOLE	
3	Gary CROFT		3	Gary COOPER ❑	
4	Peter HANDYSIDE		4	Richard FORSYTH †	
5	Ashley FICKLING		5	Andy EDWARDS	
6	Paul GROVES		6	Liam DAISH ❑	
7	Gary CHILDS †		7	Steve CASTLE	
8	Jim DOBBIN		8	Jason BOWEN	81
9	Paul JEWELL		9	Steve FINNAN ‡	
10	Ivano BONETTI		10	Ricky OTTO #	
11	Nicky SOUTHALL	65	11	Ken CHARLERY	
	Substitutes			*Substitutes*	
12	Daryle CLARE †82		12	Mark WARD †63	
13	Jack LESTER		13	Jonathan HUNT ‡63	
14	Tom WATSON		14	Steve CLARIDGE #63	

FACTFILE

Three of Birmingham's leading players, Mark Ward, Jonathan Hunt and Steve Claridge, are on the substitutes bench as Barry Fry attempts to find a new winning formation... Ian Bennett's 100th appearance for Birmingham... Grimsby have Ivano Bonetti from Torino on trial.

Steve Claridge – came on in the second half to liven things up.

Bowen blast pegs back Mariners

With a two goal advantage from the first leg Birmingham City have what appears a comfortable cushion to sit on going into the game against Grimsby.

But lurking in the background is the recent indifferent goalscoring form of the side and the decision to leave out Jonathan Hunt, Steve Claridge and Mark Ward is a calculated gamble on the part of Barry Fry.

Prior to the game there had been talk of Ward being linked with Tranmere on loan, but nothing concrete transpired as Birmingham would not consider such an arrangement for one of their key players.

On the strength of the early play it was evident that Birmingham missed the industry of Ward, while the lack of confidence, bad luck, call it what you like, was also plain to see.

As early as the sixth minute Jason Bowen failed to prosper from a mistake by Ashley Fickling when he watched his shot go across the face of the goal.

Steve Finnan and Andy Edwards both threatened the Grimsby goal, but it remained intact for the rest of the first half as the general frustration in the team began to simmer into the open.

The few bright moments of the half in fact came from the Italian striker, Ivano Bonetti, who was on trial from Torino.

Predictably the game coasted to half time without any real passion as Birmingham were never in any real danger from a neat Grimsby side that lacked strength in attack.

Early in the second half a goalline clearance by Gary Childs again kept out another effort from Andy Edwards and it was beginning to look ominous that another goalless affair was in the offing.

As is his want, Barry Fry made his customary substitutions on the hour when he sent on Claridge, Ward and Hunt to replace the once again ineffective Ricky Otto, Richard Forsyth and Finnan.

The immediate result of the re-organisation was that within a minute Grimsby had steamed ahead with a diving header from Nicky Southall following a cross from player-manager Brian Laws.

The opening goal put added pressure on Birmingham as another home goal would have taken the game into extra time with all the ramifications of a nail-biting finish.

This scenario did not materialise, as nine minutes from time a bad mistake by Paul Jewell allowed Jason Bowen to gain possession down the right and the little Welshman went hurtling forward to finish with a rasping shot on the run.

A relieved Barry Fry admitted afterwards: "The main thing is that we have got through into the third round.

"There was a lot of possession and some good crosses but no one was able to get on the end of them to finish off Grimsby."

Later there was talk of trials for the £500,000 Norwegian striker Petter Belsvik and the Peruvian, Salvo Maetri, while Bristol Rovers' front man, Marcus Stewart, was again being linked with the St. Andrew's club. It was a case of awaiting developments.

Andy Edwards – came close to scoring on several occasions.

Sunday 8th October 1995 • St. Andrew's • 2.55pm

BIRMINGHAM CITY 2   SOUTHEND UNITED 0

Half-time 1-0 • *Attendance* 17,491

Referee Billy BURNS (Scarborough)

Linesmen A.P. MONKS and B.P. POLKEY

Blue Shirts, White Shorts		Goals		Red Shirts, Red Shorts		Goals
1	Ian BENNETT			1	Simon ROYCE	
2	Gary POOLE			2	Keith DUBLIN	
3	Gary COOPER			3	Chris POWELL	
4	Steve CASTLE			4	Mike LAPPER	
5	Andy EDWARDS			5	Mike BODLEY	
6	Michael JOHNSON			6	Steve TILSON	
7	Jonathan HUNT			7	Mike MARSH	
8	Steve CLARIDGE	42, 75		8	Paul BYRNE #	
9	Steve FINNAN †			9	Paul READ †	
10	Ken CHARLERY ‡			10	Andy THOMSON ‡	
11	Jason BOWEN #			11	Julian HAILS	
	Substitutes				*Substitutes*	
12	Ricky OTTO †53			12	Dave REGIS ‡67	
13	Richard FORSYTH ‡62			13	Mark HONE #73	
14	Jae MARTIN #88			14	Gary JONES †45	

BEFORE	P	W	D	L	F	A	pts	AFTER	P	W	D	L	F	A	pts
13 Southend	10	4	2	4	10	10	14	6 Blues	11	4	4	3	18	12	16
14 Blues	10	3	4	3	16	12	13	14 Southend	11	4	2	5	10	12	14

FACTFILE

Jason Bowen is permitted to play despite a late call-up to the Welsh squad for the European Championship match against Germany... Birmingham's first win in six games... They jump from 14th to sixth place... Steve Claridge doubles his goals tally in one game... Southend are still seeking their first win at St. Andrew's.

In-form Claridge punishes United

There is a distinctly foreign atmosphere around St. Andrew's, albeit temporarily as two strikers, Flavio Maestri from Peruvian club Sporting Cristal and Petter Belsvik from Norway's IK Start, managed by Steve Perryman, check into St. Andrew's as a result of club chairman David Sullivan's eagerness to inject more fire-power into the club.

Belsvik makes one appearance for the reserves but he and Maestri depart as manager Barry Fry obviously wants to be surrounded by his own men.

It's a sink or swim attitude on a warm autumnal afternoon as Southend arrive fresh from three successive wins over Leicester, Wolves and Grimsby Town.

Steve Claridge, who reckons he has played with no less than 21 strikers since his arrival at St. Andrew's, and Jonathan Hunt are both recalled after being "rested" at Grimsby for a game televised live on Central.

Pre-match tension linking the game with the fact that manager Barry Fry was formerly with Southend did not materialise.

With no less than five former United players in Birmingham's side there was obviously a little extra keenness on the part of the players to prove the wisdom of joining the Midlands club.

This was evident in the early exchanges when Birmingham dominated the opposition, but still conspired to struggle in their quest for goals. They scorned several good opportunities and the merest sight of goal apparently turned their shooting boots to jelly.

Curiously it did not put Birmingham off their stroke and they continued to launch several dangerous raids, as Southend could make little impact as an attacking force.

The out of touch Steve Claridge headed hopelessly wide as the ball rebounded to him from a Jason Bowen effort, while Andy Edwards blasted the ball high over the bar from about ten yards.

It appeared as if the rot was in danger of getting deeper ingrained in Birmingham's play, but three minutes from half time the Blues got the opening they deserved.

Bowen made the running down the left and put the ball inside to Claridge to hit low with his left foot past goalkeeper Simon Royce.

The relief was visible on and off the field with Fry racing down the touchline with his fists raised in exhaltation.

Claridge himself was the most relieved player on the Birmingham side and continued to torment the Southend defence.

The customary second half substitutions were made by Fry, but it was Claridge who put his mark on the game with a brilliant individual goal 15 minutes from time.

He turned the American Mike Lapper and galloped away to score with a low right foot shot to the left of goalkeeper Royce to end Birmingham's miserable run without a win.

Manager Barry Fry, who has not been averse to criticising Claridge, said afterwards: "No one can fault Claridge. He always gives 150% effort but doesn't score the amount of goals he should from the chances he creates.

"But his second against Southend was magnificient. I hope this is the start of better things to come for everyone at the club.

"If we keep playing this kind of football and take a greater percentage of the chances we create, then we will have a great chance of being among the teams challenging for the league title, which I believe will be wide open until the end of the season."

Wednesday 11th October 1995 • Renato Curi Stadium • 8.30pm

AS PERUGIA 0 BIRMINGHAM CITY 1

Half time 0-0 • *Attendance* 1,200

Referee Mike BAILEY (Cambridge)

Linesmen P. MARCH and J. WESSON

Red Shirts, Red Shorts | Goals

Blue Shirts, White Shorts | Goals

1	Simone BRAGLIA	
2	Andrea CAMPIONE	
3	Andrea COTTINI ❑	
4	Claudio LOMBARDO	
5	Marco MATERAZZI	
6	Pasquale ROCCO	
7	Daniele RUSSO ‡	
8	Renzo TASSO	
9	Robero GORETTI ❑ †	
10	Davide BAIOCCO	
11	Marco NEGRI	

Substitutes

12	Salvatore TEDESCO †55
13	Adriano MEACCI ‡61
14	Paolo FABBRI
15	Paolo GROSSI
16	Giovanni CORNACCHINI

1	Ian BENNETT	
2	Gary POOLE	
3	Gary COOPER	
4	Steve CASTLE	70
5	Andy EDWARDS	
6	Michael JOHNSON	
7	Jonathan HUNT #	
8	Steve CLARIDGE	
9	Steve FINNAN	
10	Simon REA †	
11	Ricky OTTO ‡	

Substitutes

12	Paul TAIT †45 ❑
13	Richard FORSYTH
14	Scott HILEY
15	Jae MARTIN ‡80
16	Ian RICHARDSON #80

BEFORE	P	W	D	L	F	A	pts
2 Blues	1	0	0	1	2	3	0
1 Perugia	1	1	0	0	4	1	3

AFTER	P	W	D	L	F	A	pts
2 Blues	2	1	0	1	3	3	3
2 Perugia	2	1	0	1	4	2	3

FACTFILE

Birmingham's first win in the Anglo-Italian Cup... Steve Castle's winner was his first goal for Birmingham since his close season move from Plymouth... Simon Rea's debut for Blues.

Castle breeches Perugia fortress

Choosing to ignore Football League advice, Birmingham City went on an away day trip to Italy and very nearly rued the day they decided to make such a flying visit.

Everything that could go wrong went wrong in the build up to the match. It really was a catalogue of errors and Birmingham are unlikely ever again to repeat such an exercise.

Due to flight control problems the departure from Birmingham was delayed for nearly three hours.

It was a nightmare situation in which there was really no opportunity to make up for lost time.

There was not a meal on the plane for the players and then a hotel stop for further refreshments was cut out of the itinerary and the players had to make do with sandwiches and coffee at a motorway service station.

Fortunately, it was a late kick-off and a depleted Birmingham side lacking the services of skipper Liam Daish and Jason Bowen, who were both on international duty, and the injured Mark Ward, was able to complete the three hour coach trip to Perugia without any further problems.

The game itself against the struggling Serie B side was not a classic by any means. Perugia had more chances than Birmingham to have built up a commanding lead, but they lacked the finishing power to carve out a win.

Both Russo and Negri had several good chances, but their laid-back approach enabled Birmingham to survive.

Simon Rea was given a testing debut and the youngster found the going more than a little rugged and he eventually made way for Paul Tait at the interval.

This move gave Birmingham a little more composure with the industrious Tait enjoying the final 45 minutes when he linked up effectively with Jonathan Hunt.

With the game drifting to a goalless draw the game was settled in the 70th minute with a classic goal which made the trip all the more worthwhile for the few Birmingham fans who had made the journey.

Steve Claridge hooked the ball from the right way out to Ricky Otto who headed back for the onrushing Steve Castle to grab the only goal of the game with a shot on the volley as he was falling into the ground.

But Birmingham's troubles were far from over. On the coach back to Rome airport they ran into a traffic jam following an accident and it was almost 5.00am when they took off.

Barry Fry was far from amused. He said: "Luton went out to Italy for three days and Southend spent two days for their Anglo-Italian match, so how on earth everyone at the club thought we could go there and back in a day is absolutely beyond me."

Karren Brady, Birmingham's managing director, later pointed out that it was the players themselves who requested a day visit and that the club chartered a plane for £28,000 to comply with their wishes.

It was unfortunate that the trip was blighted with problems, but it could be an experience from which the club could benefit in the future.

This win puts Blues top of the English Section, being the only English club to have won a match; Port Vale are second with two points from two drawn games; Oldham lie in third place with one point; and Luton are bottom with no points.

Genoa have gone top of the Italian Section with six points after wins over Blues and Luton; Ancona are second on four points; and Perugia have dropped down to third on three points; with Cesena holding the others up with two points.

All teams have played two games.

Saturday 14th October 1995 • Fratton Park • 3.00pm

PORTSMOUTH 0 BIRMINGHAM CITY 1

Half time 0-1 • *Attendance* 10,006

Referee Ian HEMLEY (Ampthill)

Linesmen B.L. PARKER and A.J. WEBB

Blue Shirts, White Shorts	Goals	Red Shirts with Blue and White Trim, Red Shorts	Goals
1 Alan KNIGHT		1 Ian BENNETT	
2 John DURNIN		2 Gary POOLE	
3 Tony DOBSON ❏		3 Gary COOPER ❏	
4 Alan McLOUGHLIN		4 Steve CASTLE ❏	
5 Jon GITTENS		5 Andy EDWARDS	
6 Guy BUTTERS		6 Michael JOHNSON	
7 Paul WALSH		7 Jonathan HUNT ❏	
8 Fitzroy SIMPSON #		8 Steve CLARIDGE #	24
9 Paul WOOD		9 Steve FINNAN ‡	
10 Lee BRADBURY ‡		10 Jason BOWEN †	
11 Jason REES †		11 Paul TAIT	
Substitutes		*Substitutes*	
12 Bob PETHICK †52		12 Ricky OTTO †45	
13 Paul HALL #73		13 Ian RICHARDSON ‡65	
14 Carl GRIFFITHS ‡59		14 Ken CHARLERY #89	

BEFORE		P	W	D	L	F	A	pts	AFTER		P	W	D	L	F	A	pts
6	Blues	11	4	4	3	18	12	16	5	Blues	12	5	4	3	19	12	19
22	Portsmouth	11	2	4	5	14	18	10	22	Portsmouth	12	2	4	6	14	19	10

FACTFILE

Back from 'the Journey to Hell' to triumph at Pompey... Liam Daish is left out of Birmingham's side... Birmingham increase their unbeaten run to seven games... Steve Claridge returns to embarrass his home town club... The Blues are now just three points adrift of the leaders, Leicester City.

Claridge cashes in to take points

There was a big buzz around Fratton Park even before the kick-off and surprise, surprise manager Barry Fry was in the centre of all the action.

It had been hinted some 24 hours previously that club skipper Liam Daish would not be in the side, as Fry was keen to give a vote of confidence to the squad which had performed outstandingly in difficult conditions against Perugia only a few days previously.

This rumour had become fact when Fry announced his team – which did not even include Daish on the subs bench.

Fry quickly revealed that Daish had declined to be a substitute and as a result the player had been fined two weeks wages.

The Birmingham manager said: "Daish has often criticised me for changing a winning team. In this case I took notice of his comments to keep the same team – so everything has rebounded on him.

"Personally, I am very disappointed with his attitude. I have the greatest respect for him and the greatest admiration for him, but what he did today was nothing short of disgraceful."

Fry said that he badly needed Daish as a back-up for his defenders and was bitterly disappointed with the player's attitude.

As events transpired Birmingham were able to generate a great deal of confidence and enthusiasm from their trip to Italy and this was observed by the way in which Andy Edwards and Michael Johnson combined to shut out the threat of Paul Walsh.

Birmingham's task was made all the more easy by Portsmouth's predicament and no one was more pleased than Steve Claridge, who was playing in front of his family and friends on his return to his home town.

The Portsmouth man responded with a 24th minute winning goal when he collected a bad header from Pompey's John Durnin and the Birmingham striker put the ball away from less than ten yards.

Steve Finnan and Jason Bowen later had good chances, but then Birmingham began to tail off, but Portsmouth lacked the fire-power to take advantage of the situation which unfolded in the second half.

Fry admitted that there was little power left in the reserve tank in the closing stages and it was then that Gary Butters gave Birmingham a scare by heading against the post and then watching as Ian Bennett made one of his customary late saves to give his team maximum points.

It was a typical situation for Portsmouth who had won just one of their last 13 games.

Meanwhile, Daish sat in the stand and watched as his colleagues held on desperately in the closing stages in a situation which could have been made a little easier by his inclusion in the side.

Later Daish claimed that there had been a misunderstanding, but he was still drafted into the reseves for the next game against Manchester United at Old Trafford and told to prove himself capable of regaining his place in the first team.

Steve Claridge goes in for a near-post cross.

Saturday 21st October 1995 • St. Andrew's • 3.00pm

BIRMINGHAM CITY 3 GRIMSBY TOWN 1

Halft time 0-0 • *Attendance* 16,445

Referee Mike PIERCE (Portsmouth)

Linesmen J.H. GRIFFITHS and D.J. HINE

Blue Shirts, White Shorts		Goals	Black and White Striped Shirts, Black Shorts		Goals
1	Ian BENNETT		1	Paul CRICHTON	
2	Gary POOLE		2	Brian LAWS	
3	Gary COOPER		3	Gary CROFT	
4	Steve CASTLE ‡		4	Peter HANDYSIDE	
5	Andy EDWARDS ❑		5	Richard SMITH †	
6	Michael JOHNSON		6	Paul GROVES	
7	Jonathan HUNT		7	Gary CHILDS	
8	Steve CLARIDGE	52, 89	8	Jim DOBBIN	
9	Steve FINNAN †		9	Neil WOODS	77
10	Ricky OTTO #		10	Ivano BONETTI ❑	
11	Paul TAIT		11	Nicky SOUTHALL ‡	
	Substitutes			*Substitutes*	
12	Jae MARTIN ‡88		12	Jamie FORRESTER ‡67	
13	Ian RICHARDSON #88		13	Ashley FICKLING †57	
14	Ken CHARLERY †45	72	14	Craig SHAKESPEARE	

BEFORE		P	W	D	L	F	A	pts	AFTER		P	W	D	L	F	A	pts
5	Blues	12	5	4	3	19	12	19	4	Blues	13	6	4	3	22	13	22
11	Grimsby	12	4	5	3	12	12	17	12	Grimsby	13	4	5	4	13	15	17

FACTFILE

Coventry show an interest in teenagers, Jon Bass and Ben Sedgemore... Steve Claridge takes his goals tally to five goals in three games against Grimsby who last won at St. Andrew's in the 1936-37 season... Ken Charlery nets his first goal at St. Andrew's as Birmingham move into fourth place.

In-form Claridge bags a brace

Mid-week news puts Birmingham City once again on the front pages with stories of the club being investigated by the Birmingham Trading Standard officers. Apparently complaints had been made by supporters concerning aspects of the away day club.

As to be expected club owner, David Sullivan, was far from happy with the latest newspaper comments and complained very bitterly about the lack of support from the local media and business people.

Sullivan, a Welshman living in Essex, is a newcomer to the area and does not realise that the history and background of the clubs is littered with such instances.

The club has always been left to paddle its own canoe and it will take a great deal to change the relationship.

Fortunately the club's playing fortunes have taken a dramatic turn for the better and early season optimism is fully justified.

As threatened a week previously by manager Barry Fry there was no place for out of favour skipper Liam Daish, who was left to kick his heels sitting in the directors box.

Fry named an unchanged side to give his new defensive partnership of Andy Edwards and Michael Johnson a vote of confidence and another chance to show what they can do.

But the Mariners prove to be frustrating opposition on the day and the 4-2-4 formation operated by Fry struggles to break down a work-manlike Grimsby defence.

The result is that Birmimgham miserably fail to open their account in the first half despite some good work by youngster Steve Finnan who could consider himself more than a trifle unlucky to lose his place during the interval to out of form Ken Charlery.

But no one could knock Fry as this tactical change certainly had the desired effect as only seven minutes into the second half Steve Claridge obtained his first goal of the game in somewhat controversial circumstances.

Ricky Otto, under orders to provide crosses as often as possible, put in a low centre. Grimsby's goalkeeper Paul Crichton claimed he was impeded by Steve Claridge, who is hit by the ball and watches it trickle over the line for a somewhat fortuitous goal.

Claridge afterwards summed up the goal when he claimed that: "it's all going for me at the moment."

Grimsby then lost their key defender Richard Smith and while attempting to get back into the match left themselves exposed when Ken Charlery collected a Gary Cooper pass to obtain his first goal at St. Andrew's.

At this stage it appeared as if Grimsby would capsize but instead they hit back with substitute Jamie Forrester, on loan from Leeds, forcing Ian Bennett to parry a shot to Neil Woods, who scored an easy goal.

The game became a little hectic but Claridge, in bubbling form, grabbed a third goal in the last minute with a rising shot which cannoned in off the underside of the bar.

Manager Fry was delighted. He said: "With the number of players coming back into the side I know that we can get even better in the future.

"I really am looking forward to the rest of the season because it is going to be very exciting."

Gary Poole and Steve Finnan end another Grimsby attack.

Tuesday 24th October 1995 • St. Andrew's • 7.50pm

BIRMINGHAM CITY 1 TRANMERE ROVERS 1

Half time 1-0 • *Attendance* 13,752

Referee Terry HEILBRON (Newton Aycliffe)

Linesmen P. WALTON and M.A. WILLIAMS

Blue Shirts, White Shorts		Goals	Yellow and Black Striped Shirts, Black Shorts		Goals
1	Ian BENNETT		1	Danny COYNE	
2	Gary POOLE		2	Gary STEVENS	
3	Gary COOPER ❏ ▪		3	Tony THOMAS	
4	Steve CASTLE ‡		4	John McGREAL	2og
5	Andy EDWARDS		5	Shaun TEALE	
6	Michael JOHNSON		6	Gary JONES	
7	Jonathan HUNT		7	Ged BRANNAN	
8	Steve CLARIDGE		8	John ALDRIDGE	
9	Ken CHARLERY		9	Gary BENNETT †	
10	Ricky OTTO †		10	Ian MOORE	75
11	Paul TAIT		11	Pat NEVIN	
	Substitutes			*Substitutes*	
12	Jae MARTIN		12	Graham BRANCH †74	
13	Ian RICHARDSON ‡78		13	Eric NIXON (Gk)	
14	Steve FINNAN †78		14	Shaun GARNETT	

Birmingham fail at their first attempt to reach the last 16 for first time in 13 years... Gary Cooper sent off for third time as a Birmingham player... Still no place for club skipper Liam Daish... Dutch triallist goalkeeper Bart Griemink impresses in the reserves and will be given an extended trial.

Ken Charlery head to head with Gary Stevens.

The Blues Review 1996

Cooper clanger proves costly

Transfer talk still abounds, but there appears a general reluctance to inject any 'new' money into the club with the feeling that manager Barry Fry should go out and generate his own finance if he wants to strengthen his squad.

Heavy rain before the game threatens to put a damper on the proceedings. In the high wind the match is in doubt for a short period as Tranmere Rovers become stranded in heavy motorway traffic.

They eventually make St. Andrew's with about 30 minutes to spare and rush out onto the pitch to see the groundsman remarking the lines after the heavy downpour had washed away his original work.

Birmingham parade an unchanged side in the hope that they make further progress towards Wembley, which means that both Liam Daish and Mark Ward are both still on the sidelines along with several other injured key players.

Tranmere were obviously still in an agitated frame of mind at the start of the game as was highlighted when a high cross from Steve Claridge was headed down by Ken Charlery and John McGreal promptly turned the ball into his own net after only two minutes.

Birmingham were naturally in a confident attacking mode and threatened to over-run Tranmere as they once again dominated the exchanges.

It was then that an incident took place which was to ruin any hopes of a Birmingham victory. Gary Cooper inexplicably handled the ball in midfield under no pressure as if he was doing it for a lark.

The referee had no alternative but to book the Birmingham defender who then found himself in trouble again when he mistimed his tackle just inside Tranmere's half and earned himself another yellow card which was accompanied by the red card.

The disadvantage was not readily apparent as Birmingham continued to attack the Tranmere goal with Danny Coyne making good saves in particular from Jonathan Hunt and Claridge, who was supposedly being watched by Everton manager, Joe Royle.

The player more than likely attracting Royle was the Tranmere teenager, Ian Moore, who forced Ian Bennett to make the save of the game just before the break.

Amazingly Birmingham still carved out the better chances, but the finishing of Ricky Otto left a great deal to be desired as he was far too often wide of the target.

Bennett undoubtedly kept Birmimgham in the game with a fine save from Gary Bennett, who had scored twice on his previous visit to St. Andrew's when he was in the Wrexham team.

As a result of some sterling work by Andy Edwards, Michael Johnson, Paul Tait and makeshift defender Jonathan Hunt, Birmingham managed to retain their slender lead, only to surrender it in the 75th minute.

A cross from Tony Thomas found teenager Moore, son of Tranmere's coach, Ronnie, to head in a fine goal to maintain his goal a game sequence for the Merseyside club.

Afterwards, manager Barry Fry squarely attached Birmingham's failure to win on the shoulders of the hapless Gary Cooper for his needless sending off.

He said: "It would have been a cracking game of football if both teams had been eleven against eleven.

"Cooper only had himself to blame for two silly bookings which were miles away from any danger.

"After his dismissal it was always going to be an uphill battle, but we are still in the fourth round draw."

Sunday 29th October 1995 • Vale Park • 2.55pm

PORT VALE 1 BIRMINGHAM CITY 2

Half time 0-1 • *Attendance* 8,875

Referee Roger GIFFORD (Llanbradach)

Linesmen D.M. HORLICK and M.J. JONES

White Shirts with Black and Yellow Trim, Black Shorts	Goals
1 Paul MUSSELWHITE	
2 Andy HILL	
3 Allen TANKARD	
4 Ray WALKER †	
5 Gareth GRIFFITHS	
6 Dean GLOVER	
7 John McCARTHY ‡	
8 Andy PORTER	80pen
9 Tony NAYLOR	
10 Lee GLOVER #	
11 Steve GUPPY	
Substitutes	
12 Ian BOGIE †70	
13 Stuart TALBOT ‡70	
14 Lee MILLS #70	

Blue Shirts, White Shorts	Goals
1 Ian BENNETT	
2 Gary POOLE	
3 Gary COOPER	
4 Steve CASTLE	
5 Andy EDWARDS	
6 Michael JOHNSON	
7 Jonathan HUNT #	
8 Steve CLARIDGE	71
9 Ken CHARLERY ‡	
10 Jae MARTIN †	
11 Paul TAIT	8
Substitutes	
12 Steve FINNAN †45	
13 Sigurd RUSHFELDT ‡66	
14 Liam DAISH #82	

BEFORE		P	W	D	L	F	A	pts
4	Blues	13	6	4	3	22	13	22
22	Port Vale	13	2	5	6	11	15	11

AFTER		P	W	D	L	F	A	pts
2	Blues	14	7	4	3	24	14	25
24	Port Vale	14	2	5	7	12	18	11

FACTFILE

Birmingham move into second spot – their highest position for three seasons... Just three points behind the leaders Millwall... Birmingham include the Norwegian international striker, Sigurd Rushfeldt on the subs bench... Fourth successive win at Vale Park.

Johnson inspires hard fought win

Birmingham's telephone and fax bill continues to rise following transfer talk which brings in Sigurd Rushfeldt on loan from Tromso IL, and Dutch goalkeeper Bart Griemink for a trial at St. Andrew's.

Manager Barry Fry succumbs to the demand to inject some continental blood into his squad. He admits that he had been averse to such a move in the past but now recognises the benefit of such signings as British players of the same ability would invariably cost a great deal more than he was prepared to pay.

But there is still no room for two of Birmingham's stalwarts, Mark Ward and Liam Daish, who is forced to take up a position on the subs bench.

Following another Saturday off because the game was televised live by Central, Birmingham were fully aware of the task ahead of them at Vale Park where they had won their last three games.

They had been unbeaten in their ten previous matches and their spirits were high when they headed for the Potteries to face a Port Vale side that had hit a very poor playing spell.

This was reflected in the way Birmingham were able to penetrate John Rudge's side in the early stages. Paul Tait for instance went close very early in the game to force Paul Musselwhite to make a fine save.

The industrious Tait, arguably enjoying one of his best spells at the club, could not be denied and popped up after only eight minutes to put the Blues ahead.

Steve Claridge, the joker in the pack off the field but one of the most industrious players on the pitch, provided the cross from which Ken Charley headed the ball back from the far post to Tait who forced his effort over the line.

Following an impressive performance in midweek for the reserves, Jae Martin earned his reward with his first start and responded with several good runs that posed problems for Port Vale's beleagured defence.

On one occasion he set up Claridge, while shortly afterwards Charlery wasted an opening created by Steve Castle.

Port Vale gambled with a triple substitution in the 69th minute and manager John Rudge must have wondered if it had been the right decision as only two minutes later Claridge netted his seventh goal of the season with a tantilising back header which agonisingly crept over the line.

The goal produced a heavy siege by Port Vale to atone and they created numerous problems for Birmingham's defence when Ian Bennett again demonstrated his outstanding ability which attracted Joe Royle to St. Andrew's for the Tranmere game.

Ten minutes from time Blues' skipper Gary Poole handled in the area and Andy Porter, previously denied by Bennett's heroics, converted the spot kick.

Fry was later very far from being happy with the performance. He said: "We dominated them for 20 minutes and then allowed them to take control."

While bemoaning Birmingham's performance Fry announced that Mark Ward had been transfer listed at his own request – one of four players wanting to leave St. Andrew's.

The other ones being goalkeeper Ryan Price, Chris Whyte and Scott Hiley.

Ken Charlery – laid on Paul Tait's early goal.

Saturday 4th November 1995 • St. Andrew's • 3.00pm

BIRMINGHAM CITY 2 MILLWALL 2

Half time 1-0 • *Attendance* 23,016

Referee John KIRBY (Leicester)

Linesmen J.J. ASHMAN and B.J. RUDKIN

Blue Shirts, White Shorts		Goals	Green and White Halved Shirts, Green Shorts		Goals
1	Ian BENNETT		1	Kasey KELLER	
2	Gary POOLE		2	Ricky NEWMAN	
3	Gary COOPER		3	Jason Van BLERK	
4	Steve CASTLE	24	4	Bobby BOWRY ❏	
5	Andy EDWARDS		5	Tony WITTER	
6	Michael JOHNSON		6	Keith STEVENS ❏	
7	Jonathan HUNT ‡		7	Scott TAYLOR	
8	Steve CLARIDGE		8	Alex RAE	85
9	Sigurd RUSHFELDT		9	Uwe FUCHS †	
10	Ricky OTTO †		10	Chris MALKIN	
11	Paul TAIT		11	Maurice DOYLE ❏ ‡	
Substitutes			*Substitutes*		
12	Jae MARTIN †65		12	Kerry DIXON †45	58
13	Richard FORSYTH		13	Dave SAVAGE	
14	Ken CHARLERY ‡68	87	14	Ben THATCHER ‡52	

BEFORE		P	W	D	L	F	A	pts	AFTER		P	W	D	L	F	A	pts
1	Millwall	14	8	4	2	17	11	28	1	Millwall	15	8	5	2	19	13	29
2	Blues	14	7	4	3	24	14	25	4	Blues	15	7	5	3	26	16	26

FACTFILE

34-year-old defender, Chris Whyte is awarded a free transfer by the club... Birmingham fail in their bid to go to the top of the table... Millwall again fail to win at St. Andrew's... Their previous success was in 1969... Birmingham still unbeaten at home... Steve Castle scores his first league goal for the Blues.

Charlery strike salvages a point

Birmingham's dirty linen is again washed in public following a confrontation in print between the transfer seeking Mark Ward and the club's Managing Director, Karren Brady.

Both demonstrated their inexperience in such matters, while manager Barry Fry sat on the fence as he prepared for the crucial home game with Millwall, which everyone hoped would go off without any trouble.

All the silent hopes were dashed even before the game began as it transpired the Millwall coach had been attacked and the two rear windows broken.

The game itself began at a fever pitch and it was unfortunate that subsequent events should over-shadow the match as illustrated in the Daily Mail back-page lead story which contained just one paragraph (the last) on the 90 minutes play!

This is a great pity because Birmingham began, as usual, with a great deal of passion and fire that threatened to sweep Millwall aside. In the opening five minutes Steve Claridge and Ricky Otto both missed two fine chances that could easily have destroyed top of the table Millwall.

Millwall's goalkeeper, Kasey Keller, admitted afterwards: "It was a case of hanging on, because it was obvious that Birmingham would not be able to sustain the pace and pressure they displayed in the opening 20 minutes for the entire match."

The Londoners' defence, however, was suspect and were fortunate to survive. Then in the 24th minute Claridge was impeded by Bobby Bowry and Jonathan Hunt produced a perfect free-kick which was powered home by Steve Castle from about eight yards for his first league goal in Birmingham's colours.

Another goal could have settled the issue in Birmingham's favour, but Millwall held out and the introduction of veteran striker Kerry Dixon quickly paid dividends with a 58th minute equaliser following a close range header.

The game was then fought out at a frantic pace with Millwall looking the more composed the longer the game was in progress, with Birmingham's Norwegian international, Siggy Rushfeldt, struggling to make a real impact on his home debut.

It appeared curtains for Birmingham when the highly rated Alex Rae fired home a shot which took a deflection off Castle in the 85th minute. But two minutes later a mix-up between Keller and Tony Witter saw the ball drop at the feet of substitute Ken Charlery who turned to score from close range for a well merited equaliser.

Manager Fry was disappointed afterwards. "When they scored a second goal, I thought they are now six points ahead of us," he said. "But we deserved a point and I thought we should have won the game."

News of the off the field problems began to filter through with Millwall's manager, Mick McCarthy disclosing that his substitite Dave Savage had allegedly been attacked by a spectator during the game.

Then there was the violence in the crowd after the game – with both clubs denying any involvement in the outrageous scenes which were a sad throw-back to the 1970's.

An F.A. investigation was bound to follow.

Steve Claridge breaks through the Millwall defence.

Wednesday 8th November 1995 • Prenton Park • 7.45pm

TRANMERE ROVERS 1 BIRMINGHAM CITY 3

After extra time
Half time 0-0 • Full time 1-1 • Attendance 9,151
Referee Kevin LYNCH (Knaresborough)
Linesmen R.E. BOWDEN and O. DYCE

White Shirts with Blue and Green Trim, White Shorts		Goals	Black and Silver Striped Shirts, Blue Shorts		Goals
1	Danny COYNE		1	Ian BENNETT	
2	Gary STEVENS		2	Gary POOLE ❏	
3	Tony THOMAS		3	Michael JOHNSON	
4	John McGREAL		4	Mark WARD	
5	Shaun TEALE ❏		5	Andy EDWARDS	
6	Gary JONES		6	Liam DAISH	
7	Ged BRANNAN		7	Jonathan HUNT ‡	
8	John ALDRIDGE	90	8	Steve CLARIDGE	
9	Gary BENNETT †		9	Sigurd RUSHFELDT †	48
10	Ian MOORE		10	Steve CASTLE #	
11	Pat NEVIN		11	Paul TAIT	
	Substitutes			*Substitutes*	
12	Graham BRANCH †74		12	Steve FINNAN ‡90	
13	Eric NIXON (Gk)		13	Ricky OTTO #90	
14	Shaun GARNETT		14	Ken CHARLERY †69 ❏	96,115

F A C T F I L E

Birmingham make the last 16... Matchwinner Ken Charlery takes his goals tally to three in two games... Liam Daish and Mark Ward recalled following lengthy absences... Ward still transfer listed and hoping to impress the management of Tranmere, whom he is looking to join.

Siggy Rushfeldt gets in a flying header on the Rovers goal.

. . . Now it's – bring on Juninho

No one needed reminding that a trip back to Prenton Park evoked some sad memories for every Blues fan. It was back in May 1994 that Birmingham inflicted a 2-1 defeat on the Merseyside club and were still relegated to the Second Division.

But it was a game which manager Barry Fry thought should have been unnecessary because Birmingham should have won the first match at St. Andrew's.

The first half sending off at St. Andrew's of Gary Cooper, however, enabled Tranmere to earn a second chance.

Ironically, Cooper's enforced absence from the replay allowed Fry to recall Liam Daish, who only a few days previously had been sent off in a reserve game against West Bromwich Albion.

Birmingham's skipper bemoaned his bad luck which originated with his selection for the Republic of Ireland squad. Upon his return to Birmingham he found himself ousted from the team, due to the fine form of Michael Johnson and fined after failing to appear on the substitutes bench.

He was fined for that transgression and picked up a similar fine for the sending off which meant that technically he played for a month without any pay.

The pre-match talk, however, had overshadowed the game. There had been adverse comments about the Millwall game and then it was also disclosed that Birmingham were considering doing 'a Newcastle' by forming an association with Moseley Rugby Club.

But once the game was under way Birmingham still contrived to make life difficult for themselves even in the replay when they were 'gifted' a goal ten minutes before the break, but

Siggy Rushfeldt somehow failed to hit the target as a result of a desperate clearance by Tony Thomas.

Birmingham, beaten only once in 15 games, made amends three minutes into the second half and fittingly it was new-boy Rushfeldt who grabbed the vital goal when the Norwegian striker forced his way onto a Michael Johnson cross to head past Andy Coyne.

The goal appeared to be sufficient as Birmingham, never in arrears in the two games, defended their slender lead, but in the last minute of normal time the talented Ian Moore headed Pat Nevin's centre back across the goal from the far post, for the prolific John Aldridge to scramble the equaliser.

With the game going into extra time Fry's response was to send on Ken Charlery and Ricky Otto and once again these moves were richly rewarded.

Six minutes into extra time Charlery steered a Steve Claridge pass into the net and sealed Tranmere's fate with a well directed header from just outside the six yard box from an accurate left wing cross by Otto.

It was a high quality performance of which everyone in the Birmimgham club could be justly proud.

Fry was naturally well pleased with a victory which earned a fourth round trip to meet Middlesbrough and the famous Juninho.

Birmingham's boss said: "We can now look forward to making further progress, because my team can take on any side in the country and not be disgraced.

"Personally, I feel we have been vastly underrated by a lot of people. The Middlesbrough game will be interesting. What I would like is a draw at Middlesbrough and a win in the replay at St. Andrew's."

Steve Claridge was also optimistic and gave a warning to Juninho not to expect an easy ride when he comes up against the likes of Andy Edwards, Michael Johnson and Liam Daish.

Saturday 11th November 1995 • Elm Park • 3.00pm

READING 0 BIRMINGHAM CITY 1

Half time 0-0 • *Attendance* 10,203

Referee Neale BARRY (Scunthorpe)

Linesmen B.C. FISH and E.W. GREEN

Blue and White Shirts, White Shorts		Goals	Red Shirts with Blue and White Trim, Red Shorts		Goals
1	Chris WOODS		1	Ian BENNETT	
2	Ken BROWN ❑		2	Gary POOLE ❑	
3	Micky GOODING ❑		3	Michael JOHNSON	
4	Jimmy LAMBERT		4	Mark WARD ❑	
5	Andy BERNAL		5	Andy EDWARDS	
6	Keith McPHERSON		6	Liam DAISH	
7	Micky GILKES		7	Jonathan HUNT †	
8	Phil PARKINSON		8	Steve CLARIDGE	
9	Lee NOGAN		9	Sigurd RUSHFELDT ‡	
10	Stuart LOVELL †		10	Steve CASTLE #	
11	Paul HOLSGROVE		11	Paul TAIT	
	Substitutes			*Substitutes*	
12	Stephan SWALES †81		12	Steve FINNAN †45	
13	Robert CODNOR		13	Ken CHARLERY ‡45	74
14	Tom JONES		14	Ricky OTTO #45	

BEFORE		P	W	D	L	F	A	pts	AFTER		P	W	D	L	F	A	pts
4	Blues	15	7	5	3	26	16	26	3	Blues	16	8	5	3	27	16	29
17	Reading	15	4	6	5	20	22	18	17	Reading	16	4	6	6	20	23	18

FACTFILE

Gary Cooper fit again, but Fry keeps an unchanged team... Gary Poole keeps the Captain's armband... Birmingham extend their unbeaten run to 13 and the eighth in the league... Charlery grabs his fifth goal in four games... They move up into third place just three points behind the leaders, Leicester City.

Substitutions pay off again

Peace and quiet for a few days prior to the weekend game at Reading and it is accompanied by a growing belief that this is going to be another memorable season.

Surprise, surprise, past differences involving Mark Ward and Liam Daish with manager Barry Fry are patched up.

Fry quickly discounts rumours linking Daish with Wimbledon in a big money deal, while the Birmingham boss reveals that he is prepared to talk fresh terms with Ward early in the new year.

Ward is one of 21 Birmingham players who will be out of contract at the end of the season and they all face the prospect of lengthy talks with Manager, Barry Fry.

The bubbling Birmingham boss retained the team which began at Tranmere in midweek, but is obviously unhappy with the early showing of several players as the game struggles to come to life.

Jonathan Hunt lacked his usual positive approach, while Steve Castle was not so happy in a left sided role after some impressive displays when he kept Ward out of the team.

The result was that Reading created plenty of trouble and strife for Birmingham and were unlucky not to take the lead on a couple of occasions.

But Birmingham's mean machine kept out the opposition and with only 16 goals conceded in 15 games they are building a solid foundation for their promotion launch pad.

The gambling streak in Fry was revealed at the start of the second half. He usually waits until the last 30 minutes before making any substitutions, but on this occasion he plumped for naming all three substitutes after the half time break.

Castle, Hunt and Siggy Rushfeldt, who had a promising first half when he often created problems for the Reading defence, made way for Steve Finnan, Ricky Otto and of course, super sub, Ken Charlery, but it was Reading who created the more danger in the early period of the second half.

Birmingham had their moments with the industrious Steve Claridge quickly setting up goalscoring opportunities for Charlery.

The vital breakthrough, however, came in the 74th minute when Charlery took the ball from Micky Gilkes and scored with a low shot, to record his fourth goal in eight days and his fifth in four matches. This goal certainly vindicated Charlery, but still left him in the situation whereby manager Fry did not consider him as a first choice to start a match.

A jovial Fry, wise-cracking all the time, admitted afterwards: "You play Ken Charlery for 90 minutes and he's hopeless! As a substitute he's brilliant. It's little wonder he has no way of starting a game!"

Charlery admitted: "Obviously I would like to be first choice and there is not a great deal more I can do at the present time.

"I'm enjoying myself now after a shaky start and all I can do is to keep scoring goals and the rest is up to the manager."

Sigurd Rushfeldt leaves his marker for dead.

Wednesday 15th November 1995 • Conero Stadium • 2.00pm

ANCONA 1 BIRMINGHAM CITY 2

Half time 0-2 • Attendance 1,000

Referee John LLOYD (Wrexham)

Linesmen Sig. MONTAINE and Sig. RICCIARDELLI

Red Shirts, Red Shorts		Goals	Blue Shirts, White Shorts		Goals
1	Paulo ORIANDONI		1	Ian BENNETT	
2	Luigi CORINO †		2	Richard FORSYTH	
3	Vincenzo ESPOSITO ❑		3	Michael JOHNSON ❑ †	
4	Carlo CORNACCHIA		4	Steve CASTLE ‡	
5	Francesco TOMEI		5	Andy EDWARDS	29
6	Davide TENTONI	33 og	6	Liam DAISH	
7	Carlo CAVALLIERE ‡		7	Jonathan HUNT	
8	Mario SESIA	53	8	Ken CHARLERY	
9	Mario LEMME #		9	Sigurd RUSHFELDT	
10	Gincomo MODICA		10	Ricky OTTO	
11	Fabio LUCIDI		11	Paul TAIT ❑ #	
	Substitutes			*Substitutes*	
12	Roberto MAGNANI †14		12	Gary COOPER †56	
13	Matteo BARTOLINI ‡23		13	Ian RICHARDSON ‡61	
14	Edoardo ARTISTICO #31 ❑		14	Steve FINNAN #67	
15	Grabiano VINTI		15	Steve CLARIDGE	
16	Stefano RICCI		16	Jae MARTIN	

BEFORE	P	W	D	L	F	A	pts	AFTER	P	W	D	L	F	A	pts
2 Blues	2	1	0	1	3	3	3	1 Blues	3	2	0	1	5	4	6
3 Ancona	2	1	0	1	1	2	3	4 Ancona	3	1	0	2	2	4	3

FACTFILE

Birmingham's win puts them on top of their group ahead of Port Vale...
Ken Charlery starts the match as a reward for his goalscoring performances...
Skipper Gary Poole and Steve Claridge are not in the starting line-up.

First half goals set up victory

Birmingham did not attempt a repeat of their travel arrangements from the previous tie. Instead they flew out the day before the re-arranged game because it was an afternoon kick-off.

On this occasion everything went to plan – until the start of the match.

What should have been a low-key game turned out to be a major incident with both clubs claiming the other was to blame for the unfortunate fracas.

The real problem was that Birmingham took control, following a rather tame start to the match, when Andy Edwards moved up to head home an accurate free-kick from Jonathan Hunt.

Only four minutes later Siggy Rushfeldt's cross was diverted into the Ancona net by Davide Tentoni and this was too much for the home side.

A few minutes later Paul Tait and Mario Sesia clashed with both players retaliating. Quickly there was a lot of pushing between players and then the Ancona coach, Edoardo Cacciatori, raced onto the pitch and attacked Tait.

Surprisingly, referee John Lloyd of Wrexham did not take any action other than to book Tait. It was hardly a decision to calm down the players and the Italians responded with a series of offences which did little to enhance their reputation.

Ancona pulled back a goal in the 53rd minute through Sesia and it should, in normal circumstances, have set up the match for an exciting finish.

Unfortunately, the game was a shambles with Tait, Steve Castle, Rushfeldt and physiotherapist, Neil McDiarmid, all involved in skirmishes with the Italians.

Even substitute Jae Martin did not escape the wrath of the Ancona coach, late in the game he headed a ball away from the dugout area and Cacciatori was so annoyed by this action that he confronted the Birmingham player, only to be prevented from any act of aggression by coach David Howell.

The final whistle saw the Italians go down the tunnel first with manager Barry Fry and Tait the last two off the field accompanied by the referee.

It was at this point that matters allegedly got out of hand.

Cacciatori sustained a broken cheek-bone and had to be taken to hospital, while referee Lloyd damaged his hand, which also required treatment.

Birmingham officials and players vigorously denied any involvement, but serious accusations were later made by the Italians.

Fry said after the game: "It was an absolute disgrace what happened. The Ancona coach ran on to the pitch and grabbed both Tait and Ricky Otto.

"I almost died when I saw it because if I had done that sort of thing in England I would have been kicked out of football."

It later transpired that the police requested the passports of Michael Johnson, Jae Martin and David Howell. They were copied and returned to all three.

Over 24 hours later the Italians were still complaining bitterly, with threats of making a request to extradite some of the Birmingham players, demonstrating the lack of tact which had prevailed from the start of the sorry incident-packed game, which was further inflamed by the intrusion of Cacciatori onto the field to attack Tait.

In the aftermath of allegations and counter allegations Kevin Keegan revealed that Cacciatori had been involved in a similar incident two years previously in a game against his side, Newcastle United.

Saturday 18th November 1995 • Kenilworth Road • 3.00pm

LUTON TOWN 0 BIRMINGHAM CITY 0

Half time 0-0 • *Attendance 7,920*

Referee Jim RUSHTON (Stoke-on-Trent)

Linesmen J.R. HUBBARD and T.J. POLLARD

White Shirts with Blue Sleeves, Blue Shorts	Goals	Red Shirts with Blue and White Trim, Red Shorts	Goals
1 Ian FEUER		1 Ian BENNETT	
2 Trevor PEAKE ❏		2 Scott HILEY	
3 Marvin JOHNSON		3 Gary COOPER ❏	
4 Julian JAMES		4 Mark WARD	
5 Ceri HUGHES		5 Andy EDWARDS ❏	
6 Paul McLAREN †		6 Michael JOHNSON	
7 Graham ALEXANDER ❏		7 Jonathan HUNT ❏	
8 Scott OAKES		8 Steve CLARIDGE	
9 Vidar RISETH		9 Ken CHARLERY ‡	
10 Dwight MARSHALL ‡		10 Ricky OTTO #	
11 Richard HARVEY		11 Paul TAIT †	
Substitutes		*Substitutes*	
12 Stuart DOUGLAS †73		12 Steve FINNAN †45	
13 Tony THORPE ‡84		13 Sigurd RUSHFELDT ‡58	
14 David OLDFIELD		14 Jae MARTIN #63	

BEFORE	P	W	D	L	F	A	pts	AFTER	P	W	D	L	F	A	pts
3 Blues	16	8	5	3	27	16	29	3 Blues	17	8	6	3	27	16	30
23 Luton	16	3	4	9	11	23	13	23 Luton	17	3	5	9	11	23	14

FACTFILE

Birmingham's fifteenth game without defeat... Only the third goalless draw of the season... Liam Daish misses the first of three games due to suspension... Gary Cooper returns from a one match ban... Scott Hiley is a twelfth hour replacement for skipper Gary Poole.

Non-stop pressure draws a blank

After the shenanigans in Italy it was a relief to travel the few miles down the M1 to Luton for what is almost a home game for manager Barry Fry.

The Battle of Ancona still rumbles on, but it is back to the bread of butter of the Endsleigh League and a bid to close the gap on the league leaders.

Birmingham go into the game against the struggling Hatters in third spot, but it is their fourth successive away game (the previous three all having been won) and a few players have collected some injuries, whilst others have been taken ill.

Skipper Gary Poole was ruled out and Richard Forsyth was to continue in the number two shirt, but he went down with flu and Scott Hiley was rushed to Kenilworth Road to make his first appearance since September.

Steve Claridge was not 100 per cent fit either after having picked up a tummy bug during the trip to Italy.

Earlier in the week Luton had indicated that the game was in doubt because nine of their players had flu. But it was Luton who made the early running with Dwight Marshall looking particularly dangerous.

Luton, however, were never able to break through Birmingham's defence to test Ian Bennett, who had one of his easiest games of the season.

By the same token Birmingham lacked drive and penetration. Claridge, the former Luton player, was not his usual sparkling self, while Ken Charlery began the game and again failed to score.

It only supported the theory of manager Fry that Charlery's biggest asset is sitting on the bench before making a belated entry into the game to emerge onto the pitch to score the winning goal.

Second half substitutions failed to do the trick on this occasion as the game tailed off badly despite Mark Ward's industrious display in midfield.

Jonathan Hunt, who had a quiet spell in recent games, moved into a midfield role alongside Ward.

He produced several good passes and on one occasion sent Claridge clear, but no one was able to get on the end of the cross, an event which generally summed up Birmingham's performance on the day.

The best chance fell to substitute Jae Martin in the closing minutes when the Birmingham player's shot was deflected wide by Ian Feuer and justice was done.

Manager Fry, reluctant to make too many comments about the mid-week trip to Italy, did quip: "At least the game was trouble-free, but my lads didn't know what to expect afterwards when they saw the Luton players at the end of the tunnel.

"It turned out they wanted to say 'well done' so that was a pleasant change after Ancona.

"But the match and the trip took a lot out of the players and with games coming up thick and fast it is good that we have a big squad of players available to step in when required."

Ken Charlery takes evasive action.

Tuesday 21st November 1995 • St. Andrew's • 7.45pm

BIRMINGHAM CITY 1 DERBY COUNTY 4

Half time 1-2 • *Attendance* 19,417

Referee Kevin BREEN (Liverpool)

Linesmen A.N. BUTLER and J. HOLBROOK

Blue Shirts, White Shorts		Goals
1	Ian BENNETT	
2	Scott HILEY	
3	Gary COOPER	
4	Mark WARD	43 pen
5	Andy EDWARDS	
6	Michael JOHNSON	
7	Steve FINNAN †	
8	Steve CLARIDGE	
9	Sigurd RUSHFELDT ‡	
10	Ricky OTTO	
11	Paul TAIT #	

Substitutes

12	Jae MARTIN #47	
13	Jonathan HUNT †45	
14	Ken CHARLERY ‡45	

White Shirts, Black Shorts		Goals
1	Russell HOULT ❏	
2	Gary ROWETT	
3	Chris BODEN	
4	Daryl POWELL †	73
5	Dean YATES ❏	
6	Igor STIMAC	
7	Robin VAN DER LAAN ‡	
8	Dean STURRIDGE ❏	5
9	Ronnie WILLEMS	40
10	Marco GABBIADINI	47
11	Lee CARSLEY	

Substitutes

12	Paul SIMPSON ‡86	
13	Steve SUTTON (Gk)	
14	Sean FLYNN †85	

BEFORE		P	W	D	L	F	A	pts	AFTER		P	W	D	L	F	A	pts
3	Blues	17	8	6	3	27	16	30	3	Blues	18	8	6	4	28	20	30
10	Derby	17	6	6	5	22	23	24	8	Derby	18	7	6	5	26	24	27

FACTFILE *A flu bug is sweeping the club – Swedish triallist, Dan Sahlin, is draughted into the squad... Birmingham become the last team in the First Division to lose their record of not having lost at home... It also ended a run of fifteen games without defeat... League leaders Millwall and Leicester both drop vital away points.*

"Men against boys" says Fry

The ramifications of the Ancona affair still lingered over St. Andrew's with the Football League awaiting reports from Italy and St. Andrew's before deciding on what action, if any, to take.

It is not a happy situation, but the problem facing manager Barry Fry was the dwindling number of players at his disposal because of injuries and illness.

The performance at Luton in the previous game was of great concern, as Birmingham looked as if they were in danger of becoming a little frayed at the edges.

Fry, however, was hoping that a return to St. Andrew's after four successive away games would give his side the necessary lift to regain some of their best form.

But they were facing a Derby side beaten only once in their previous eight games and reportedly showing a big improvement after sorting out their early season problems.

Jim Smith's influence on the side has been readily apparent, while Birmingham's high profile off the field has only added to internal problems.

As early as the fifth minute Birmingham were exposed and a vibrant Derby County side, looking yards faster and far better organised, put their mark on the game with an astutely taken goal that should be noted by the stereotype coaches.

It is hardly a coincidence that Smith is of the old school and obviously a keen believer in making the ball do most of the work.

Robin Van Der Laan was the mid-field inspiration for the opening goal described in one quarter as 'simple' – the person concerned failing completely to understand the basics of wrong-footing the opposition.

Van Der Laan engineered the goal by slipping his pass on the inside of Scott Hiley and Dean Sturridge ran through to hit the ball to the left of Ian Bennett.

Sturridge, brother of the former Birmingham player, Simon, who is also having a good goalscoring spell at Stoke City, gave a real live-wire performance for the Potters, highlighted by his ability to make good use of space and a quick turn of speed.

Birmingham were completely under a cloud and Derby increased their lead five minutes before the break when Johnson headed clear, but the ball only went to Van Der Laan who quickly headed it back in the direction from which it had come.

Johnson was unable to head the ball out and Sturridge raced through to square a low pass to Ron Willems to score from the edge of the six yard box.

Two minutes before the break Steve Claridge was bundled over in the penalty area by Gary Rowett and Mark Ward calmly converted the spot kick.

The lack of application by Birmingham was exposed again two minutes into the second half when Van der Laan, once again, produced an adroit pass to Sturridge who was unmarked as he made a run down the left and his high cross to the far post was headed in by Marco Gabbiadini.

Birmingham might have got back into the game when Ken Charlery went through, but he could only fire straight at Russell Hoult and that was the end of any hope of salvaging their unbeaten run.

Daryl Powell scored another 'simple' goal by moving onto a Gabbiadini pass to complete Birmingham's horror show, described by manager Barry Fry as "men against boys and we were the boys".

He added: "We could have gone top, but if we play like we have for the last two games we could finish bottom."

Sunday 26th November 1995 • St. Andrew's • 2.55pm

BIRMINGHAM CITY 2 LEICESTER CITY 2

Half time 1-2 • *Attendance* 17,350

Referee David ALLISON (Lancaster)

Linesmen D.S. BREMNER and A.C. HOWELLS

Blue Shirts, White Shorts		Goals	Yellow Shirts, Yellow Shorts		Goals
1	Ian BENNETT		1	Kevin POOLE	
2	Richard FORSYTH		2	Simon GRAYSON ❑	15
3	John FRAIN ❑		3	Mike WHITLOW	
4	Steve CASTLE †		4	Frank ROLLING	
5	Chris WHYTE ❑		5	Brian CAREY	
6	Michael JOHNSON		6	Garry PARKER	
7	Jonathan HUNT	30, 49 pen	7	David LOWE	
8	Steve CLARIDGE		8	Scott TAYLOR	
9	Kevin FRANCIS ‡		9	Mark ROBINS †	
10	David PREECE		10	Iwan ROBERTS	9
11	Danny HILL ❑ #		11	Colin HILL	
	Substitutes			*Substitutes*	
12	Dan SAHLIN #75		12	Julian JOACHIM	
13	Kenny LOWE †68		13	Richard SMITH	
14	Ken CHARLERY ‡68		14	Emile HESKEY †89	

BEFORE	P	W	D	L	F	A	pts	AFTER	P	W	D	L	F	A	pts
3 Leicester	18	9	4	5	28	20	31	4 Leicester	19	9	5	5	30	22	32
6 Blues	18	8	6	4	28	20	30	5 Blues	19	8	7	4	30	22	31

FACTFILE

Eight Birmingham players missing from the side which played Derby County... Kevin Francis makes his first senior appearance of the season following a close season operation... New on loan signings, David Preece (Derby) and Danny Hill (Spurs) go straight into the side.

Heroic display by makeshift side

Injuries, illness and loss of form took their toll of Birmingham City – and manager Barry Fry reacted in the only way he knows – wholesale changes.

He called up John Frain for the first time since the Charlton defeat in September and immediately made him captain – the fourth different player to wear the armband this season.

Veteran transfer-listed Chris Whyte is also back in the side, while David Preece checks in on loan from Derby County and Danny Hill of Spurs is also included in the team.

On the subs bench is Dan Sahlin, a recruit from Hammarby IF, while Kenny Lowe is recalled from his on loan spell at Hartlepool.

The end result in Fry's own words is "a Mickey Mouse side".

It was hardly surprising that such a makeshift side should be completely disorganised at the outset – a dangerous predicament when faced by a side that would go to the top of the table if they were to record a win.

With no obvious game-plan and a side which was lop-sided, Birmingham were at an immediate disadvantage against a team which had, in Iwan Roberts, a potential match winner.

The danger of Roberts was quickly highlighted when the Leicester striker gained possession from a Simon Grayson cross. He appeared to be as surprised as the Birmingham defence because his first effort hit the post but he put away the rebound to give Leicester a shock 9th minute advantage.

When Grayson collected a Garry Parker right wing corner to fire a rising cross shot past Ian Bennett six minutes later it appeared as if Birmingham were to suffer a second successive home humiliation.

Pride and determination added to a moment of sheer magic rescued Birmingham from the brink of disaster.

In the 30th minute a Steve Claridge cross from the left was brought down by Jonathan Hunt with his right foot and before the ball touched the ground he had hammered his 30 yard left footed shot past Leicester's 'keeper, Kevin Poole.

The goal ended a personal barren spell of 15 games for Hunt – which surprisingly corresponded with Birmingham's commendable unbeaten run.

An outstanding save by Bennett from Roberts prevented a further Leicester goal before the interval, when Birmingham were able to regroup and earn some hard-won praise from Fry.

Fired up by their interval pep-talk Birmingham surged at Leicester and it was Frain who went galloping into the opposition area only to be brought down by Scott Taylor.

Hunt moved up to take the 49th minute spot kick to put Birmingham on level terms – a situation which was to remain unchanged for the rest of the game.

On the over-all play it was a result which neither side could complain about on the day. Leicester's manager, Mark McGhee, did give vent to his feelings about the linesman flagging before Birmingham's first goal and then taking no action, but generally a draw was a fair result for both teams.

Fry admitted: "It was a bit of a Mickey Mouse team, but they played like heroes. After being two down in the first 15 minutes, I was more than delighted to get a point."

Kevin Francis rises to the occasion.

Wednesday 29th November 1995 • Riverside Stadium • 7.45pm

MIDDLESBROUGH 0 BIRMINGHAM CITY 0

Half time 0-0 • *Attendance* 28,031
Referee Billy BURNS (Scarborough)
Linesmen M.J. DOUGLAS and C.H. WEBSTER

Red Shirts, White Shorts		Goals	Black and Silver Striped Shirts, Blue Shorts		Goals
13	Gary WALSH		1	Ian BENNETT ❏	
2	Neil COX		2	Richard FORSYTH	
3	Chris MORRIS		3	Michael JOHNSON †	
4	Steve VICKERS		4	Steve CASTLE	
5	Nigel PEARSON		5	Andy EDWARDS	
6	Craig LIDDLE ❏		6	Liam DAISH	
7	Nick BARMBY		7	Jonathan HUNT ❏	
8	Jamie POLLOCK		8	Steve CLARIDGE	
9	Jan Aage FJORTOFT †		9	Kevin FRANCIS	
10	JUNINHO		10	John FRAIN ❏	
11	Phil STAMP		11	Danny HILL	
	Substitutes			*Substitutes*	
1	Alan MILLER (Gk)		12	Chris WHYTE	
12	Craig HIGNETT †72		13	Louie DONOWA †45	
14	Jaime MORENO		14	Ken CHARLERY	

FACTFILE

Birmingham are accompanied to the North East by 2,600 of their supporters... Liam Daish back in action after a three match suspension... Andy Edwards returns to the side after missing the Leicester game with illness... Birmingham's first visit to the new Riverside Stadium.

Jonathan Hunt just fails to make contact.

Daish inspires wonder show

There was a pre-match shock with news that Barry Fry had listed 14 players in a clear-out aimed at making the playing staff more flexible.

Ken Charlery was one of the 14 and he ruefully admitted: "Going into training you never know who you will meet. Invariably you are being introduced to yet another new signing."

Others on the list included Mark Ward, Ricky Otto, Steve Castle, John Frain, Chris Whyte and Kenny Lowe. It was obvious that Fry was under orders to clear the decks following the arrival of some players from the Continent.

Whether the continental flavour will change the St. Andrew's aroma is debatable, but on the strength of recent visits to Italy, club officials might well have been strongly recommended to steer another course.

Despite uncertainty in some quarters, Birmingham still arrived in Middlesbrough determined to prove themselves hardy cup fighters of the highest quality.

Blackburn and Liverpool may have been casualties at the new Riverside Stadium, but Birmingham tackled their task with a keen spirit and were determined to brush aside the highly talented Juninho.

The result was that Middlesbrough ran headlong into opposition that was in no mood for turning and found themselves in a dour battle.

Fry's fighters were the more dangerous in a first half which took a long time to come alive. Then, in quick succession, John Frain forced Gary Walsh to make an acrobatic save and Steve Claridge tested the former Manchester United 'keeper.

Birmingham's luckiest let-off occurred when goalkeeper Ian Bennett dashed from his goal and handled the ball outside his area.

This earned the 'keeper a yellow card when it was a red card job. Birmingham prospered from this let off and were indebted to some outstanding saves by Bennett.

The best chance of an upset occurred early in the second half when Louie Donowa, back in action following a lengthy spell on the side lines, on the 'disability list' as they say in the USA, missed a good chance at the far post.

Donowa, who took over at the break from Michael Johnson, was unable to control the ball after Walsh had been beaten by a long cross from Jonathan Hunt and missed the chance from just three yards.

Juninho faded from the game and it was often Jan Fjortoft who was the main danger to Birmingham's chances of earning a replay.

But Birmingham survived with growing optimism and the prospect of another big night of cup soccer back at St. Andrew's was a major spur. Following the disappointment of previous games, Fry was delighted with the performance and in particular the displays of Bennett and Liam Daish.

He said: "I defy anyone to show me a better goalkeeper than Bennett or a better central defender than Daish in the Premier Division.

"The team were great. They battled for the entire game and also produced some good football. Everyone enjoyed a fine game and I am looking for a repeat in the replay and naturally a win to take us into the fifth round."

Andy Edwards gets shirty with Juninho.

Saturday 2nd December 1995 • Roots Hall • 3.00pm

SOUTHEND UNITED 3 BIRMINGHAM CITY 1

Half time 2-1 • *Attendance 7,700*

Referee Richard POULAIN (Huddersfield)

Linesmen M.R. HALSEY and F.R. CRICK

Blue Shirts, Blue Shorts		Goals
1	Simon ROYCE	
2	Keith DUBLIN	
3	Chris POWELL	
4	Mike LAPPER	
5	Mick BODLEY	44
6	Phil GRIDELET	
7	Mike MARSH	
8	Paul BYRNE	70
9	David REGIS	45
10	Gary JONES	
11	Julian HAILS	
	Substitutes	
12	Andy THOMSON	
13	Steve TILSON	
14	Paul READ	

Red Shirts with Blue and White Trim, Red Shorts		Goals
1	Ian BENNETT	
2	Richard FORSYTH	
3	John FRAIN	
4	Steve CASTLE †	
5	Andy EDWARDS	
6	Liam DAISH	
7	Jonathan HUNT #	
8	Steve CLARIDGE	29
9	Kevin FRANCIS	
10	David PREECE ‡	
11	Danny HILL	
	Substitutes	
12	Louie DONOWA †18	
13	Gary POOLE ‡56	
14	Ken CHARLERY #56 ❑	

BEFORE	P	W	D	L	F	A	pts
5 Blues	19	8	7	4	30	22	31
15 Southend	19	6	6	7	19	24	24

AFTER	P	W	D	L	F	A	pts
6 Blues	20	8	7	5	31	25	31
13 Southend	20	7	6	7	22	25	27

FACTFILE *Barry Fry puts 14 players on the open-to-offers list, including record signing, Ricky Otto... Michael Johnson sidelined with a groin strain... Birmingham's third game in seven days... Birmingham's second league defeat in three matches... Last win at Reading on 11 November... Steve Claridge grabs his ninth goal of the season.*

Out-of-sorts City given a lesson

Following the high profile Middlesbrough game the trip to Roots Hall was certainly low key, considering the number of former Southend personnel in the Birmingham camp.

The general uncertainty among the players following the decision to release 14 of the squad created a delayed reaction, as was evident on the strength of the over-all performance.

There had been a genuine desire on the part of Barry Fry to introduce the Danish international, Ronnie Ekelund, into his side at Southend, but the transfer did not materialise with the Birmingham club expressing the view that to all intents and purposes the deal was dead.

As events turned out, it was Southend who were more fired up on the day, with a lethargic Birmingham suffering an early set-back when Steve Castle, one of the 14 informed that he has no future at the club, sustained a facial injury which required seven stitches.

That accident occurred as early as the eleventh minute, but Blues hopes were raised when Steve Claridge prodded the ball home after Kevin Francis had seen his shot bounce off the goalkeeper's legs.

The ungainly Francis struggled to make any impact and to make matters worse Southend staged a grandstand finish to the first half to add to Birmingham's anxiety.

They scored twice in two minutes with both of the goals coming from players who ironically appeared in the Blue of Birmingham City last season.

Birmingham's defence was sadly at fault when they allowed Mick Bodley a free-header from Paul Byrne's free-kick to notch the equaliser that proved to be the turning point of the game.

A minute later goalkeeper Ian Bennett had a nightmare when a snap shot from Byrne, a £50,000 bargain buy from Glasgow Celtic, bounced awkwardly in front of him, hit his chest and bounced back to Dave Regis to convert the rebound.

Byrne was to torment Birmingham's defence again mid-way through the second half when he waltzed his way through without a serious tackle from the Midlanders' defence to score with a low drive.

The main worry for Fry was that so many players were out of form at the same time and the mediocrity of the side was exposed by a Southend team not exactly noted for its high skill factor.

Jonathan Hunt had one of his least inspired games and even Fry's customary second half substitutions, when he sent on Ken Charlery and Gary Poole, failed to ignite a revival.

Fry was fully aware that his side had been well beaten at the end of the day. His blunt comment on the match was that he had no excuses.

Fry added: "We had no zip, no spark and no ideas. I was disappointed with Ian Bennett making such a bad mistake which allowed Dave Regis to get their second goal.

"Now its a case of trying to sort out this mess because we can't allow it to continue, that's for sure."

Steve Castle – his early departure with a nasty facial wound forced a reshuffle.

Saturday 9th December 1995 • St. Andrew's • 3.00pm

BIRMINGHAM CITY 1 WATFORD 0

Half time 0-0 • Attendance 16,970

Referee Clive WILKES (Gloucester)

Linesmen C. JONES and I.A. MADGE

Blue Shirts, White Shorts	Goals		Yellow Shirts with Red and Black Trim, Black Shorts	Goals
1 Ian BENNETT		1	Kevin MILLER	
2 Gary POOLE ❑		2	Darren BAZELEY	
3 John FRAIN		3	Richard JOHNSON	
4 David PREECE ❑		4	Colin FOSTER	
5 Andy EDWARDS		5	David HOLDSWORTH	
6 Liam DAISH		6	Steve PALMER	
7 Jonathan HUNT		7	Andy HESSENTHALER	
8 Steve CLARIDGE		8	Paul WILKINSON	
9 Kevin FRANCIS ❑	51	9	Tom MOONEY	
10 Steve CASTLE		10	Geoff PITCHER †	
11 Danny HILL †		11	Kevin PHILLIPS	
Substitutes			*Substitutes*	
12 Louie DONOWA ‡85		12	Nathan LOWNDES	
13 Steve FINNAN †30 ‡		13	Robert PAGE	
14 Ken CHARLERY		14	Gary PENRICE †76	

BEFORE	P	W	D	L	F	A	pts	AFTER	P	W	D	L	F	A	pts
7 Blues	20	8	7	5	31	25	31	4 Blues	21	9	7	5	32	25	34
19 Watford	20	4	8	8	24	29	20	22 Watford	21	4	8	9	24	30	20

FACTFILE

Birmingham's first win in five games after collecting just two points from a possible 12... But they are still in a group of six clubs on 34 points just three behind the leaders, Sunderland... Kevin Francis scores his first goal of the season in his fourth comeback game.

Blues endeavour wins the day

The Ronnie Ekelund saga is seemingly over, with the Danish international being introduced before the match by Bob Matthews.

On Birmingham's form of the previous few games it would appear that Barry Fry badly needs his inclusion in the side.

Several players, including the transfer listed Mark Ward, are still absent for a game played on treacherous conditions.

Birmingham, as usual, made all the early running but in a goalless first half were thwarted by another inspired performance from their former goalkeeper, Kevin Miller.

The Hornet's 'keeper saved well from the gangling Kevin Francis, but neither side could gain the upper hand in a game where there was very little to choose between either side.

But the tempo and excitement mounted early in the second half and it was the popular Francis who set the game alight with his vital goal after 51 minutes.

The build up occurred when the ball found on-loan Dave Preece some 30 yards from the Watford goal.

He attempted a snap shot which Miller, who has a habit of palming his saves instead of attempting to hold the shot, could only knock down and Francis was in like a shot to head home the rebound from inside the six-yard area.

The 6ft 7ins tall striker was highly delighted with the goal, as were the relieved Birmingham fans.

It was only the fourth game he has played since all his problems began with his knee injury sustained in the Auto Windscreens Shield final at Wembley.

His belated return to the side was welcomed and if Birmingham use his attributes correctly then he could be a menace to the opposition and open the door to more goal opportunities for Steve Claridge.

Birmingham, however, were in luck after their recent struggling performances when Kevin Phillips produced a fast, low centre across the face of the goal, only for on-loan striker Paul Wilkinson to narrowly miss by inches with a connection.

Ian Bennett was in action late in the match, but Birmingham managed to hold on for a win that could easily have been snatched from their grasp, in a game from which Watford manager, Glenn Roeder, felt they should have gained at least a point.

With Fry tied up yet again in talks with Ekelund he did not make his post-match press conference, but on this occasion it was Kevin Francis who held centre stage.

He admitted: "It was an important win for us and from a personal point of view it was great to score after nearly eight months on the sidelines following my knee operation.

"There have been a lot of frustrations and I would have expected to have been eased back into the side through the reserves and not rushed as I have been into the first team.

"But there have been a lot of injuries and I have no complaints, although I feel I need another month before I am fully fit and sharp.

Steve Finnan heads just over the bar.

Wednesday 13th December 1995 • St. Andrew's • 7.45pm

BIRMINGHAM CITY 3   CESENA 1

Half time 1-0 • Attendance 7,813

Referee Gennaro BORRIELLO (Italy)

Linesmen A. LAZZARIN and G. MASSEI

Blue Shirts, White Shorts	Goals	White Shirts, Black Shorts	Goals
1 Ian BENNETT †		1 Andrea SARDINI	
2 Gary POOLE		2 Gianluca ZANETTI	
3 John FRAIN		3 Juri TAMBURINI	75og
4 Richard FORSYTH		4 Filippo MEDRI	
5 Andy EDWARDS #		5 Fabrizio ALBONETTI	
6 Ian RICHARDSON		6 Simone FARABEGOLI	
7 Jonathan HUNT	78	7 Vincenzo MAENZA	
8 Steve CLARIDGE	27	8 Adriano PIRACCINI ‡	
9 Kevin FRANCIS ‡		9 Gianni COMANDINI #	47
10 David PREECE		10 Fabio FAVI †	
11 Louie DONOWA		11 Alessandro TEODORANI	
Substitutes		*Substitutes*	
12 Gary COOPER		12 Davide MICILLO	
13 Bart GRIEMINK (Gk) †59		13 Angelo AFFATIGATO †45	
14 Simon REA #86		14 Andrea FARABEGOLI	
15 Steve FINNAN		15 Emanuele CHIARETTI #65	
16 Ken CHARLERY ‡59		16 Paolo PONZO ‡45	

BEFORE	P	W	D	L	F	A	pts
1 Blues	3	2	0	1	5	4	6
2 Cesena	3	1	2	0	4	3	5

AFTER	P	W	D	L	F	A	pts
1 Blues	4	3	0	1	8	5	9
2 Cesena	4	1	2	1	5	6	5

FACTFILE

Birmingham reach the domestic semi-finals with a home game against West Brom... Bart Griemink becomes 32nd player in 32nd game to be used since the season started... Claridge and Hunt take their goals tally into double figures.

Oh! so easy as Italians collapse

Pre-match talk was the decision of the Italian League and the Football League to ban Birmingham's skipper Liam Daish from all future Anglo-Italian Cup games following the 'Battle of Ancona'.

Birmingham were forced to comply with the order, but were far from happy with the implications of such an instruction.

Barry Fry said: "By their action they indicate that Daish was guilty of the accusations made in Ancona when he is not guilty. It is a dangerous precedent and a situation which we are not very happy about."

There were obvious instructions to Birmingham's players to be on their best behaviour and to their credit they conducted themselves impeccably throughout the entire 90 minutes.

In the absence of Daish manager Fry drafted in Ian Richardson for his first start.

The middle line of Richard Forsyth, Andy Edwards and Richardson are comparatively inexperienced, but this was not shown in the general play on the night.

Cesena put out their stall from the kick-off with a loose line of five defenders – an indication that they would have little inclination to go on the attack.

Kevin Francis emerged as an early danger with a header from a David Preece free kick, only to see Andrea Sardini produce the first of several impressive saves.

Sardini, however, could not hold a Forsyth block-buster in the 27th minute and the razor sharp Steve Claridge was on hand to tap home the rebound.

Very little was seen of the Italians as an attacking unit although Alessandro Teodorani did manage to test Ian Bennett a couple of minutes before the interval.

Two minutes after the break Cesena made a quick movement through the middle with Gianni Comandini streaking forward to hammer home a shot from just outside the penalty area for a surprise equaliser.

But even this goal failed to inspire Cesena to any concentrated attacking play and Birmingham were accorded a lot of space and in particular Louie Donowa.

He gained possession from a Claridge pass and put in a low drive which Juri Tamburini attempted to clear but only succeeded in firing the ball into his own net in the 75th minute.

Two minutes later Claridge set up Jonathan Hunt and he jinked his way through to score with a low angled shot from the left to put the issue beyond doubt and confirm a place in the domestic semi-final.

Fry, who was being interviewed on local radio almost before his players had reached the dressing room, said: "The eyes of the world were on us against Cesena and I thought we conducted ourselves in a proper manner and thoroughly deserved to win.

"To be honest, I told the players to take things easy because I didn't want any trouble.

"Cesena hadn't lost in the competition before facing us, so I was delighted to beat them considering we had so many of our better quality players missing for one reason or another."

Kevin Francis 'Splits' the Cesena defence.

Saturday 16th December 1995 • Boundary Park • 3.00pm

OLDHAM ATHLETIC 4 BIRMINGHAM CITY 0

Half time 1-0 • *Attendance 6,602*

Referee Steve BAINES (Chesterfield)

Linesmen C. BASSINDALE and A.C. HARTEVELD

Blue Shirts, Blue Shorts		Goals	Red Shirts with Blue and White Trim, Red Shorts		Goals
1	Paul GERRARD		1	Ian BENNETT	
2	Ian SNODIN		2	Gary POOLE †	26 og
3	Chris MAKIN		3	John FRAIN	
4	Andrew HUGHES		4	Richard FORSYTH	
5	Richard GRAHAM		5	Andy EDWARDS	
6	Steve REDMOND		6	Liam DAISH	
7	Gunner HALLE	69	7	Jonathan HUNT	
8	Paul RICKERS		8	Steve CLARIDGE	
9	Sean McCARTHY		9	Kevin FRANCIS ‡	56 og
10	Stuart BARLOW	58	10	Ian RICHARDSON	
11	Mark BRENNAN		11	Louie DONOWA	
	Substitutes			*Substitutes*	
12	Darren BECKFORD		12	Kenny LOWE †61	
13	Jon HALLWORTH (Gk)		13	Gary COOPER	
14	David BERESFORD		14	Ken CHARLERY ‡61	

BEFORE		P	W	D	L	F	A	pts	AFTER		P	W	D	L	F	A	pts
4	Blues	21	9	7	5	31	25	34	8	Blues	22	9	7	6	31	29	34
16	Oldham	21	6	9	6	30	26	27	12	Oldham	22	7	9	6	34	26	30

FACTFILE

Blues take squad of 19 to Boundary Park as cover for flu virus sweeping club... Birmingham's heaviest defeat of the season... Ian Richardson makes his first league start... Birmingham crash to their third defeat in five league games and slip four places in the league chart, four points behind the leaders, Sunderland.

Oldham given two goal start

The farcical transfer saga involving Ronnie Ekelund finally collapsed because of a hotel room!

Barry Fry revealed that Birmingham had met all of Ekelund's many demands when it was announced that the Dane was not happy having to swop from the Hyatt Hotel to the New Cobden.

This was the last straw for Fry who had been hoping to include the Barcelona player in the side at Oldham.

Fry said: "The board had been prepared to push the boat out to sign Ekelund and make him our highest paid player. But now I've washed my hands of him."

Ekelund, ironically signed, on loan, a day later for Manchester City who, with the arrival of the midfielder, took their tally of Continental players to four.

Fry, meanwhile, was forced to make two enforced changes for the match at Boundary Park with Danny Hill and Steve Castle the latest flu victims making way for Ian Richardson and Louie Donowa.

Following the goalless draw between the two clubs earlier in the season another hard battle was on the cards, with Birmingham finding themselves under pressure.

The lack of midfield dominance was quickly evident in Bimingham's play and this appeared to restrict the front men against a team which had not won in its previous five league games.

Gary Poole came to Blues' rescue when he headed a Stuart Barlow effort off the line as the former Everton striker quickly indicated his potential danger.

Barlow's persistence was finally rewarded, but in a bizarre way as Poole scored an own goal in the 26th minute with a tremendous header

after Ian Bennett had pushed out a shot from the Oldham striker.

Neither Kevin Francis or Steve Claridge could make much impression against Oldham's defence, but Birmingham were still very much in contention going into the second half.

Barlow wasted a fine chance of beating Bennett, but then in the 56th minute Francis demonstrated to the Oldham players just how easy it was to beat the Birmingham goalkeeper when a corner from Mark Brennan skidded off his head and into his own net.

It was bad enough to be two goals behind but to have given both of them on a plate took a great deal of forgiveness on the part of Barry Fry.

The implications were quickly apparent as Barlow increased Oldham's lead a couple of minutes after the blunder from Francis, when he scored easily after a good cross from Paul Rickers had been put into the path of the Oldham striker by Sean McCarthy.

The goal only confirmed Birmingham's worst performance of the season and raised the question whether the uncertainty of the future of 14 players and the aborted big money signing of Ekelund had taken its toll.

Oldham certainly took advantage of the situation and Gunner Halle notched their fourth after the dangerous Barlow had cleverly headed the ball into the direction of the Norwegian.

Four goals was bad enough, but Oldham could very easily have added to their tally – such was the lack lustre Birmingham performance which was disturbing in the extreme just days before the visit of Middlesbrough.

John Frain is cut down.

Wednesday 20th December 1995 • St. Andrew's • 7.45pm

BIRMINGHAM CITY 2 MIDDLESBROUGH 0

Half time 2-0 • *Attendance* 19,878

Referee Micky PIERCE (Portsmouth)

Linesmen M. CARRINGTON and G. EDGELEY

Blue Shirts, White Shorts		Goals	Red Shirts, White Shorts		Goals
1	Ian BENNETT		13	Gary WALSH	
2	Gary POOLE		2	Neil COX	
3	John FRAIN		3	Curtis FLEMING †	
4	Richard FORSYTH		4	Steve VICKERS	
5	Andy EDWARDS		5	Nigel PEARSON	
6	Liam DAISH		6	Derek WHYTE	
7	Jonathan HUNT		7	Phil STAMP	
8	Steve CLARIDGE		8	Jamie POLLOCK	
9	Kevin FRANCIS ❑ †	11,17	9	Jan Aage FJORTOFT	
10	Danny HILL ‡		10	JUNINHO	
11	Ian RICHARDSON ❑		11	John HENDRIE	

Substitutes			*Substitutes*		
12	Steve BARNES ‡87		1	Alan MILLER (Gk)	
13	Sigurd RUSHFELDT		12	Craig LIDDLE	
14	Louie DONOWA †72		14	Alan MOORE †45	

FACTFILE

Loan star Danny Hill returns after flu... 19-year-old winger Steve Barnes comes in for the first time... Birmingham reach the quarter finals for the first time in 15 years and earn a trip to Norwich, who beat Bolton on penalties at Burnden Park in their replay... Middlesbrough suffer only their fifth defeat of the season.

Kevin Francis scores an eleventh minute goal.

Big Kev blasts Boro out of Cup

The night began on the right note for Birmingham City as they were presented with the Midlands BBC "team of the year" award by Steve Lee before the start of the match.

Overnight snow had to be cleared from the St. Andrew's pitch and conditions were far from ideal when the game started.

Juninho, wearing gloves, was an obvious stranger to such a situation, but the young Brazilian still conspired to show some good touches.

Birmingham, a little shell-shocked after the 4-0 defeat at Boundary Park, in the previous game, went into the match with a miserable record of gaining only five points from their six previous League outings.

Prospects against a Premier League club with only four defeats were not in Blues favour and early Middlesborough dominance indicated that the Midlanders were in for a hectic night against Bryan Robson's side.

There was a claim for a penalty when both Juninho and Jan Fjortoft were brought down at the same time by Ian Bennett, but the referee took the view that the two Middlesbrough players had, in fact, jostled themselves into collision.

It proved to be a crucial turning point, as in Birmingham's first attack in the eleventh minute they took the lead with a fine goal from their giant striker, Kevin Francis.

Jamie Pollock made a mistake and Steve Claridge gained possession to send Francis racing towards the Middlesbrough goal, the lanky striker took the ball into the box before hitting a superb right-foot shot across Walsh and into the far corner of the net.

Francis later claimed: "When I crossed the penalty area white line I simply did what I always do by trying a shot on goal. The ball kept low and went into the far corner of the net."

The Claridge-Francis partnership once more produced the goods six minutes later. A right wing cross again found Francis surprisingly unmarked and he rose high to head home past Gary Walsh.

Manager Barry Fry did one of his dashes of delight down the touchline and it was fully justified as Birmingham dramatically turned the tables on the North East club.

It was a dream start for Birmingham and as the game wore on it was patently obvious that Middlesbrough were not going to break down the spirited resistence of the home side.

Fjortoft was a persistent striker but his efforts, thanks to the excellent work of Daish and Co, were invariably long range shots which Ian Bennett was able to deal with quite easily.

Juninho attempted to revitalise Middlesbrough but to no avail as Birmingham went on to record another smart win.

Fry was highly delighted and Bryan Robson admitted afterwards that he could have no complaints about the result and said afterwards that Blues deserved their victory.

The Birmingham manager admitted: "All the players were marvellous. 'Tiny' Francis came up trumps with another performance which justified me signing him last season.

"He is an awkward player and puts any defence in trouble. He creates situations which make openings for other players.

"Only a crazy manager like myself would have rushed him back into the side after such a long lay off, but I was desperate for another goalscorer to play alongside Claridge.

"Another plus for me was the form of Richard Forsyth and Ian Richardson. They were both in the non-league last season, but they proved that they will run their hearts out for you because they realise the great opportunity they have been given."

Saturday 23rd December 1995 • St. Andrew's • 3.00pm

BIRMINGHAM CITY 1 TRANMERE ROVERS 0

Half time 0-0 • *Attendance* 18,439

Referee Scott MATHIESON (Stockport)

Linesmen G.M. LEE and R. SMITH

Blue Shirts, White Shorts		Goals	White Shirts with Blue and Green Trim, Blue Shorts		Goals
1	Ian BENNETT		1	Danny COYNE	
2	Richard FORSYTH		2	Alan ROGERS	
3	John FRAIN		3	Tony THOMAS	
4	David PREECE		4	Dave HIGGINS	
5	Andy EDWARDS		5	Shaun GARNETT	
6	Liam DAISH		6	Gary JONES	
7	Jonathan HUNT	75	7	Ged BRANNAN	
8	Steve CLARIDGE		8	John ALDRIDGE	
9	Kevin FRANCIS ‡		9	Gary BENNETT ❑	
10	Danny HILL †		10	Ian MOORE	
11	Ian RICHARDSON		11	Pat NEVIN	
Substitutes			*Substitutes*		
12	Steve BARNES		12	Liam O'BRIEN	
13	Sigurd RUSHFELDT ‡80		13	Eric NIXON (Gk)	
14	Louie DONOWA †45		14	Steve MUNGALL	

BEFORE		P	W	D	L	F	A	pts	AFTER		P	W	D	L	F	A	pts
8	Blues	22	9	7	6	32	29	34	4	Blues	23	10	7	6	33	29	37
13	Tranmere	20	8	6	6	32	24	30	14	Tranmere	21	8	6	7	32	25	30

FACTFILE

Only Birmingham's second win in seven games... They move back up into fourth place just three points behind the new leaders, Derby County... Jonathan Hunt takes over as Birmingham's leading marksman with 11 goals... It was Tranmere's fifth successive defeat.

Hit-man Hunt sees off Rovers

On a high from their well merited success over Middlesbrough in mid-week, there was justified optimism that Birmingham would maintain the form they displayed in the Coca-Cola Cup.

But Tranmere are doughty fighters and the pattern of the game was entirely different with the Merseyside club, desperate to get out of a losing streak of four matches, making all the early running.

Gary Bennett, who notched a hat-trick for Wrexham at St. Andrew's last season, was an early problem roving wide on the right.

He collected a ball and produced a low centre which went across a packed goalmouth only two yards from the goal line without anyone getting a touch.

It was a let-off for Birmingham as Tranmere mounted several good attacks before the home side were able to swing forward, only for the Middlesbrough match hero, Kevin Francis, to shoot hopelessly wide following an astute pass from the rapidly improving Ian Richardson.

If Birmingham had any doubts about the outcome they were dispelled in the 20th minute of the match when a Pat Nevin corner hit Andy Edwards on the legs and Ian Bennett had to make a reflex goal line save that, in the end, was worth three points to the Blues.

Bennett was again in action five minutes later pushing away a John Aldridge header as Tranmere did everything but score and break their dismal run of form which has prevented them challenging the league leaders.

In this hectic period it was a chronicle of Tranmere chances and Bennett rising to the occasion to demonstrate his ability as one of the best goalkeepers in the country.

He saved another Niven effort and right on the stroke of half time he denied both Bennett

and teenager Ian Moore with two quick saves in a matter of seconds which must have demoralised the Northern club.

Birmingham's good luck continued in the second period to the misfortune of Tranmere, who were terribly unlucky as was highlighted when Jonathan Hunt put the Blues ahead in the 75th minute.

Hunt collected a lose ball some 25 yards out from Tranmere's goal and let fly with a powerful low shot which took a wicked deflection off the unfortunate Gary Jones to plunge the Merseysiders to their fifth successive defeat, which left the likeable Tranmere manager, John King, speechless.

It was a fortunate goal, but as Barry Fry later reflected, it is often these kind of situations which are the difference between winning a league title or being among the also-rans.

He said: "It wasn't a good performance but a great result. If you are going to win championships, you are going to need that little bit of luck we had in the first half.

"I think we can build upon this performance and when all the players are fully fit we should really be able to turn on the gas.

"At the present time we are not scoring enough goals, but these will come when we hit our best form."

Ian Richardson cuts out a Tranmere attack.

Tuesday 26th December 1995 • Bramall Lane • 12.15pm

SHEFFIELD UNITED 1 BIRMINGHAM CITY 1

Half time 1-1 • Attendance 17,688

Referee Ian CRUIKSHANKS (Hartlepool)

Linesmen D. CHARLTON and P. CALLOW

Red and White Shirts, Black Shorts		Goals	Blue Shirts, White Shorts		Goals
1	Alan KELLY		1	Ian BENNETT	
2	Paul ROGERS		2	Richard FORSYTH	
3	Roger NILSEN		3	John FRAIN	
4	John GANNON †		4	David PREECE	
5	Scott FITZGERALD		5	Andy EDWARDS	
6	David TUTTLE		6	Liam DAISH	
7	David WHITE		7	Jonathan HUNT ❑	
8	Mark PATTERSON	42	8	Steve CLARIDGE	
9	Phil STARBUCK ‡		9	Kevin FRANCIS ‡	27
10	Glyn HODGES		10	Danny HILL †	
11	Mitch WARD		11	Ian RICHARDSON #	
	Substitutes			*Substitutes*	
12	Adrian HEATH †73		12	Steve CASTLE #60	
13	Simon TRACEY (Gk)		13	Sigurd RUSHFELDT ‡60	
14	Mark FORAN ‡84		14	Louie DONOWA †45	

BEFORE		P	W	D	L	F	A	pts	AFTER		P	W	D	L	F	A	pts
4	Blues	23	10	7	6	33	29	37	3	Blues	24	10	8	6	34	30	38
23	Sheffield U.	23	5	6	12	30	42	20	23	Sheffield U.	24	5	7	12	31	43	21

FACTFILE

Kevin Francis grabs third goal in four games... Despite an indifferent run Blues are still in title-chasing pack, moving into third spot behind Derby and Charlton... Sheffield United increased their unbeaten run to three games under the control of new manager Howard Kendall, who took over from long serving 'Harry' Bassett.

Awayday form shows promise

Lack of consistency was the problem facing Barry Fry going into this game and it was a feature which was to emerge again at Bramall Lane. He is still trying to put his finger on why his players cannot reproduce their cup form in the league.

Rather surprisingly, the manager had not been linked with the transfer market before the match and he had himself failed to unload any of his own players.

The result was that he retained the side which had scrambled to a narrow home win over Tranmere.

A sudden upsurge in interest at Sheffield United caught the Yorkshire club a little unawares and they were forced to delay the kick-off for 15 minutes.

Midfielder Jonathan Hunt was prominent in the opening exchanges, but the game quickly developed into a drab, uninteresting encounter which was surprising, because both teams had something to prove.

The crowd's expectation quickly evaporated and there were few highlights of note.

Ian Richardson and Steve Claridge both tested United's Republic of Ireland international goalkeeper, Alan Kelly, without anyone being on hand to capitalise when both efforts were blocked.

The persistent Claridge then emerged with a determined run which ended with a shot which Kelly again could only parry. This time the ball ran invitingly into the path of Kevin Francis for the Birmingham giant to tap home into an empty net.

This gave Birmingham fresh heart, but they were unable to really capitalise upon the situation. They had the upper hand, but Sheffield United, a better team than their league record

suggested going into the match, were always capable of hitting back.

They demonstrated their danger three minutes before the break when Richardson headed out Glyn Hodges' corner straight to newcomer Mark Patterson, who equalised with a looping header into the top right hand corner of the net with Ian Bennett simply unable to even make an effort to keep out the ball.

From Birmingham's point of view the game went downhill, following this equaliser, for a long spell in the second period.

Bennett, who has to keep a careful eye on his own players following two own goals in the previous away game at Oldham, was in action keeping out a back-header from Richardson.

Liam Daish, under pressure, also went close to notching an own goal after Bennett had pushed David White's cross against the crossbar.

Richardson and Francis made way for Steve Castle and Siggy Rushfeldt on the hour and in isolated raids Birmingham went very close to snatching a win with an effort from Claridge hitting the outside of the post with Kelly well beaten.

This was definitely a better away performance than the previous two games, both of which were lost with the concession of seven goals.

Credit for this goes to Andy Edwards and Liam Daish for keeping a close eye on David White and to Ian Bennett for a brave display.

Fry gave a fair assertion of the match afterwards when he said: "We have had two heavy defeats away from home and it was important to get a result.

"In saying that, the result was better than the performance.

"Sheffield United were the better team in the first half and deserved their goal. If we had nicked it then it would have been an injustice.

"After two away defeats I've got to be happy with a point, but we are still struggling to get a good service from the wings."

Saturday 6th January 1996 • St. Andrew's • 3.00pm

BIRMINGHAM CITY 1 WOLVES 1

Half time 0-1 • *Attendance* 21,349

Referee Robbie HART (Darlington)

Linesmen P. WALTON and M. WILLIAMS

Blue Shirts, White Shorts		Goals	Old Gold Shirts with Black Trim, Black Shorts		Goals
1	Ian BENNETT		1	Mike STOWELL	
2	Gary POOLE ❑	72	2	Andy THOMPSON ❑	
3	John FRAIN		3	Eric YOUNG	
4	Richard FORSYTH		4	Mark ATKINS	
5	Andy EDWARDS		5	Neil EMBLEN †	
6	Liam DAISH ❑		6	Dean RICHARDS	
7	Jonathan HUNT †		7	Mark WILLIAMS	
8	Steve CLARIDGE		8	Don GOODMAN	
9	Kevin FRANCIS ‡		9	Steve BULL	25
10	Ian RICHARDSON		10	Simon OSBORN	
11	Louie DONOWA ❑		11	Dennis PEARCE ‡	
Substitutes			*Substitutes*		
12	Jason BOWEN †70		12	Mark RANKINE †45 #	
13	Gary COOPER		13	Dominic FOLEY #65	
14	Gary BULL ‡70		14	Darren FERGUSON ‡62	

New rule regarding loan players in the FA Cup means Hill and Preece must stand down... It was only the third meeting between the two Midlands clubs in the FA Cup... The first was in 1889-90 when Wolves won 2-1 and on February 19, 1954, again at Molineux, when Birmingham won 2-1.

Ian Richardson goes past Darren Ferguson.

The Blues Review 1996

Poole strike earns a replay

Once again incidents not involving the players took centre stage in the build-up to the vital third round tie.

Wolves should have appeared at St. Andrew's on New Year's Day in an Endsleigh League Division One match, but the game was postponed because of the ice-bound pitch. Comments attributed to Barry Fry, later vigorously denied by Birmingham's manager, were aimed at Wolves for not agreeing to re-arrange the game two days later.

Wolves felt this was not a viable proposition and declined, in view of their own hectic programme over the next few weeks which contains a more than usual number of local derbies, most of them away from home.

Birmingham fans were disgruntled when it was announced that ticket money for the game, other than in exceptional circumstances, would not be refunded.

This was followed by an announcement that Birmingham intended to purchase a club in Ireland to enable them to maintain a flow of players into the club at a low cost.

At the same time some of the youth teams in the community scheme were being disbanded because of the high cost to Birmingham, who thought the money could be better used for first team affairs.

Other than that it was just like normal times at St. Andrew's in preparation for the Wolves tie – the first time that the Molineux men had played at the ground in an FA Cup tie.

They arrived with a depressing record and still seeking their first win under the managerial guidance of Mark McGhee.

Birmingham attempted to swamp Wolves and it was a big surprise when Steve Bull put his side ahead in the 25th minute in an incident in which there appeared to be no apparent trouble to the home side.

Gary Poole, attempting to clear his lines, only succeeded in smashing the ball into Don Goodman. The ball bounced high off the ground and Steve Bull was on hand to head the ball over a stranded Ian Bennett.

Wolves were then subjected to a spell of defensive pressure and in one incident Neil Emblen was injured in a clash with Ian Bennett and had to be taken to hospital with a shoulder injury.

This disrupted Wolves and for much of the second half it was one way traffic, but it was not until the 72nd minute that Birmingham deservedly equalised – with Poole making amends for his earlier miss.

South African international Mark Williams was alleged to have conceded a foul which was quickly taken by Poole. His pass found Steve Claridge and his shot rebounded back into the path of Poole to score with a left foot shot.

Surprisingly it was then that Wolves escaped from their defensive shell to produce a rare attacking spell. But it was to no avail and the game finished all square, despite a late appearance of Bull's cousin, Gary, who very nearly grabbed a winner for Birmingham following his free-transfer move from Nottingham Forest, the striker coming close to scoring on a couple of occasions

The pace of the Wolves substitute, Dominic Foley, caused the Blues defence some problems and he very nearly scored for Wolves from their only worthwhile chance of the match.

Fry was quietly reserved after the match when he said: "I wasn't happy with a draw. We created the chances but our finishing was poor.

"Credit to Wolves. They did their homework well and deserved a second chance.

"I know Mark McGhee thought there was something wrong with our equaliser, but it was only that we took it too quickly for their defence to get organised at the back."

Wednesday 10th January 1996 • Carrow Road • 7.45pm

NORWICH CITY 1 BIRMINGHAM CITY 1

Half time 0-0 • *Attendance 13,208*

Referee Richard POULAIN (Huddersfield)
Linesman P.M. ROBERTS and K.D. Hill

Yellow Shirts, Green Shorts		Goals	Black and Silver Striped Shirts, Blue Shorts		Goals
1	Bryan GUNN		1	Paul SANSOME	
2	Carl BRADSHAW		2	Gary POOLE	
3	Mark BOWEN		3	John FRAIN	
4	Jan MOLBY		4	Richard FORSYTH	
5	Jon NEWSOME †		5	Andy EDWARDS	
6	John POLSTON		6	Liam DAISH	
7	Neil ADAMS ❏		7	Jonathan HUNT ❏ †	
8	Robert FLECK	69	8	Steve CLARIDGE	
9	Darren EADIE		9	Kevin FRANCIS	66
10	Ashley WARD ‡		10	Ian RICHARDSON ❏ ‡	
11	Keith O'NEILL #		11	Louie DONOWA ❏	
Substitutes			*Substitutes*		
12	Spencer PRIOR †23		12	Jason BOWEN †52	
13	Keith SCOTT ‡85		13	Gary COOPER ‡64	
14	Robert ULLATHORNE #88		14	Gary BULL	

FACTFILE

Birmingham's 14th cup match of the season – and still on course for honours... Veteran goalkeeper Paul Sansome, on loan from Southend, because Ian Bennett (broken bone in hand) and Bart Griemink (ankle injury) are both sidelined, becomes the 35th different player used in Birmingham's side this season.

Kevin Francis gives Blues the lead.

The Blues Review 1996

Penalty miss lets Canaries off hook

It transpired that Birmingham City paid a heavy price for their F.A. Cup draw with Wolves. Goalkeeper Ian Bennett sustained a broken finger to rule him out of action for at least a month.

The injury could not have come at a worse time in view of Birmingham's heavy fixture list and the absence of Bennett was compounded when his deputy, Bart Griemink, damaged his ankle while training a couple of days before the trip to Norwich.

With both goalkeepers out of action manager Barry Fry had to launch a hectic search for a replacement and resorted to his trusty, well-tried method of picking up a player who had been a member of one of his previous teams.

On this occasion the choice was Paul Sansome, who had not played in Southend's first team this season and had, in fact, turned out for the reserves against Barnet two days before facing the Norwich attack.

It was a massive gamble for obvious reasons but Fry only had Hobson's choice – he had to take whatever was available.

But Birmingham are old hands at the cup game this season and it was just yet another tough tie. They acquitted themselves exceptionally well in a tie which turned out to be a thriller from start to finish.

They rattled Norwich and only the skill and expertise of Bryan Gunn kept the East Anglia side in the match, as was highlighted when Jon Newsome handled a cross from the ever improving Richard Forsyth.

Jonathan Hunt, who scored a hat-trick against Norwich early in the season and has been very reliable from the spot kick, produced a weak effort which Gunn saved without too much trouble.

Norwich, without a win since 24 November and obviously short of confidence, were encouraged by this save and hit Birmingham with a series of attacks which certainly tested Sansome.

Gangling Kevin Francis conspired to trouble the Norwich defence at every opportunity and demonstrated his potential danger with one effort which hit the post.

A minute later, in the 66th minute, Francis followed up to notch an easy goal after John Polson had blocked a Steve Claridge shot to give Birmingham a well deserved lead which was quickly cancelled out.

Fleck, back at Carrow Road following a far from successful spell with Chelsea, mishit a shot, but was still on target to beat Sansome as the ball bounced over the head of the stranded goalkeeper.

So in the end it was a game which Birmingham could have won but by the same token could have lost.

Barry Fry, on local radio within five minutes of the match being completed, claimed: "I'm gutted that we didn't win.

"The penalty depressed us and gave them a lift, but I thought we should still have won at the end of the day.

"But we are still in the draw for the semi-final and that should give a big lift for the replay. It isn't as if it will be a new experience.

"We appear to make winning a cup tie very difficult for ourselves."

Steve Claridge fights for possession.

Sunday, 14th January 1996 • St. Andrew's • 3.00pm

BIRMINGHAM CITY 3 CHARLTON ATHLETIC 4

Half time 1-3 • *Attendance* 18,539

Referee Phil RICHARDS (Preston)

Linesmen L. BAKER and R. OSBORNE

Blue Shirts, White Shorts		Goals	Red Shirts, Black Shorts		Goals
1	Paul SANSOME		1	Mike SALMON	
2	Gary POOLE		2	John HUMPHREY	
3	John FRAIN †		3	Jamie STUART	
4	Richard FORSYTH	81	4	Paul MORTIMER	
5	Andy EDWARDS ❏	18og, 75	5	Richard RUFUS	
6	Liam DAISH		6	Stuart BALMER	
7	Jonathan HUNT ❏ ‡	1 pen	7	Shaun NEWTON	
8	Steve CLARIDGE #		8	Carl LEABURN	70
9	Gary BULL		9	John ROBINSON ❏	44
10	David PREECE		10	Kim GRANT †	36
11	Louie DONOWA		11	Lee BOWYER	
	Substitutes			*Substitutes*	
12	Kevin FRANCIS #45		12	David WHYTE	
13	Gary COOPER †45		13	Gary NELSON †77	
14	Jason BOWEN ‡45		14	Mike AMMANN (Gk)	

BEFORE		P	W	D	L	F	A	pts	AFTER		P	W	D	L	F	A	pts
4	Charlton	24	10	9	5	31	24	39	2	Charlton	25	11	9	5	35	27	42
6	Blues	24	10	8	6	34	30	38	7	Blues	25	10	8	7	37	34	38

FACTFILE

The last time Charlton won at St. Andrew's was in the 1938-39 season and the score was 4-3!... Birmingham's defeat means that they collected only nine points from nine games... Paul Sansome makes his home debut in place of the injured Ian Bennett... Charlton move into second place.

Comeback too little too late

Alan Curbishley arrived at St. Andrew's with his young team that has cost in total the sum of £275,000. What they lack in experience they more than make up in skill and flair that has made them dark horses for promotion.

The former Birmingham player has been quietly pleased with the form of his London side, but he was to suffer an early set-back as Charlton made a disastrous start.

Louie Donowa made the running down the left and cut inside, only to be tapped on his ankles by Stuart Balmer.

It was the mildest of interceptions so that Donowa attempted in vein to retain his balance only to slip to the floor. Referee Paul Richards awarded a penalty and the game was only 26 seconds old.

Despite his vital penalty miss at Norwich in the previous game Jonathan Hunt determinedly picked up the ball, placed it on the spot and hammered it past Mike Salmon.

This was a perfect start for Birmingham and their fans in front of the television cameras but suddenly the early lead appeared to be a little precarious and there was a feeling that everything was not going according to plan.

Charlton won a corner on the left and Balmer floated the ball goalwards where their talented young striker Carl Leaburn back headed and beat Paul Sansome, only to see the ball smack against the post.

Both Paul Frain and Andy Edwards raced back in an attempt to prevent the ball going over the line and it was the unfortunate Edwards, unable to avoid the rebound, who watched in sheer horror as the ball went into the net for the 18th minute equaliser.

This was a definite warning bell which should have been heeded. Unfortunately, no one appeared to notice and a long ball found a struggling Liam Daish all at sea and the pass went unchecked to the isolated Kim Grant who went forward to score with a low cross shot from the left.

The own goal was bad enough, but without the inspirational form of Ian Bennett, who was nursing a broken finger, Birmingham appeared to be a ragged team.

Worse was to follow a minute before the break when Lee Bowyer, on the right, appeared to be yards off-side, but the linesman who was within a few feet, had a different opinion and allowed play to continue with Birmingham's defence completely stranded.

Bowyer produced a low cross which John Robinson hammered home to leave a bemused Birmingham wondering what had happened.

Predictably Barry Fry responded by taking off John Frain, Hunt and Steve Claridge and replacing them during the break with Gary Cooper, Jason Bowen and Kevin Francis.

But it all appeared to be a fruitless task when Paul Mortimer put over a low left wing cross which Leaburn turned past Sansome in the 70th minute. This goal signalled a positive response from Birmingham and within five minutes Edwards turned in a Gary Poole cross to reduce the arrears.

The rapidly improving Richard Forsyth, worth a great deal more than the £50,000 paid to Kidderminster, demonstrated his growing confidence when he finished off a four man move with a cracking 25-yard drive.

Birmingham very nearly scrambled to a draw but Charlton held on to record their fourth successive away win and move into second place.

Fry, concerned with his defence, said: "My lads have played a tremendous number of games and I think they are now beginning to feel the effects.

"In saying that, if the three officials have a look at the video of the game they will have red faces for some of their decisions."

Wednesday 17th January 1996 • Molineux • 7.45pm

WOLVES 2 BIRMINGHAM CITY 1

Half time 1-0 • *Attendance* 28,088

Referee Robbie HART (Darlington)

Linesmen P.J. JOSLIN and P.WALTON

Old Gold Shirts with Black Trim, Black Shorts		Goals	Black and Silver Striped Shirts, Blue Shorts		Goals
1	Mike STOWELL		1	Bart GRIEMINK	
2	Mark RANKINE		2	Gary POOLE	
3	Andy THOMPSON		3	John FRAIN	
4	Eric YOUNG		4	Richard FORSYTH	
5	Mark VENUS		5	Andy EDWARDS ❑	
6	Brian LAW ❑ ∎		6	Liam DAISH ❑	
7	Simon OSBORN		7	Steve CASTLE †	
8	Don GOODMAN ❑		8	Steve CLARIDGE	
9	Steve BULL	61	9	Kevin FRANCIS ❑ #	
10	Darren FERGUSON ❑	17	10	Ian RICHARDSON ‡	
11	Mark ATKINS		11	Michael JOHNSON ❑	
	Substitutes			*Substitutes*	
12	Dominic FOLEY		12	Jason BOWEN ‡45	
13	Dennis PEARCE		13	Jonathan HUNT †45	51
14	Tony DALEY		14	Gary BULL #69	

F A C T F I L E

Michael Johnson makes his first appearance since November after only one reserve team outing... Birmingham go out in the third round for the second successive season and again after a replay... Mike Stowell's penalty save was his second in the space of five days – and both were taken by a player named Hunt.

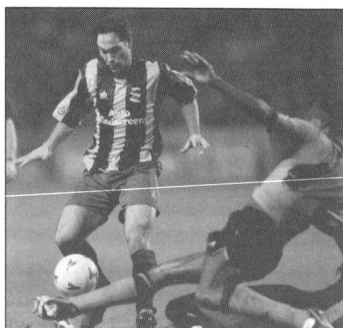

Richard Forsyth beats Eric Young to the ball.

Another Hunt penalty miss

With matches coming thick and fast Barry Fry's main concern is that his team will fall between three stools and fail to achieve anything from the main competitions.

This explains his renewed transfer activity in an attempt to inject some fresh life into the side although other people have different views of the situation.

Goalkeeper Fred Barber is obtained on loan to provide cover in the absence of Ian Bennett, but there are obviously more urgent team places in need of attention.

Blues travel to Molineux facing a Wolves side that had not won under the managership of Mark McGhee, indicating that their problems are deep-seated.

As a tactical ploy Fry comes up with the surprise inclusion of Michael Johnson following a ten game absence. He said: "I sent him out in the number eleven shirt and he dropped back into a central defensive role!"

Despite his flippant remark it was a calculated gamble for Johnson to occupy this position in an attempt to nullify the danger of Steve Bull and Don Goodman.

As events transpired it was a move which badly misfired and one which should not have been taken as the Wolves duo, despite their reputations, had not been producing the goods on a regular basis.

Fry was obviously concerned with matters at the heart of his defence as he later explained that he thought Andy Edwards and Liam Daish were "a bit dodgy" and needed some extra support in that area.

These fears were highlighted when Birmingham went behind in the 17th minute and it all came from an aimless punt forward by Daish.

Wolves goalkeeper, Mike Stowell, gained possession and his long clearance was headed on by Bull for Darren Ferguson to slip through the middle and score only his second goal for the club.

This was a set-back and it took Birmingham some time to recover in a game which became a little untidy – which was highlighted by seven bookings made by referee Robbie Hart in the first half.

Typically, Fry responded to the situation at half time by taking off Ian Richardson and Steve Castle and sending on Jonathan Hunt and Jason Bowen.

Fry's explanation was: "I put out the battlers in the first half and replaced them with the footballers for the second."

Hunt justified his inclusion with a 51st minute equaliser, but ten minutes later Bull put Wolves ahead with a shot from the inside-right channel, after being put through by Simon Osborn, which was deflected past debut boy Bart Griemink.

Unfortunately, Hunt blackened his copybook with a penalty miss, his second in successive cup ties, which would seemingly have given Birmingham the edge.

Brian Law, who was sent off for a handling offence which prevented Claridge from scoring, rewarded Wolves with a fourth round tie and a lucrative pay-day at Spurs.

Birmingham attempted to repair the damage but Stowell was in inspired form as he demonstrated with another late save, diving full length to tip over a stinging drive to prevent the ever improving Richard Forsyth from equalising.

Fry was unusually downcast afterwards. He admitted: "We had no one to blame but ourselves. We had enough chances to have won handsomely. Steve Claridge should have put the his shot low into the net when Law flicked the ball high over the bar. A player with 20 odd goals a season should not put in shots like that from close range."

Saturday 20th January 1996 • Portman Road • 3.00pm

IPSWICH TOWN 2 BIRMINGHAM CITY 0

Half time 1-0 • *Attendance* 12,540

Referee Ian HEMLEY (Ampthill, Beds)

Linesmen A.C. HARVEY and A.R. LEGG

Blue and White Shirts, Blue and White Shorts	Goals	Red Shirts with Blue and White Trim, Red Shorts	Goals
1 Richard WRIGHT		1 Bart GRIEMINK	
2 Gus UHLENBEEK		2 Scott HILEY ‡	
3 Tony VAUGHAN		3 John FRAIN	
4 Claus THOMSEN		4 Richard FORYSTH	
5 Tony MOWBRAY		5 Andy EDWARDS	
6 Geraint WILLIAMS		6 Liam DAISH	
7 Paul MASON †		7 Jonathan HUNT	
8 Steve SEDGLEY		8 Steve CLARIDGE	
9 Alex MATHIE		9 Kevin FRANCIS	
10 Neil GREGORY ‡		10 Jason BOWEN #	
11 Simon MILTON	22,55	11 Michael JOHNSON †	
Substitutes		*Substitutes*	
12 James SCOWCROFT ‡86		12 Steve FINNAN ‡57	
13 Craig FORREST (Gk)		13 Paul TAIT †45	
14 Frank YALLOP †75		14 Gary BULL #71	

BEFORE		P	W	D	L	F	A	pts	AFTER		P	W	D	L	F	A	pts
7	Blues	25	10	8	7	37	34	38	10	Blues	26	10	8	8	37	36	38
13	Ipswich	25	8	10	7	45	37	34	11	Ipswich	26	9	10	7	47	37	37

FACTFILE

Blues lose out to Man. City in bid to sign Nigel Clough... Darren Ferguson, Vinny Samways and Vinny Jones are names mentioned as Barry Fry widens the net... City's third defeat in space of seven days... They have picked up only nine points from last ten games but are only seven points adrift of second placed Charlton.

Weary players firing blanks

Birmingham City's two games a week programme which has not abated since the hectic pre-season programme appears to have finally caught up with everyone and suddenly the panic button is being pushed like someone stuck in a lift which will not move.

Manager Barry Fry is, as usual, bustling around, trying to inject yet more spirit into, it has to be said, a willing horse.

Still no Ian Bennett and Gary Poole was forced to miss the trip to Suffolk which allowed Scott Hiley to make a rare appearance at a time when his old Exeter City boss, Alan Ball, had indicated an interest in taking him to Manchester City on trial.

Birmingham still conspired to rush the opposition off their feet, but they faced a different Ipswich side than that which appeared at St. Andrew's earlier in the season.

They have not been beaten in the league since November and their confidence is sky high following their win at Blackburn Rovers in an F.A. Cup replay.

Ipswich have developed around the dominance of their two central defenders, Claus Thomsen and Tony Mowbray, and this was quickly made obvious as Steve Claridge and Kevin Francis struggled to make their mark.

The inability to prise open the Ipswich side was compounded when Simon Milton produced a 20-yard rocket which left Bart Griemink transfixed.

Fry's decision to take off the tiring Michael Johnson, still struggling for full match fitness, at the break, signalled a significant improvement and a better balanced side operating a 4-4-2 formation.

But Ipswich appeared to be having the breaks at just the right moment and ten minutes into

the second period a pass from Neil Gregory found the elusive Milton, who chipped the ball over the inexperienced Griemink.

Although Richard Forsyth had yet another impressive performance, Birmingham's lack of fire power sadly let them down and suddenly games are getting harder by the minute.

Fry appeared from the dressing room to comment: "At the moment I am more worried about relegation than promotion.

"We are going through a silly little spell when everything appears to be going in favour of the opposition. It is one of those situations from which we have got to work our way out, by any means possible.

"No one needs to tell me that nine points out of 30 is relegation form, but I have players in the side who are capable of picking up the club and getting us back to where we were before this mini-slump.

"But in saying that, we do need some quality. You cannot expect to win this division and compete in the Premier League with players costing less than a £1m.

"My board recognised this situation and are prepared to again dig deep into their pockets to enable me to bring in these quality players.

"It would, of course, help if I could finance some of the deals with money raised on the transfer market."

Richard Forsyth – gave another fine midfield performance.

Wednesday 24th January 1996 • St. Andrew's • 7.45pm

BIRMINGHAM CITY 2 NORWICH CITY 1

Half time 0-0 • *Attendance* 21,097

Referee Roger GIFFORD (Llanbradach)

Linesmen A.J. GREEN and D.C. MADGWICK

Blue Shirts, White Shorts		Goals	Yellow Shirts, Green Shorts		Goals
1	Bart GRIEMINK		1	Bryan GUNN	
2	Gary POOLE ❑ ■		2	Carl BRADSHAW ❑	
3	John FRAIN		3	Mark BOWEN	
4	Richard FORSYTH		4	Jan MOLBY	78
5	Andy EDWARDS		5	John POLSTON	
6	Liam DAISH ❑	88	6	Spencer PRIOR	
7	Louie DONOWA		7	Neil ADAMS	
8	Steve CLARIDGE		8	Robert FLECK	
9	Kevin FRANCIS #		9	Ashley WARD	
10	Steve CASTLE ‡		10	Darren EADIE †	
11	Neil DOHERTY †		11	Keith O'NEILL	
Substitutes			*Substitutes*		
12	Gary BULL #80 ❑		12	Andy JOHNSON †63	
13	Jason BOWEN †45	53	13	Andy MARSHALL (Gk)	
14	Paul TAIT ‡63		14	Rob NEWMAN	

FACTFILE

Birmingham reach the League Cup semi-final for the first time in 29 years... It is their first major semi-final in 21 years... Jonathan Hunt starts suspension... Neil Doherty starts his first game in 13 months... Gary Poole back from injury... Skipper Liam Daish nets only his second goal of the season.

Kevin Francis puts the Norwich defence under pressure to get in an attempt on goal.

Captain Marvel kills off Canaries

The pre-match talk surrounds Birmingham's reported interest in Vinny Samways from Everton and even more surprisingly, Wimbledon's Vinny Jones.

Samways attends the game with his agent, but Birmingham are unable to reach any agreement on personal terms.

The Jones story surrounds an approach to Wimbledon about Andy Clarke and in turn Birmingham are duly informed that the tough tackling defender is available.

Although manager Fry plays down the move, it transpires that Birmingham offered Wimbledon £300,000 for Jones – a lot of money for a player in whom manager Fry was apparently not interested.

Fry is looking for quality players and feels he needs to unload some of his squad – hardly the best preparation going into such an important tie after an indifferent spell of league form.

In their tenth Coca-Cola Cup tie of the season Birmingham were far from assured in any of their early play and if Robert Fleck, in particular, had shown better finishing power, the Blues could have been in serious trouble.

Norwich were the more dangerous on several occasions and, without the inclusion of the suspended Jonathan Hunt, Birmingham's attack appeared to be very disjointed.

There was one bright moment for Birmingham when winger Neil Doherty produced an inswinging corner which thudded against the face of the Norwich crossbar and away to safety.

On the other hand there was an anxious moment in the Birmingham penalty area when Ashley Ward was brought down in a joint operation between John Frain and Liam Daish, who were later to join up in a lucrative match winning move.

Richard Forsyth, with his intelligent use of the ball, continued to be the pick of Birmingham's team as Steve Claridge, in particular, was inconspicuous in a goalless first half.

Welsh international Jason Bowen took over from Doherty at the interval and promptly put his mark on the game with a beautiful first time volley on the run in the 53th minute from an inventive Steve Castle pass to give Birmingham a surprise lead.

But Birmingham put themselves in a desperate position when Gary Poole, booked in the first half for a foul on Keith O'Neill, collected a second booking for a handling offence and the dreaded red card.

Suddenly Norwich applied some concentrated pressure and on-loan Jan Molby fired in an unstoppable 25-yard shot off the right-hand post of Bart Griemink's goal, having first sidestepped two defenders, to bring the tie alive, the flying 'keeper having no chance.

Birmingham were on the ropes and reeling as Norwich set-up the knock-out blow, but two minutes before the end of the game John Frain advanced and won a corner on the left. He took the kick himself and found Liam Daish running in at the far post to head back across goal and into the far corner of a strangely unguarded net.

Daish later paid credit to Frain's corner. He said: "Everything was right about the corner. In saying that I thought I was due for a goal after a lot of near misses in previous games."

Manager Fry claimed: "When I came here, people asked me why did I think I could succeed where far better managers than me couldn't. And I said because I am a lucky so and so. And that says everything about the result against Norwich.

"We were lucky to get through but we battled and took our chances. It was a tremendous performance on the night and we have put a few more hundred thousand pounds into the owners' pockets with a two leg semi-final against Leeds United."

Tuesday 30th January 1996 • St. Andrew's • 7.45pm

BIRMINGHAM CITY 2 WEST BROMWICH A. 2

After extra time • Albion won 4-1 on penalties
Half time 0-1 • 90 minutes 2-2 • Attendance 9,113
Referee Jim RUSHTON (Stoke-on-Trent)
Linesmen M. CARRINGTON and K.J. HAWKES

Blue Shirts, White Shorts		Goals	Yellow Shirts with Blue Sleeves, Yellow Shorts		Goals
1	Bart GRIEMINK		1	Stuart NAYLOR	
2	Gary POOLE	47	2	Paul HOLMES	
3	John FRAIN		3	David SMITH	
4	Richard FORSYTH		4	Shaun CUNNINGTON #	
5	Andy EDWARDS		5	Daryl BURGESS	
6	Michael JOHNSON		6	Paul RAVEN	80
7	Jonathan HUNT		7	Kevin DONOVAN	
8	Jason BOWEN #		8	David GILBERT ‡	
9	Gary BULL	59	9	Tony REES †	18
10	Ricky OTTO †		10	Andy HUNT	
11	Steve FINNAN ‡		11	Julian DARBY	
	Substitutes			*Substitutes*	
12	Steve CLARIDGE †45		12	Bob TAYLOR †66	
13	Fred BARBER (Gk)		13	Paul REECE (Gk)	
14	Paul TAIT ‡45		14	Ian HAMILTON	
15	Steve BARNES #63		15	Stacy COLDICOTT #78	
16	Gary COOPER		16	Lee ASHCROFT ‡66	

FACTFILE

Blue's dismal penalty taking record gets worse... They have missed 14 of the 24 taken... Albion win first game in 16 matches... The last was against Brescia in the Anglo-Italian Cup... Birmingham again banned from including Liam Daish.

PENALTY SHOOT-OUT

Lee Ashcroft	scored	0-1
John Frain	hit crossbar	0-1
Andy Hunt	scored	0-2
Gary Bull	saved	0-2
Bob Taylor	scored	0-3
Paul Tait	scored	1-3
David Smith	scored	1-4

Off-target Blues pay the penalty

Three ground inspections were required before the game was given the green light by referee Jim Rushton and the lateness of his final decision obviously had an important impact on the attendance on a cold January evening.

But following the trials and tribulations of previous cup ties the reward for victory was the prospect of a two-legged English final against Port Vale (4-2 winners at Ipswich in the other semi-final) and a possible Wembley appearance.

Facing a West Bromwich Albion side which had last won on December 13 against Brescia in the Anglo-Italian Cup and had picked up just one point from a possible 39 in the league, Birmingham were made obvious pre-match favourites.

On a treacherous icy surface both teams conspired to produce an exciting game with Ricky Otto, back for his first game since the Derby defeat in December, quickly emerging as a potential danger.

It was Otto who latched onto a John Frain corner and hammered in a shot which hit Albion's woodwork. If Otto had scored Birmingham could quite conceivably have romped to a big win against an Albion side woefully short of self-confidence.

In Birmingham's eagerness to dominate Albion they left themselves exposed, particularly down their left flank where Kevin Donovan emerged as a potential threat.

He demonstrated his danger when he shrugged off a Michael Johnson tackle only to see his effort also hit the woodwork. Unlike Birmingham the Albion hit back and in the next minute a lofted cross from their right found the unmarked Tony Rees on hand to head home his first goal of the season in his first game since the Brescia match.

To say it was a shock to the system was putting it mildly, but it was just the opening shot on a night of set-backs.

A double substitution at the break resulted in Steve Claridge and Paul Tait making their entrance with Tait, as usual, quickly making things happen.

Tait put Jonathan Hunt in possession and he rolled the ball back for acting captain Gary Poole to power in a rising shot past Stuart Naylor two minutes into the second half.

Whatever confidence Albion possessed visibly drained out of the team and when Gary Bull nonchalantly put Blues ahead in the 59th minute they were seemingly heading for another defeat. The move was started by Claridge who sent a neat back-header into the path of Forsyth, who immediately sent Bull away with a delightful pass, to beat Naylor with a low left-foot shot just inside the near post

But suddenly it was Blues turn to be on the defensive in the face of some desperate attacks which culminated in a brilliant header by Paul Raven ten minutes before the end of normal time from Lee Ashcroft's corner, producing the equaliser and 30 minutes of extra time that took the game into a dramatic penalty shoot-out to the dismay of the home fans.

They had every reason to be apprehensive in the light of Blues' record from the penalty spot and these fears were quickly justified after Lee Ashcroft converted Albion's first spot kick.

John Frain blasted his effort against the bar and Naylor saved Bull's effort and suddenly Blues were out, beaten 4-1 on penalties.

Typically Fry was forthright in his views when he said: "I am delighted to be out of the competition. It has brought us nothing but misery, problems and injury.

"The game itself need not have gone to penalties with our record. We could score 88 out of 88 on the training ground, but it is in front of a stadium full of people where it really matters."

Sunday 4th February 1996 • Carrow Road • 3.00pm

NORWICH CITY 1 BIRMINGHAM CITY 1

Half time 0-0 • Attendance 12,612
Referee Alan BUTLER (Sutton-in-Ashfield)
Linesmen M. HAIR and P. WING

Yellow Shirts, Green Shorts	Goals	Blue Shirts, White Shorts	Goals
1 Bryan GUNN		1 Bart GRIEMINK	
2 Carl BRADSHAW		2 Gary POOLE	
3 Mark BOWEN †		3 John FRAIN	
4 Ian CROOK		4 Richard FORSYTH	
5 John POLSTON		5 Michael JOHNSON	
6 Spencer PRIOR		6 Liam DAISH	
7 Neil ADAMS		7 Jason BOWEN †45	
8 Robert FLECK		8 Steve CLARIDGE	
9 Ashley WARD	74	9 Kevin FRANCIS ❑	
10 Andy JOHNSON #		10 Gary COOPER	
11 Ade AKINBIYI ‡		11 Paul TAIT ‡	
Substitutes		*Substitutes*	
12 Rob NEWMAN †20		12 Ricky OTTO ‡61	76
13 Jeremy GOSS #87		13 Steve BARNES †45	
14 Keith SCOTT ‡68		14 Gary BULL	

BEFORE		P	W	D	L	F	A	pts	AFTER		P	W	D	L	F	A	pts
11	Norwich	28	10	8	10	39	34	38	10	Norwich	29	10	9	10	40	35	39
12	Blues	26	10	8	8	37	26	38	11	Blues	27	10	9	8	38	27	39

FACTFILE

Striker Sigurd Rushfeldt has returned to Tromso, Norway and midfielder David Preece has gone back to Derby after loan spells... The fourth meeting of the season between the two clubs... Andy Edwards misses only his second game of the season because of a suspension... Ricky Otto obtains his second goal of the season.

Super-sub Otto to the rescue

As usual, transfer activity emanating from St. Andrew's occupied many inches of column space in the Evening Mail and Birmingham Post in the build up to the game at Norwich City; when Blues made a slight detour to slip in a friendly game at Harwick.

Included in the Blues side against Harwick was Dzoni Novak, a Croatian international with 33 caps to his credit, and he impressed in a smart win to earn considerable praise from the management team.

But of more immediate concern was the game at Norwich where Michael Johnson took over from the suspended Andy Edwards and there were quickly signs that any hopes of improving upon their league position was going to be a very difficult task.

Norwich, seeking their first win of the season over Birmingham, were the more penetrative side and for long spells the Blues were under considerable pressure attempting to keep out the Canaries attack.

Ashley Ward, in particular, was a lively striker and was always a potential match-winner. Twice he hit the woodwork as Birmingham's bid to revive their promotion aspirations took a buffeting.

A win would have taken Birmingham into a challenging sixth position, but Norwich were not a side to roll over and goalkeeper Bart Griemink had to be on his best form to keep the home side at bay.

Robert Fleck, too, was a danger and Johnson experienced considerable trouble attempting to quell a dangerous Norwich strikeforce.

The game flared up when Kevin Francis was involved in an incident with Mark Bowen which resulted in the Norwich player leaving the field on a stretcher with a rib injury.

Francis collected a yellow card when some observers were of the opinion that the offence warranted even firmer action.

Steve Claridge, who continued to struggle, went close on one occasion as did Francis, but generally it was Norwich who were in control and went ahead with a goal from Ward after 74 minutes with a simple tap-in after a Fleck shot had been deflected.

It was then that the Blues displayed a great deal of character when Ricky Otto, who had replaced Paul Tait on the hour, grabbed an equaliser two minutes later.

Claridge put Francis in possession and the striker hammered his effort against the crossbar only for Otto to pick up the loose rebound to fire in his second goal of the season.

The final 15 minutes were rather frantic with both teams appearing to lose their cool. The final whistle resulted in unfortunate scenes with Liam Daish appearing to take exception to an earlier incident involving Keith Scott.

Barry Fry later said: "I had to tell Daish to leave the field before he got us into even more trouble. He is already suspended for the next match."

The Birmingham manager admitted he was disappointed with the result, as a draw did little to improve their league position, but he added that Norwich were the better team on the day and did not deserve to lose the game.

Steve Claridge comes off second best this time.

Sunday 11th February 1996 • St. Andrew's • 4.00pm

BIRMINGHAM CITY 1 LEEDS UNITED 2

Half time 1-0 • *Attendance* 24,781

Referee Keith COOPER (Pontypridd)

Linesmen E.W. GREEN and P.M. ROBERTS

Blue Shirts, White Shorts   Goals

White Shirts, Navy Blue Shorts   Goals

	Birmingham City	Goals		Leeds United	Goals
1	Bart GRIEMINK		1	John LUKIC	
2	Jon BASS		2	Gary KELLY	
3	John FRAIN		3	Tony DORIGO	
4	Richard FORSYTH †		4	Carlton PALMER	
5	Chris WHYTE	73 og	5	Paul BEESLEY	
6	Michael JOHNSON		6	David WETHERALL ❏	
7	Jonathan HUNT		7	Mark FORD ‡	
8	Steve CLARIDGE		8	Rod WALLACE †	
9	Kevin FRANCIS	27	9	Tony YEBOAH	54
10	John SHERIDAN #		10	Gary McALLISTER	
11	Gary COOPER ‡		11	Gary SPEED	
	Substitutes			*Substitutes*	
12	Ricky OTTO †66		12	Brian DEANE †85	
13	Jason BOWEN #77		13	Mark BEENEY (Gk)	
14	Louie DONOWA ‡66		14	Lucas RADEBE ‡89	

Birmingham's first League Cup semi-final in 29 years... Blues were without the services of Ian Bennett, Gary Poole, Andy Edwards and Liam Daish... John Sheridan, on loan from Sheffield Wednesday, made his first appearance but Vinny Samways from Everton is cup-tied... Jon Bass makes only his second senior outing... Leeds were back to full strength for the game.

Steve Claridge beats off Paul Beesley.

Francis strike gives hope

A capacity crowd packed St. Andrew's for the first time since the F.A. found the club guilty of misconduct following crowd trouble before, during and after the game with Millwall in November.

Club owner David Sullivan expressed his concern about the situation and stated that it was the opinion that a hard core of about 100 were to blame for the position in which Birmingham found themselves.

He hoped for a trouble free match on such an important day, but his plea was not observed as, late in the game, a coin and another object were thrown at the Leeds United skipper Gary McAllister. It was an isolated incident – but one which could result in the ground being closed for one game at a cost to Birmingham City of approximately £200,000.

Once again it was a makeshift Birmingham side in action against one of the big spenders. To their credit Birmingham acquitted themselves brilliantly in the circumstances.

Young Jon Bass was called up for only his second senior game and it was nearly twelve months after his previous appearance, also in the Coca-Cola Cup, against Blackburn.

Chris Whyte was recalled from his on loan spell at West Ham and it was to turn out to be an occasion that he will never forget.

With McAllister controlling the Leeds side in mid-field and attack, Leeds were marginally the stronger side, but Birmingham's tremendous spirit, backed by the vocal support, enabled them to compete almost on level terms.

The game came alight in dramatic fashion in the 27th minute when John Sheridan put Steve Claridge in possession and a quick through ball found the gangling Kevin Francis advancing on the Leeds goal.

It felt like an age before the ball finally settled down in front of the striker and ended with Francis unleashing a ferocious shot from the edge of the area to easily beat John Lukic via the inside of his right-hand post.

There was a lucky let off for Blues when Bart Griemink parried a Mark Ford shot and from the rebound Tony Yeboah hit the crossbar.

Leeds, always dangerous, deservedly equalised when the luckless Whyte saw the ball go through his legs from a Yeboah shot in the 54th minute following a long clearance from Lukic.

The two players were again directly involved in what turned out to be the winning goal in the 73rd minute. Gary Kelly pumped over a cross which Yeboah headed goalwards. There was no danger of a goal until Whyte popped up to head the ball into his own net.

Birmingham strived for the equaliser with Louie Donowa turning Leeds' defence inside out in the closing stages but the vital goal would not materialise.

The best chance fell to another substitute, Jason Bowen, just two minutes from the end. A long clearance from Griemink was headed on by Francis, but the Welsh international appeared to be a little casual with his shot and the ball drifted wide of the post with only Lukic to beat.

The depressed Whyte was full of remorse afterwards. He said: "It was a sickener, The ball took a horrible bounce and I had to try to get it over the bar but it looped into the net."

It could well have been Whyte's last appearance for the club as manager Barry Fry snapped up Gary Breen, the Republic of Ireland international from Peterborough, a couple of days before the Leeds match.

On the game, Fry said: "I'm bitterly, bitterly disappointed. We played against a side packed full of internationals and matched them for 90 minutes. It was a performance of which I am proud.

"Although we trail 2-1 we will have a go at them at Elland Road, make no mistake."

Saturday 17th February 1996 • Victoria Ground • 3.00pm

STOKE CITY 1 BIRMINGHAM CITY 0

Half time 1-0 • *Attendance* 15,716
Referee Terry HEILBRON (Co. Durham)
Linesmen A. McGHEE and R. RUSSON

Red and White Striped Shirts, White Shorts		Goals	Blue Shirts, Blue Shorts		Goals
1	Mark PRUDHOE		1	Bart GRIEMINK	
2	Ian CLARKSON		2	Jon BASS	
3	Lee SANDFORD		3	John FRAIN	
4	Larus SIGURDSSON		4	Vinny SAMWAYS ❑	
5	Ian CRANSON		5	Andy EDWARDS	
6	Graham POTTER †		6	Michael JOHNSON	
7	Carl BEESTON ‡		7	Jonathan HUNT †	
8	Ray WALLACE ❑		8	Jason BOWEN ‡	
9	Mike SHERON		9	Kevin FRANCIS	
10	Simon STURRIDGE	26	10	John SHERIDAN	
11	Nigel GLEGHORN		11	Louie DONOWA ❑ #	
	Substitutes			*Substitutes*	
12	John DREYER †88		12	Gary BREEN †45	
13	Kevin Keen ‡89		13	Gary BULL ‡45	
14	John GAYLE		14	Ricky OTTO #45	

BEFORE		P	W	D	L	F	A	pts	AFTER		P	W	D	L	F	A	pts
7	Stoke	28	11	9	8	40	34	42	3	Stoke	29	12	9	8	41	34	45
13	Blues	27	10	9	8	38	37	39	13	Blues	28	10	9	9	38	38	39

FACTFILE

Vinny Samways makes his debut for Birmingham City following his on-loan move from Everton... Gary Breen, signed from Peterborough in part-exchange for Ken Charlery, is also in the squad... Jonathan Bass's league debut... Birmingham have produced just two wins in twelve League games.

Blues lose their cutting edge

Birmingham City fans are rocked by the news that their popular striker Steve Claridge is having talks with Leicester City about a possible move – the first of several crisis developments to take place over 24 hours.

Claridge had expressed his dissatisfaction with his current financial terms with Birmingham. He also found himself two weeks wages lighter after refusing to play for the reserves in a private game against Coventry City.

It would have been an occasion for Coventry manager, Ron Atkinson, to decide whether to put in a bid for the striker. Instead, Claridge went to Filbert Street to discuss terms with Martin O'Neill.

Manager Barry Fry made a quick dash up the motorway and had a few more surprises in store. He left out acting skipper Gary Poole and Richard Forsyth, who had been one of the most consistent players in the side.

Instead he gave young Jonathan Bass his first league game and introduced Vinny Samways from Everton. Skipper Liam Daish was also absent because of suspension, although he did play against Coventry and sparked off a subsequent offer from Atkinson.

Poole was not happy to be side-lined and later requested a transfer as an indication of his dissatisfaction with the whole affair.

Unfortunately for Fry the changes did not have the desired effect and to rub salt into the wounds a Birmingham old boy, Simon Sturridge, one of six in Stoke's squad, scored the only goal of the game in the 26th minute.

Graham Potter, another former Birmingham player, produced a long ball down the left which Sturridge collected to fire home with a fierce cross shot past Bart Griemink, who did his best to narrow the angle.

There was little doubt that Birmingham sadly lacked the services of Claridge, while Samways struggled to slot in and Sheridan was unable to make a strong contribution.

Fry, as usual, responded by sending on his three substitutes at the interval with Jonathan Hunt particularly aggrieved. Stoke still posed problems and should have increased their lead through Mike Sheron and Sturridge.

On the other hand Birmingham had their opportunities to salvage at least one point as Andy Edwards highlighted when his header smashed against the bar in the closing minutes of the game.

Fry admitted after the game: "We have been struggling for several weeks, if not months. Something has to be done very quickly or we could find ourselves in serious trouble.

Afterwards there were conflicting reports that Birmingham were interested in old boy Paul Peschisolido rejoining the club from Stoke and this was the explanation why he had been left out of the Potters side.

A fee in the region of £1.5m was mentioned but Birmingham thought this was excessive in view of the fact that Stoke only paid £600,000 for the Canadian.

Later there were unsubstantiated stories of a rift between Fry and owner David Sullivan. It was subsequently claimed by Fry, in a fax to national newspapers, that Sullivan in no way interferes with team affairs.

Kevin Francis in full flight.

Tuesday 20th February 1996 • St. Andrew's • 7.45pm

BIRMINGHAM CITY 0 BARNSLEY 0

Half time 0-0 • Attendance 14,168

Referee Kevin LYNCH (Knaresborough)

Linesmen S. CASTLE and G.A. STONES

Blue Shirts, White Shorts		Goals
1	Bart GRIEMINK	
2	Gary POOLE	
3	John FRAIN	
4	Richard FORSYTH †	
5	Gary BREEN	
6	Michael JOHNSON	
7	Jonathan HUNT ‡	
8	Steve CLARIDGE	
9	Jason BOWEN	
10	Ricky OTTO #	
11	Vinny SAMWAYS	

Substitutes

12 Louie DONOWA #64

13 Gary BULL ‡64

14 John SHERIDAN †64

Red Shirts, Black Shorts		Goals
1	David WATSON	
2	Nicky EADEN	
3	Peter SHIRTLIFF	
4	Martin BULLOCK	
5	Steve DAVIS	
6	Arjan de ZEEUW	
7	Andy LIDDELL	
8	Neil REDFEARN	
9	Brendan O'CONNELL	
10	Andy PAYTON	
11	Darren SHERIDAN	

Substitutes

12 Charlie BISHOP

13 Adam SOLLITT

14 Glynn HURST

BEFORE		P	W	D	L	F	A	pts
7	Barnsley	29	11	10	8	40	44	43
13	Blues	28	10	9	9	38	38	39

AFTER		P	W	D	L	F	A	pts
6	Barnsley	30	11	11	8	40	44	44
13	Blues	29	10	10	9	38	38	40

FACTFILE

Gary Breen makes his home debut for Blues on the day Liam Daish agrees to join nearby Coventry City for £1.5 million... Birmingham's last win was December 23 when they beat Sheffield United... They have won just two games in 13 league matches... Barnsley unbeaten in eight games.

Tyke terriers hold out for a point

St. Andrew's is vibrating with the news of the departure of Liam Daish and the likelihood of Steve Claridge joining Leicester City.

Daish has been a big man of huge presence in Birmingham's revival and to allow him to leave the club in such circumstances has posed a number of probing questions which the management neatly side-stepped.

He has been a stable figure and a player of his stature would, many people thought, have been invaluable in a side preparing for a League Cup semi-final.

Manager Barry Fry came out with some well worn cliches such as "no player is bigger than the club," and "the time is right for the player and club to part company."

The Claridge saga was apparently unrelated, but what Birmingham's fans could not understand was losing their two key players at the same time.

Fry claimed that in the Claridge case it was simply a case of money. He said: "Mark Ward is the highest paid player in the club and Claridge is the second best paid.

"There are players in the side receiving ten times less than Claridge and they are not knocking on my door to complain."

But Fry did recall Claridge after leaving him out of the team to play at Stoke and despite the fact that the popular striker had not trained since the previous Thursday.

Recent signings, John Sheridan and Vinny Samways had been drafted into the squad, but without any apparent impact.

It may have been due to the cold weather and the unattractiveness of the opposition, but Blues were watched by their smallest league crowd of the season.

With the crowd singing "there is only one Stevie Claridge", the game itself struggled to come alive. Barnsley, unbeaten in seven league games, were a compact, well organised side who were capable of playing some good football under the managership of Danny Wilson and the game quickly settled down into a battle for midfield supremacy.

Conditions were far from ideal and this posed problems throughout the 90 minutes, but was no real excuse for a low key game. Birmingham lacked their usual passion and it was illustrated by their inability to apply any concentrated pressure.

There was no real definition in their play and the only real chance of grabbing all three points occurred mid-way through the first half when the experienced John Frain, not without his experience of the ups and downs of being part of the Birmingham set-up, burst through the right-hand flank of the Barnsley defence and saw his cross-shot hit the far post.

Typically, Fry responded to the situation with a triple substitution in the 64th minute when he sent on Gary Bull, Louie Donowa and John Sheridan.

In the circumstances it was more a panic move than anything else and the total result was that there was no improvement what so ever in Birmingham's low key performance when they rarely appeared capable of chalking up a win.

Fry, obviously very upset by the treatment handed out by some national newspapers, responded by refusing to attend the post-match press conference and subsequently lying low for a couple of days.

This was totally out of character for the usually expansive manager, but it illustrated the upheaval at the club when the situation was likened to a powder keg that was likely to explode.

Everyone was hoping that, like the Gunpowder Plot, the danger could be averted before anyone put a match to the fuse.

Sunday 25th February 1996 • Elland Road • 12.00 mid-day

LEEDS UNITED 3 BIRMINGHAM CITY 0

Leeds United win 5-1 on aggregate

Half time 0-0 • Attendance 35,435

Referee Roger DILKES (Mossley)

Linesmen S.P. DEVINE and D.M. HORLICK

White Shirts, White Shorts		Goals	Black and Silver Striped Shirts, Blue Shorts		Goals
1	John LUKIC		1	Bart GRIEMINK	
2	Gary KELLY		2	Gary POOLE	
3	Tony DORIGO †		3	John FRAIN	
4	Carlton PALMER		4	Richard FORSYTH †	
5	Paul BEESLEY		5	Andy EDWARDS ❑	
6	David WETHERALL		6	Michael JOHNSON	
7	Phil MASINGA ‡	54	7	Ian RICHARDSON	
8	Rod WALLACE		8	Steve CLARIDGE	
9	Tony YEBOAH	58	9	Kevin FRANCIS ‡	
10	Gary McALLISTER		10	John SHERIDAN	
11	Brian DEANE	86	11	Chris WHYTE #	
	Substitutes			*Substitutes*	
12	Lucas RADEBE †18		12	Louie DONOWA †45	
13	Tomas BROLIN ‡84		13	Jason BOWEN ‡61	
14	Mark BEENEY (Gk)		14	Jonathan HUNT #61	

Birmingham's Coca-Cola Cup run ends after no less than 12 games in the competition... Transfer seeking Steve Claridge misses Birmingham's 15th spot kick from 25 awards... Ian Richardson, recalled from an on loan spell at Notts County, is a surprise selection... Leeds reach their first Wembley final in 23 years.

John Frain is brought down by Gary Kelly.

Chances created but not taken

Nearly 6,000 Blues fans made the trek North on the M1 in the hope of a major upset. It would have been a tremendous achievement – but events over the previous fortnight created a nagging doubt and the possibility of winning by more than two goals appeared to be a formidable task for another makeshift side.

In a reflective mood Blues fans required no reminding that the indifferent performances began to occur when goalkeeper Ian Bennett was forced to drop out of the team with a finger injury.

But for 45 minutes Birmingham battled hard and with Gary McAllister unable to make the same kind of impression as in the first leg there were no goals in the first period.

The vital turning point occurred just four minutes into the second half when Ian Richardson, recalled from a month on loan at Notts County and suddenly selected for the first team, should have put Birmingham ahead in the game and squared the tie 2-2.

It was certainly an expensive miss which Leeds fully exploited over the following eleven minutes when first Phil Masinga and then Tony Yeboah scored the goals that assured Leeds of their victory and a place in the final against Aston Villa at Wembley.

Yeboah snapped up a weak clearance by Michael Johnson and produced a shot which fortuitously looped straight to McAllister to shoot from close range. Bart Griemink pushed out the effort to Masinga who had the simple task of nudging in the opening goal.

Heads immediately dropped and they sagged uncharacteristaly to the floor four minutes later when Yeboah scored the second goal with an excellent scissors kick into the corner of the net wide of Griemink's left hand.

But there was still hope when Gary Kelly floored John Sheridan for a penalty; up stepped the unsettled Steve Claridge, who hammered his shot against the foot of Lukic's left-hand post to add another miserable chapter to the missed penalty saga.

A goal at that stage could have lifted the Blues. Instead, four minutes from time, Brian Deane rose to head home a third goal from Gary McAllister's left wing cross and Blues were in tatters.

In the after-math of defeat Barry Fry's re-action was typical as he dismantled his side in a matter of minutes, claiming that the Claridge-Kevin Francis partnership was finished and that he was still keen to acquire another striker.

He added: "All that matters now is the league. Even a team like Birmingham City can go up. The fans deserve it and that is why the players have got to double their efforts and see that it happens.

"There are no excuses. There are 16 games to play and we have to aim for top spot, second or the play-offs to get into the Premier League.

"What is worrying is that Steve Claridge, who hasn't scored for 15 games, wants to get away, while Jonathan Hunt is out of form.

"We do not have a player like Dwight Yorke who scores goals for fun. What I would like is to sign Marcus Stewart from Bristol Rovers for £1m – because we really are desperate to win some games."

Jonathan Hunt shrugs off a challenge from Gary Kelly.

Tuesday 27th February 1996 • Selhurst Park • 7.45pm

CRYSTAL PALACE 3 BIRMINGHAM CITY 2

Half time 1-1 • *Attendance* 12,965

Referee Steve BAINES (Chesterfield)

Linesmen R. COXHEAD and C.J. FRANCIS

Red and Blue Shirts, Red Shorts		Goals	Blue Shirts, White Shorts		Goals
1	Nigel MARTYN		1	Bart GRIEMINK	
2	Mark EDWORTHY		2	Andy EDWARDS ❑	
3	Leif ANDERSEN		3	John FRAIN ❑	
4	Andy ROBERTS		4	Gary POOLE †	
5	Gareth DAVIES	55	5	Gary BREEN ❑	
6	Dale GORDON		6	Michael JOHNSON	
7	Ray HOUGHTON		7	Jonathan HUNT	
8	David HOPKIN		8	Gary BULL	
9	George NDAH †		9	Kevin FRANCIS ‡	
10	Dougie FREEDMAN		10	Vinny SAMWAYS	
11	Bruce DYER	7,83	11	Jason BOWEN	30,77
	Substitutes			*Substitutes*	
12	Steve TAYLOR		12	Richard FORSYTH †28	
13	Simon RODGER †86		13	Ricky OTTO ‡60 #	
14	Jeroen BOERE		14	Steve FINNAN #75	

BEFORE	P	W	D	L	F	A	pts	AFTER	P	W	D	L	F	A	pts
11 Palace	30	10	12	8	39	38	42	6 Palace	31	11	12	8	42	40	45
13 Blues	29	10	10	9	38	38	40	13 Blues	30	10	10	10	40	41	40

FACTFILE

Birmingham continue to struggle and now have only two wins from their last 14 games... No Steve Claridge... He was late arriving at Selhurst Park... On loan John Sheridan again dropped... Crystal Palace chalk up only their fourth league home win of the season... The search for a striker continues.

Slack defending proves costly

Birmingham City announce that they have agreed a £1.2m fee with Leicester City for Steve Claridge, but at mid-day the deal falls through for a third time when the striker fails to agree personal terms.

As a result, he is summoned to London for the match with Crystal Palace. Making his own way to the ground Claridge is 25 minutes late arriving and his name was scrubbed off the team-sheet.

Manager Barry Fry reacts by announcing that Claridge has been fined two weeks wages – the second time in a month that he has suffered this fate.

Fry claims that the deal with Leicester has been aborted and that Claridge had been too greedy in his wage demands. He went on: "Claridge will now play out the rest of his 18 months with Birmingham City."

On past events this appears to be unlikely as Claridge has made it clear that it is his intention to leave the club in a period when the team had just failed to make the Coca-Cola Cup Final and were in a reasonable position to challenge for the play-offs.

But everything was going drastically wrong, with Fry being linked with an assortment of players. The general opinion that the numerous changes, once a fillip to some players, was beginning to wear thin, with most of the side wondering if they had any kind of a future at St. Andrew's.

Fry also suffered another two pre-match set-backs when he was informed that goalkeeper Ian Bennett's broken finger had failed to mend and that the hand had been put back into plaster for a further month, and Mark Ward was again suffering from back-trouble.

In the circumstances it was hardly surprising that everyone was fraught. Kevin Francis had a wonderful chance to give Blues an early lead but ballooned the ball high over the bar as is his want on occasions.

Palace were more precise in their finishing, when, in their first attack in the seventh minute Bruce Dyer pulled Breen out of position, turned and shot from the edge of the box to open the Londoners' account.

Gary Poole was then forced to limp off and be replaced by Richard Forsyth – a move which resulted in an immediate equaliser from Jason Bowen.

It was against the run of play at the time but the Welshman collected a cross from the un-settled Jonathan Hunt to hammer his shot past Nigel Martyn and into the roof of the net after 30 minutes.

There was some fire in Birmingham's play for a short period but Palace again assumed control much to the consternation of Fry. But their sec-ond goal did not arrive until ten minutes into the second half when George Ndah headed against the bar and Gareth Davies slotted home the rebound.

Birmingham vehemently protested that Bart Griemink had been fouled, but referee Steve Baines, the former Walsall central defender, allowed the goal to stand.

Bowen grabbed his second equaliser of the night when he ran in to head firmly past Martyn after a superb run and cross from Gary Bull, another unsettled player, but it was not enough to earn Blues a point as Birmingham hit the panic button again when Dyer grabbed the decisive winner seven minutes from time.

Gareth Davies flicked on a long throw-in from David Hopkin and Dyer clashed with Griemink before scoring, Blues protested vehe-mently, but no avail.

The defeat meant that Birmingham were just six points above the relegation area – food for thought as manager Barry Fry embarked on yet another round of transfer negotiations.

Saturday 2nd March 1996 • St. Andrew's • 3.00pm

BIRMINGHAM CITY 0 SHEFFIELD UNITED 1

Half time 0-0 • *Attendance* 16,799

Referee Scott MATHIESON (Stockport)

Linesmen J.H. HOLBROOK and A.C. HOWELLS

Blue Shirts, White Shorts		Goals	Red and White Shirts, Black Shorts		Goals
1	Bart GRIEMINK		1	Alan KELLY	
2	Andy EDWARDS		2	Chris SHORT	
3	John FRAIN		3	Roger NILSEN	
4	Vinny SAMWAYS		4	Gordon COWANS	
5	Gary BREEN		5	Doug HODGSON	
6	Michael JOHNSON		6	Gary ABLETT	
7	Jonathan HUNT †		7	David WHITE	
8	Andy LEGG		8	Mitch WARD ❏	
9	Gary BULL ‡		9	Phil STARBUCK	
10	Paul DEVLIN		10	Don HUTCHISON ❏	
11	Jason BOWEN #		11	Dane WHITEHOUSE †	
Substitutes			*Substitutes*		
12	Paul TAIT ‡45 ❏		12	Andy WALKER †72	78
13	Jae MARTIN #73		13	Simon TRACEY (Gk)	
14	Richard FORSYTH †26		14	Mark BEARD	

BEFORE		P	W	D	L	F	A	pts	AFTER		P	W	D	L	F	A	pts
14	Blues	30	10	10	10	40	41	40	15	Blues	31	10	10	11	40	42	40
21	United	34	8	11	15	40	50	35	17	United	35	9	11	15	41	50	38

Steve Claridge joins Leicester City in a £1.2m deal... Latest signings, Paul Devlin and Andy Legg from Notts County, made their first appearances... Birmingham have failed to win any of their last nine league games... Sheffield United had last won at St. Andrew's in the 1972-73 season.

"We were a shambles" – Fry

Steve Claridge departed St. Andrew's amidst a great deal of animosity when he finally linked up with Leicester City in a much protracted deal that was worth £1.2m.

The transfer left a great number of Birmingham fans totally bemused in view of the club's precarious league position after a disastrous spell since Christmas.

Barry Fry reacts in the only way he knows – buying yet more new players. The arrival of Paul Devlin and Andy Legg for £200,000 took his total to 52 players he had signed since his own arrival from Southend.

The novelty has long since worn off and it appears as if it has got to the players in the team because they are struggling to raise their game to cope with the present situation.

Injuries have not helped and the continued absence of Ian Bennett is the major concern, but if he had been fit would he still be with the club?

Sheffield United arrive at St. Andrew's hoping to maintain their revival under the new managership of Howard Kendall, who was fully aware that a victory would take the Blades to within just two points of Birmingham, who are struggling at present to amass points.

The game itself struggled to reach an acceptable standard – although Birmingham did attempt to find some attacking form. Sheffield United generally appeared to be more dangerous than Blues' lightweight attack which was even lacking the presence of their giant striker, Kevin Francis.

Jonathan Hunt, who had been expected to join Sheffield Wednesday in midweek, in a part-exchange deal involving Guy Whittingham, was replaced after only 26 minutes – the third time in four games that he had been substituted. Along with on-loan Vinny Samways he failed to control midfield which subsequently allowed the Sheffield side plenty of scope.

Birmingham had a lucky let off in the last minute of the first peirod when Phil Starbuck completely missed David White's cross. Bart Griemink fumbled the ball which ran loose for Starbuck to hook his shot on the turn, high over the bar in an incident which summed up a low key affair.

Gary Bull lost his place at the interval to be replaced by Paul Tait who then conspired to produce another bad miss. Gary Ablett, on loan to the Blades from Everton, made a poor clearance to Gary Breen who put Jason Bowen clear down the right-hand side.

Tait gained possession but hurriedly hit his shot against the post and United's keeper, Alan Kelly, quickly grabbed the rebound to prevent Birmingham having a second chance to redeem themselves.

In the 78th minute United's substitute, Andy Walker, a recent £500,000 capture from Celtic, got his head to a corner taken by Gordon Cowans and turned the ball into the net after it took a deflection off a defender.

This left an abject Barry Fry bemoaning the fact that the club could forget all about making the promotion play-offs this season if this was the level of performance of which his team was capable.

Fry added: "We were a shambles. I put on the ball players, but it never worked out. They required too long to bring the ball down and pass it."

United's manager, Howard Kendall, summed up the position at Birmingham when asked if it was difficult to plan his tactics against a Barry Fry team.

"Not really," said Kendall, "because he has so many players you never know what he is going to do, so you don't even bother to watch his team in action!"

Tuesday 5th March 1996 • St. Andrew's • 7.45pm

BIRMINGHAM CITY 2 WOLVES 0

Half time 2-0 • *Attendance* 22,051

Referee Eddie LOMAS (Manchester)

Linesmen B.P. ELLICOTT and D.P. MORRISON

Blue Shirts, White Shorts		Goals	Old Gold Shirts with Black Trim, Black Shorts		Goals
1	Bart GRIEMINK		1	Mike STOWELL	
2	Jonathan BASS		2	Andy THOMPSON	
3	John FRAIN		3	Mark ATKINS †	
4	Paul TAIT ❏		4	Eric YOUNG	
5	Gary BREEN		5	Neil EMBLEN	
6	Michael JOHNSON		6	Brian LAW ‡	
7	Jonathan HUNT ‡		7	Steve CORICA	
8	Paul DEVLIN	27pen,39	8	Don GOODMAN	
9	Paul BARNES †		9	Steve BULL	
10	Vinny SAMWAYS		10	Darren FERGUSON ❏	
11	ANDY LEGG		11	Simon OSBORN	
Substitutes			*Substitutes*		
12	Jason BOWEN ‡72		12	Mark VENUS	
13	Gary COOPER		13	Mark WILLIAMS ‡66	
14	Richard FORSYTH †65		14	Steve FROGGATT †56	

BEFORE	P	W	D	L	F	A	pts	AFTER	P	W	D	L	F	A	pts
13 Wolves	32	10	11	11	43	42	41	13 Blues	32	11	10	11	42	42	43
15 Blues	31	10	10	11	40	42	40	15 Wolves	33	10	11	12	43	44	41

FACTFILE

Birmingham's first win of the year and Paul Devlin's first goals since his arrival from Notts County... Paul Barnes' debut following his transfer from York City in a deal which took Gary Bull to the Northern club... Birmingham's first win of the three meetings between the two clubs this season.

Devlin the destroyer

Keeping track of the comings and goings at St. Andrew's was the chief talking point between fans before the re-arranged local derby which had been postponed at the end of the year because of bad weather.

While Paul Barnes became Barry Fry's 52nd signing since he himself arrived from Southend, the departure of Louie Donowa to Swansea City was held up when a medical examination suggested that the winger had a heart condition.

It was only two weeks previously that Kevin Francis revealed that he had a hole in the heart, while Steve Claridge has to take regular medication for a heart condition.

There was also news that John Sheridan would not be staying with the club and that he was returning to Sheffield Wednesday, while Chris Whyte was heading for Charlton on a free transfer.

Paul Tait, meanwhile, had rejoined the Blues from a trial at Coventry City and Barry Fry was more than pleased because he feels that the local-born player has a lot of potential which should be an asset at St. Andrew's.

With Blues anxious to improve their somewhat precarious position it was therefore a vastly different team that went into action against Wolves determined to make amends for the F.A. Cup defeat at Molineux when Jonathan Hunt's penalty miss proved so costly.

Wolves made the early running and a clever lob from Steve Bull nearly gave the Molineux men an early lead when Bart Griemink was stranded outside the penalty area.

But gradually Birmingham began to move back into the game and were infinitely much better than against Sheffield United in the previous game which resulted in a punitive Sunday morning training session.

There was, nevertheless, a measure of good fortune about the opening goal after 27 minutes when new boy Andy Legg blasted a shot against Neil Emblen which resulted in a penalty which Paul Devlin slotted away for his first goal.

With Barnes posing considerable trouble to Wolves defence the match was building up into a good game and the highlight came in the 39th minute when Barnes, on the right, produced a fast, low cross which Devlin hooked home at the near post.

In the second half Wolves hit Blues with a series of attacks, but the home side held firm with Gary Breen and Michael Johnson building up a solid front.

Jonathan Hunt, linked with a move to Sheffield Wednesday, was substituted for the fourth time in five games and was obviously far from pleased as he left the field.

Six minutes from time Wolves had a glimmer of hope when Jason Bowen handled in the area but Andy Thompson, usually so reliable, produced a weak effort which was easily saved by Griemink, who had put off the Wolves player by going on a walk about, causing the spot kick to be retaken. Even after this miss Bull had a great effort go just inches wide.

It was little wonder that Fry was later back to his old high spirits. He shouted: "What a difference a day makes!

"We played with a lot of pride, passion and commitment. But I was beginning to think we wouldn't win another game this season."

Two-goal Paul Devlin beats Eric Young to the ball.

Saturday 9th March 1996 • Prenton Park • 3.00pm

TRANMERE ROVERS 2 BIRMINGHAM CITY 2

Half time 1-1 • *Attendance* 8,696

Referee Mike RILEY (Leeds)

Linesmen A.B. OLDHAM and R. SUTTON

White Shirts with Blue and Green Trim, White Shorts		Goals	Red Shirts with Blue and White Trim, Red Shorts		Goals
1	Danny COYNE		1	Fred BARBER	
2	Gary STEVENS †		2	Jonathan BASS	
3	Alan ROGERS	70	3	JOHN FRAIN	
4	Dave HIGGINS		4	Paul TAIT	
5	Shaun GARNETT		5	Gary BREEN	
6	Paul COOK		6	Michael JOHNSON	
7	Ged BRANNAN		7	Jonathan HUNT	62
8	John ALDRIDGE	40	8	Paul DEVLIN †	
9	Ian MOORE		9	Paul BARNES	
10	Pat NEVIN		10	Vinny SAMWAYS	
11	Graham BRANCH ‡		11	Andy LEGG	39
	Substitutes			*Substitutes*	
12	Gary BENNETT		12	Jason BOWEN †58 ❑	
13	Kenny IRONS †45		13	Richard FORSYTH	
14	John MORRISSEY ‡69		14	Ian RICHARDSON	

BEFORE		P	W	D	L	F	A	pts	AFTER		P	W	D	L	F	A	pts
13	Blues	32	11	10	11	42	42	43	12	Blues	33	11	11	11	44	44	44
15	Tranmere	32	10	10	12	42	38	40	16	Tranmere	33	10	11	12	44	40	41

FACTFILE

Birmingham lead twice but share the points for the 11th time in 33 starts...
A masked Fred Barber makes his debut in goal for the injured Bart Griemink...
Birmingham are Barber's 14th club of his career... John Aldridge scores his 21st
goal of the season for Tranmere.

Barber puts a happy face on it

Fred Barber emerges as the early talking point as he takes the field on his debut wearing a horror mask. Birmingham fans hope it is not a foretaste of what is in store.

Barber, who has been wearing the mask to enter the field since his days at Walsall when David Kelly made the purchase as a dare, was making what could be his first and last appearance for Blues following a £25,000 move from Luton. He said: "I got a good reception the first time I used the mask and I've carried on ever since. It takes some of the seriousness out of the game."

Following the mid-week win over Wolves the team in general was in better spirits at Prenton Park and this was quickly illustrated as Blues appeared to have had a weight lifted off their shoulders.

Paul Tait's aggressive midfield play, allied to the subtle touches of Vinny Samways, gave Birmingham a much sharper look.

They conspired to produce some highly entertaining football that should have enabled them to build up a commanding lead. But Tranmere themselves are no push-overs in the skill market and matched Blues for long spells.

At times there was a feeling that Blues were about to break out and completely dominate the game when Andy Legg notched his first goal for the club with a 30-yard drive which took a deflection off Shaun Garnett six minutes before the break.

Any hopes of an avalanche of goals quickly disappeared as Birmingham's bubble of joy was pricked in the very next minute when the ever dangerous John Aldridge converted a cross from Ian Moore with a neat header past Barber.

It was the former Liverpool striker's 141st goal in 219 games for Tranmere and his spell at

Prenton Park must be one of the most productive in the club's history.

It's the kind of finishing which has eluded the Blues strikers this season and explained why the club were in mid-table.

Birmingham, with Hunt playing one of his better games than of late, were again the more impressive and deservedly regained the lead.

Paul Barnes, who had a quiet match, sent Jason Bowen clear, but the ball ran through for Hunt to gain possession and drive his shot home after a deflection off Alan Rogers.

But it was Rogers who had the last laugh with a mis-hit cross which completely deceived Barber. Blues stand-in goalkeeper was a couple of yards off his line and Rogers' shot looped into the net.

Barber then made his mark with a couple of saves from Kenny Irons and Aldridge in a late flurry, but Birmingham emerged with a point from a game when it was a win which would have taken them to within six points of Huddersfield Town in the fourth play-off place.

Fry's after the match comment was: "We were the pits against Sheffield United, but we sorted ourselves out against Wolves and again looked the business playing Tranmere.

"We looked capable of scoring from almost any position against Tranmere and this must be promising for the closing games of the season when anything can happen."

Paul Tait in midfield action.

Tuesday 12th March 1996 • St. Andrew's • 7.45pm

BIRMINGHAM CITY 2 HUDDERSFIELD TOWN 0

Half time 1-0 • *Attendance* 15,296

Referee John LLOYD (Wrexham)

Linesmen J.J. ASHMAN and J.D. WESSON

Blue Shirts, White Shorts		Goals	Yellow Shirts, Yellow Shorts		Goals
1	Bart GRIEMINK		1	Steve FRANCIS	
2	Jonathan BASS		2	Steve JENKINS	
3	John FRAIN		3	Tom COWAN	
4	Paul TAIT		4	Darren BULLOCK	
5	Gary BREEN		5	Lee SINNOTT	
6	Michael JOHNSON		6	Kevin GRAY	
7	Jonathan HUNT		7	Rob EDWARDS	
8	Paul DEVLIN	12	8	Lee MAKEL	
9	Paul BARNES	61	9	Andy BOOTH	
10	Vinny SAMWAYS †		10	Ronnie JEPSON	
11	Andy LEGG		11	Ben THORNLEY	
	Substitutes			*Substitutes*	
12	Richard FORSYTH		12	Iain DUNN	
13	Ian RICHARDSON †45		13	Tony NORMAN (Gk)	
14	Jason BOWEN		14	Jon DYSON	

BEFORE		P	W	D	L	F	A	pts	AFTER		P	W	D	L	F	A	pts
6	Huddersfield	33	14	10	9	46	37	52	6	Huddersfield	34	14	10	10	46	39	52
12	Blues	33	11	11	11	44	44	44	11	Blues	34	12	11	11	46	44	47

FACTFILE

Bart Griemink back from groin injury... Birmingham gain revenge for 4-2 defeat suffered in August... Paul Barnes scores his first goal for Blues... Paul Devlin grabs his third in three games... Only Huddersfield's third defeat in 14 games... Blues give themselves a realistic chance of a play-off place.

Super strikers topple Terriers

With the news that Ian Bennett was likely to be out of action for the rest of the season it was a relieved Barry Fry who welcomed back his young Dutch goalkeeper, Bart Griemink, for what was a most important match, against promotion challengers, Huddersfield Town.

The Yorkshire club were in sixth spot and it was imperative for Birmingham not to lose further ground if they were to have the slightest chance of making the play-offs.

Birmingham also had an old score to settle as they slumped to a 4-2 defeat at the hands of Huddersfield earlier in the season.

Significantly Birmingham made few changes from the side which had battled so hard at Tranmere in the previous game as Fry gave a welcome vote of confidence to the players who were unlucky not come away from Prenton Park with all three points.

Fry announced that he had also decided not to involve himself again in the transfer market before the end of the season; a fact which many Birmingham fans found hard to believe.

But the upshot of the game against Huddersfield Was that Birmingham hit the Northern club with a wave of attacks which had the opposition reeling against the ropes.

Andy Legg very nearly scored in the opening minute as Huddersfield were taken aback by such a sudden surge of attacks. Paul Devlin was a lively raider as was Paul Barnes and they formed a dangerous strike force.

It was Devlin who forced the Huddersfield goalkeeper to make a fine save when he pushed out an accurate shot. From the corner taken by Vinny Samways, Paul Tait headed the ball down and what appeared to be in slow motion Devlin turned and scored his third goal in three games from close range.

The whirlwind start could not be sustained and Huddersfield, an impressive side under the eager managership of Brian Horton, slowly worked their way back into the game.

Darren Bullock and Rob Edwards were always industrious and Birmingham found themselves under intensive pressure. Edwards clipped the bar two minues before the break, but it always appeared to be Birmingham's night.

This was clearly demonstrated when Barnes obtained his first goal for his new club in the 61st minute and it was one of the best executed this season. John Frain found Devlin down the left flank and he pulled the ball back into the path of Barnes to hit a screaming left foot shot into the net.

Barnes later admitted that the goal had given him a great deal of satisfaction. He said: "I can always score goals. It's never been a problem, but I cannot remember striking such a good shot. It was a goal as soon as it left my foot."

Huddersfield then launched a series of attacks which saw both Andy Booth and Ronnie Jepson miss good opportunities. Manager Horton was very disappointed and decribed it as Huddersfield's "worst performance of the season."

This did little justice to Birmingham's performance and manager Fry later emphasised the need to maintain the winning form to give themselves a reasonable chance of the play-offs in a real roller coaster season.

Paul Devlin knocks in Blues first goal.

Sunday 17th March 1996 • St Andrew's • 3.00pm

BIRMINGHAM CITY 0 SUNDERLAND 2

Half time 0-1 • *Attendance* 23,251
Referee Billy BURNS (Scarborough)
Linesmen C. Jones and I.A. MADGE

Blue Shirts, White Shorts	Goals	Red and White Striped Shirts, Black Shorts	Goals
1 Bart GRIEMINK		1 Shay GIVEN	
2 Jonathan BASS †		2 Dariusz KUBICKI	
3 John FRAIN		3 Martin SCOTT	
4 Paul TAIT		4 Paul BRACEWELL	
5 Gary BREEN		5 Kevin BALL	
6 Michael JOHNSON		6 Andy MELVILLE	64
7 Jonathan HUNT		7 Michael GRAY	
8 Paul DEVLIN ‡		8 Richard ORD	
9 Paul BARNES		9 Craig RUSSELL †	
10 Vinny SAMWAYS #		10 Paul STEWART ‡	
11 Andy LEGG		11 Steve AGNEW ❏	16
Substitutes		*Substitutes*	
12 Richard FORSYTH †64		12 Gareth HALL #89	
13 Ian RICHARDSON ‡64		13 Micky BRIDGES †78	
14 Jason BOWEN #64		14 Phil GRAY ‡81 #	

BEFORE		P	W	D	L	F	A	pts	AFTER		P	W	D	L	F	A	pts
2	Sunderland	35	17	12	6	46	26	63	1	Sunderland	36	18	12	6	48	26	66
11	Blues	34	12	11	11	46	44	47	11	Blues	35	12	11	12	46	46	47

FACTFILE

Birmingham's first defeat in four games... Sunderland record their seventh successive win, a new club record, to go back to the top of the division... It was only Sunderland's second win at St. Andrew's in 13 years... Chief scout Lil Fuccillo takes over as assistant manager after the sacking of Edwin Stein.

Griemink saves keep score down

The biggest league crowd of the season was attracted to St. Andrew's on a sunny afternoon which was in sharp contrast to the weather over the previous month.

They turned up in their numbers to watch in-form Sunderland because the admission prices had been dramatically slashed to £3. The fans, including nearly 3,000 from Sunderland, attended despite the game being televised.

But there was a cloud over the proceedings following yet another newspaper revelation that it had been alleged manager Barry Fry's two assistants, Edwin Stein and David Howell, had been reprimanded.

It was claimed that the two had been playing a late night game of cards with on loan signing, Vinny Samways – a situation, along with other instances, which apparently had not pleased managing director Karren Brady.

Whether this uneasy off-the-field situation had a bearing on the game it is hard to determine, other than that Birmingham produced one of their most indifferent performances for a long time.

Sunderland were a confident, efficient team and they conspired to make Birmingham look very ordinary. But it was interesting to note that of the team which opened the campaign with an impressive 3-1 home win over Ipswich, there were only two players, John Frain and Paul Tait, playing against Sunderland.

The highly mobile North East outfit hit Birmingham with a series of attacks and even in the early stages it was obvious that the Blues had a difficult task on their hands.

Only a goal-line clearance prevented Paul Stewart giving Sunderland the lead in a hectic spell of pressure on Birmingham's goal, but a minute later the Blues found themselves a goal in arrears. The defence had been pulled out of position and a through ball from Kevin Ball went between the legs of Andy Melville to the unmarked Steve Agnew, who slotted home a neat goal in the 16th minute.

Birmingham's best spell of attacking football occurred after this set-back, but Sunderland were never really threatened and only a fine save by Bart Griemink from Melville prevented a second goal for Peter Reid's team.

Man of the match Melville then kept out a Paul Barnes effort, but it never appeared to be Birmingham's day as the game always drifted in Sunderland's favour as highlighted in the 64th minute when Melville again moved up to head home a second goal for the visitors from an accurate cross from near the right hand corner flag by Dariusz Kubicki.

It was another men against boys situation according to Fry, who had no complaints about the result because Sunderland were the better outfit.

He added: "We were beaten by a superior team and if this is what it takes to reach the top then we have a long, long way to go to reach that standard."

Fry, however, is fully aware that he needs to resolve his off-the-field problems, because an unhappy ship operates on a short fuse that can explode at any moment with disastrous results.

Paul Devlin fights for possession.

Wednesday 20th March 1996 • St. Andrew's • 7.45pm

BIRMINGHAM CITY 1 WEST BROMWICH A. 1

Half time 0-1 • *Attendance* 19,147

Referee Neale BARRY (Scunthorpe)

Linesmen D.J. ADCOCK and D.J. HINE

Blue Shirts, White Shorts		Goals	Yellow Shirts with Blue Sleeves, Yellow Shorts		Goals
1	Bart GRIEMINK		1	Stuart NAYLOR	
2	Richard FORSYTH		2	Paul HOLMES	
3	Andy LEGG		3	Shane NICHOLSON	
4	Paul TAIT †		4	Richard SNEEKES	16
5	Gary BREEN		5	Daryl BURGESS ❏	
6	Michael JOHNSON		6	Paul RAVEN	
7	Jonathan HUNT	81	7	Julian DARBY ❏ †	
8	Paul DEVLIN ❏		8	Paul MARDON	
9	Paul BARNES #		9	Bob TAYLOR	
10	Vinny SAMWAYS		10	Andy HUNT ‡	
11	Jason BOWEN ‡		11	Ian HAMILTON	
	Substitutes			*Substitutes*	
12	Kevin FRANCIS †52		12	David GILBERT	
13	Andy EDWARDS #75		13	Lee ASHCROFT ‡81	
14	Ricky OTTO ‡58		14	Stacy COLDICOTT †53	

BEFORE		P	W	D	L	F	A	pts	AFTER		P	W	D	L	F	A	pts
11	Blues	35	12	11	12	46	46	47	11	Blues	36	12	12	12	47	47	48
18	Albion	35	11	7	17	44	57	40	19	Albion	36	11	8	17	45	58	41

FACTFILE

First game without assistant manager Edwin Stein and coach David Howell, who is suspended... Jonathan Hunt grabs his 15th goal of the season... Richard Sneekes scores his third goal in three games in the space of eight days for Albion... Player/coach Mark Ward linked with a free-transfer move to Huddersfield.

Hunt strike salvages point

Birmingham drop the bombshell of parting company with assistant manager Edwin Stein and delaying a decision for a fortnight on the future of Dave Howell.

Sadly, it is yet another indication of the turmoil within the club, where there is little consistency on or off the field.

It explains why Birmingham appear locked in a middle of the table position without any real sign of a major improvement, with the only normality being the coming and going of the players.

There is talk of Martin O'Connor joining from Walsall and Ian Richardson moving to Notts County to finance the deal.

But what was more important after the Sunderland game was for Birmingham to regain their winning ways to give a glimmer of hope to make the play-offs. Unfortunately it was Albion who made the early running in their bid to climb out of the danger area.

Jon Bass and John Frain were both missing from the team defeated by Sunderland. They were replaced by Richard Forsyth, who was later linked with Albion, and Jason Bowen with Andy Legg dropping into a defensive role.

With the club's former chief scout, Lil Fuc-

cillo, on the bench as Fry's new assistant, Birmingham made a hesitant start and were punished when Richard Sneekes pushed home a Paul Holmes cross after 16 minutes.

Albion, with only three points from their previous ten away games, battled hard and later built up a defensive barrier that Blues found difficult to penetrate.

Paul Devlin was a busy type of player but the end product was never any problem to Albion's three man central defensive partnership of Mardon, Burgess and Raven.

There were very few plus points from Birmingham's point of view and a lot of the early season excitement and passion had been replaced by a team of mediocrity.

Gary Breen was the exception. The bean-pole built defender again impressed with his determination to break up Albion's attacks but Birmingham could have had no complaints if Albion had added to their lead.

Andy Hunt carelessly wasted a couple of chances, while Ian Hamilton slammed one effort into the post.

It was Hunt's second miss which was to prove expensive. Fry sent on Andy Edwards and switched Breen into an attacking role which was an admission that Blues attack was lacking in several sections.

The impact was immediate. Breen headed a ball down and it took a deflection off Mardon and fell into the path of Jonathan Hunt who quickly turned and hammered a left foot shot into the roof of the net for a face saving equaliser.

Fry later said: "It shows the lad has talent but we have got to get some consistency from him."

Fry, who had been prepared to part with Hunt to Sheffield Wednesday a few weeks earlier, admitted: "Draws are no use to us.

"We've got to do what we did last season and finish with a string of wins, otherwise we are going to stay in the middle of the table."

Paul Tait rises to meet a near-post corner.

Saturday 23rd March 1996 • Molineux • 3.00pm

WOLVES 3 BIRMINGHAM CITY 2

Half time 1-1 • *Attendance* 26,256

Referee John KIRKBY (Sheffield)

Linesmen M. JOY and B.L. POLKEY

Old Gold Shirts with Black Trim, Black Shorts		Goals	Blue Shirts, White Shorts		Goals
1	Mike STOWELL		1	Bart GRIEMINK	
2	Jamie SMITH		2	Richard FORSYTH	
3	Andy THOMPSON	86pen	3	Andy LEGG ❑	
4	Eric YOUNG †		4	Vinny SAMWAYS	
5	Neil EMBLEN		5	Gary BREEN ❑	
6	Dean RICHARDS		6	Michael JOHNSON	
7	Steve CORICA		7	Jonathan HUNT	
8	Don GOODMAN	40	8	Paul DEVLIN	7,84pen
9	Steve BULL	89	9	Kevin FRANCIS	
10	Steve FROGGATT		10	Paul BARNES	
11	Simon OSBORN		11	Steve CASTLE	
Substitutes			*Substitutes*		
12	Mark ATKINS †79		12	Louie DONOWA	
13	Mark WILLIAMS		13	Jason BOWEN	
14	Dennis PEARCE		14	Andy EDWARDS	

BEFORE	P	W	D	L	F	A	pts	AFTER	P	W	D	L	F	A	pts
11 Blues	36	12	12	12	47	47	48	12 Blues	37	12	12	13	49	50	48
14 Wolves	36	11	12	13	46	48	45	13 Wolves	37	12	12	13	49	50	48

FACTFILE

Blues and Wolves finish the game with identical playing records... Wolves record their 34th home win in 49 league encounters with Birmingham... Paul Devlin takes his tally to five goals in seven games – four against Wolves... Steve Castle, back from a loan spell at Gillingham, is included in the Blues line-up.

Points disappear in late goal rush

Birmingham were unable to make the short trip across the Midlands without making further team changes. Paul Tait was injured, while Jason Bowen was dropped to the substitutes bench to make way for the return of Steve Castle.

Everyone in the Blues camp was determined to make amends for the F.A. Cup exit at Molineux a few weeks previously and this explained why they made a 'flyer' from the starting whistle.

But soccer matches are not a sprint and this was to become painfully obvious as the game progressed.

Fortunately off-the-field problems were put on one side and the team hit Wolves with an opening barrage which earned Paul Devlin a seventh minute goal.

The former Notts County player, who keeps a snake as a hobby, scored twice in the league game at St. Andrew's and picked up where he left off in that encounter.

Jonathan Hunt, showing signs of recapturing his best form, pulled back the ball to Kevin Francis who transferred his pass into the direction of Devlin to score from about ten yards.

Birmingham were boosted by this start but were unable to capitalise upon the goal and allowed Wolves back into the game five minutes before the break when Don Goodman scored with a cross shot past Bart Griemink.

For a long period it appeared as if that would be the result as both teams tested each other without success.

But the game is never over until the final whistle as was vividly exemplified in this local derby when all the action came in an electric final six minutes play.

The game exploded when the gangling Kevin Francis gained possession and completely missed his kick yards away from goal. It was alleged by the referee that Francis had been impeded by Dean Richards but this view was discounted, even by Barry Fry.

He didn't think it was a penalty either which enabled Wolves to equalise just four minutes later through long serving Andy Thompson after acting skipper Gary Breen was said to have handled a shot.

But worse was to follow for Blues, who had twice led in the game only to have the fruits of success grabbed from their eager hands in the last minute of the game.

Steve Bull produced a typical solo effort when he careered through Birmingham's defence to hammer a shot past Griemink after Michael Johnson had failed to cut out the Wolves striker.

Fry was magnanimous in defeat as was acknowledged by Mark McGhee, who admitted that he would have been gutted in similar circumstances.

He said: "One minute we were counting the three points and two minutes later, we had nothing. It's a hard game but we only had ourselves to blame.

"We deserved something from the match but Wolves battled hard and kept going right until the final whistle and Steve Bull was magnificent. He never knows when he is beaten and yet again he was their match-winner."

Kevin Francis wins a penalty.

Saturday 30th March 1996 • Blundell Park • 3.00pm

GRIMSBY TOWN 2 BIRMINGHAM CITY 1

Half time 2-1 • *Attendance* 5,475
Referee David ALLISON (Lancaster)
Linesmen M.J. MOUNTAIN and K. POWELL

Black and White Striped Shirts, Black Shorts		Goals	Red Shirts with Blue and White Trim, Red Shorts		Goals
1	Paul CRICHTON		1	Bart GRIEMINK	
2	John McDERMOTT		2	John FRAIN †	
3	Tony GALLIMORE		3	Martin GRAINGER	
4	Richard SMITH		4	Vinny SAMWAYS	
5	Graham RODGER		5	Gary BREEN	
6	Paul GROVES	35	6	Michael JOHNSON	
7	Mark FLATTS		7	Jonathan HUNT ‡	
8	Craig SHAKESPEARE		8	Paul DEVLIN	
9	Jamie FORRESTER		9	Paul BARNES #	5
10	Steve LIVINGSTONE	40	10	John CORNFORTH	
11	Nicky SOUTHALL		11	Andy LEGG	
	Substitutes			*Substitutes*	
12	Neil WOODS		12	Paul TAIT †63	
13	Ashley FICKLING		13	Kevin FRANCIS ‡63	
14	Brian LAWS		14	Paul PESCHISOLIDO #63	

BEFORE	P	W	D	L	F	A	pts	AFTER	P	W	D	L	F	A	pts
12 Blues	37	12	12	13	49	50	48	13 Blues	38	12	12	14	50	52	48
18 Grimsby	36	11	12	13	42	51	45	15 Grimsby	37	12	12	13	44	52	48

FACTFILE

Blues included their two latest signings, Martin Grainger and John Cornforth, in the side with Paul Peschisolido on the subs bench following his return from Stoke City... There were no less than eight newcomers in the team since the start of the new year... Birmingham extended their run to eleven away games without a win.

Bennett missed as Blues miss out

Birmingham City boss, Barry Fry, simply could not miss out on the transfer deadline activity and snapped up Martin Grainger from Brentford for £400,000, John Cornforth from Swansea City for £350,000 and surprise, surprise Paul Peschisolido returned to St. Andrew's from Stoke City for £400,000.

It all added to the confusion and uncertainty which existed in the club, made worse by the departure of assistant manager Edwin Stein and coach David Howell.

Only John Frain and Jonathan Hunt remained from the side which opened the year a few weeks previously, indicating the almost complete transformation made by Fry.

In the circumstances it was hardly surprising that such a disjointed team went into the Grimsby game with a record of not having won any of its previous ten league away games.

Birmingham's middle of the table position was a fair reflection of their form which is all the more surprising that in the previous twelve months they had reached the semi-finals of the Coca-Cola Cup and won the Second Division title and also the Auto Windscreens Shield.

Unfortunately there was again somewhat of an air of mediocrity about the team at Grimsby despite making a fast, attacking start which resulted in Paul Barnes snapping up a fifth minute goal with a low shot from the edge of the penalty area.

There were several wasted chances as Grimsby survived several spells of pressure. They were boosted by their ability to contain a less than positive Birmingham side and made the Midlanders pay dearly before the comfort of the half time whistle.

Paul Groves, the centre of attention from West Bromwich Albion, equalised in the 35th minute when Birmingham's defence hit the panic button following a long throw-in from Richard Smith.

Birmingham were in trouble five minutes later when Smith flashed a header against the post and before anyone in the Blues defence could react to clear their lines Steve Livingstone dived in for the winner.

The game progressed to just past the hour mark before Fry made the now usual triple substitution of a desperate gambler.

Gangling Kevin Francis conspired to upset the Grimsby defence, but Paul Peschisolido never had the kind of service he needs for his darting runs at the opposition.

As a result Birmingham could have few complaints. Cracks in the team were obvious. New-boys Grainger and Cornforth made little impact, while goalkeeper Bart Griemink's lack of experience was again exposed.

It left Fry bemoaning the absence of Ian Bennett. He said: "If Benno had been in the side this year we would have won at least three away games and that would have put us in the play-off zone.

"As it is, we need to win at least two games to make certain that we are not sucked into the relegation area."

Paul Barnes – put Blues into an early lead.

Tuesday 2nd April 1996 • St. Andrew's • 7.45pm

BIRMINGHAM CITY 2 PORTSMOUTH 0

Half time 1-0 • *Attendance* 14,886

Referee Eddie WOLSTENHOLM (Blackburn)

Linesmen A.J. GREEN and M.L. SHORT

Blue Shirts, White Shorts		Goals	Red Shirts with Black Stripes, Black Shorts		Goals
1	Bart GRIEMINK		1	Alan KNIGHT	
2	Andy EDWARDS		2	Danny HINSHELWOOD ❏	
3	Martin GRAINGER		3	Andy AWFORD †	
4	Vinny SAMWAYS		4	Alan McLOUGHLIN	
5	Gary BREEN		5	Andy THOMSON	
6	Michael JOHNSON		6	Russell PERRETT	
7	Jonathan HUNT		7	Martin ALLEN	
8	Paul TAIT		8	Fitzroy SIMPSON ‡	
9	Paul BARNES	19	9	Deon BURTON	
10	Paul PESCHISOLIDO †		10	Paul HALL	
11	Paul DEVLIN	80pen	11	John DURNIN	
	Substitutes			*Substitutes*	
12	Jason BOWEN		12	Lee RUSSELL †45	
13	Kevin FRANCIS †77		13	Sammy IGOE ‡75	
14	John CORNFORTH		14	Lee BRADBURY	

BEFORE		P	W	D	L	F	A	pts	AFTER		P	W	D	L	F	A	pts
13	Blues	38	12	12	14	50	52	48	13	Blues	39	13	12	14	52	52	51
18	Portsmouth	39	11	12	16	56	61	45	19	Portsmouth	40	11	12	17	56	63	45

FACTFILE

Paul Barnes produces his third goal in six games to turn Birmingham's relegation fears into hopes of making the play-offs... Portsmouth slump to their third successive defeat against Midland opposition following wins by Port Vale and West Bromwich Albion.

Terrific Tait leads the way

Rumours concerning the future of manager Barry Fry abound, but the jovial Birmingham boss denies that he is leaving the club as he is firmly committed to taking the Blues into the Premier League.

He claims that his buying and selling policy is geared to this end and that he wanted people in the club not to panic.

Fry said: "If we win a few games it eases all the tension around the place. I'm the first to admit that no one is more disappointed that we have not done much better.

"I still say that if Ian Bennett had been in goal we could have won three away games and who knows what we might have achieved."

Portsmouth's visit, therefore, was of vital importance to both clubs. Birmingham required victory to assure their mid-table slot, while Portsmouth needed to improve their record after picking up just six points from their last eight games.

Pompey were the more positive in the early stages when John Durnin and Alan McLoughlin were unfortunate not to score. They proved to be expensive misses as Paul Barnes, earlier jeered by the fans for his indifferent ball control, silenced his critics.

In the 19th minute a short free kick by Vinny Samways to Jonathan Hunt resulted in an accurate cross that found Barnes rushing in to head home a fine goal off the underside of the bar.

Barnes had been on target to give Blues the lead in the previous game at Grimsby only for Fry's team to lose. Fears of a repeat were always at the back of the fans' minds as the young Portsmouth side strived manfully to get back into contention.

One disturbing feature was the poor contribution made by Paul Peschisolido. In his first home game since his return from Stoke he struggled to get involved and was substituted late in the game.

Barnes, meanwhile, continued to be a busy player as he contrived to put Portsmouth under pressure. He should have had a second goal early in the second half, but Portsmouth's veteran goalkeeper Alan Knight, in his 17th season at the club, cleverly blocked the effort.

Portsmouth often looked threatening as was highlighted when Martin Allen smashed a 25-yard free-kick against the post with Griemink well beaten.

Fry then decided to pull off Peschisolido and send on Kevin Francis. Within a minute Birmingham increased their lead, although it was a little fortuitous.

Man of the match Paul Tait was going through when Lee Russell put in what appeared to be a sound tackle only for substitute referee Mr. Short, who took over from the injured Eddie Wolstenholm at the interval, to award a penalty.

Paul Devlin despatched the spot kick with vigour to confirm that he was the club's penalty expert following the poor record of other players earlier in the season.

Fry's reaction to the welcome win was that it did little to enhance the club's play-off prospects. "We have as much chance as I have of getting the Manchester United manager's job tomorrow," he quipped.

Paul Barnes aims to block a Pompey attack.

Saturday 6th April 1996 • St. Andrew's • 3.00pm

BIRMINGHAM CITY 3 PORT VALE 1

Half time 2-0 • *Attendance* 17,469

Referee George CAIN (Bootle)

Linesmen D.N. CAMPBELL and A.D. MILLS

Blue Shirts, White Shorts		Goals	White Shirts with Black and Yellow Trim, Black Shorts		Goals
1	Bart GRIEMINK		1	Paul MUSSELWHITE ❏	
2	Gary BREEN		2	Andy HILL	
3	Martin GRAINGER		3	Dean STOKES	
4	John CORNFORTH		4	Ian BOGIE #	
5	Andy EDWARDS		5	Randy SAMUEL	
6	Michael JOHNSON		6	Neil ASPIN	
7	Jonathan HUNT		7	Jon McCARTHY ‡	
8	Paul DEVLIN		8	Andy PORTER	68
9	Paul BARNES	16	9	Martin FOYLE	
10	Paul PESCHISOLIDO	44	10	Tony NAYLOR †	
11	Paul TAIT	59	11	Steve GUPPY	
	Substitutes			*Substitutes*	
12	John FRAIN		12	Ray WALKER #73	
13	Kevin FRANCIS		13	STUART TALBOT ‡61	
14	Steve BARNES		14	Lee MILLS †36	

BEFORE		P	W	D	L	F	A	pts	AFTER		P	W	D	L	F	A	pts
11	Port Vale	37	13	13	11	48	47	52	9	Blues	40	14	12	14	55	53	54
13	Blues	39	13	12	14	52	52	51	12	Port Vale	38	13	13	12	49	50	52

FACTFILE

Port Vale still without a win at St. Andrew's since their last success in the 1954-55 season... The North Staffordshire side lose their first league game in 13 outings... Barnes opens the scoring for the third successive match and Paul Peschisolido nets his first goal upon his return to the club.

Barnes-storming display by Paul

High riding Port Vale arrive keen to improve their league position at the expense of a new look Birmingham side that contained players who had only made a handful of appearances in the blue shirts.

With an unbeaten league run of 12 games, the Vale were worthy opponents to test Barry Fry's latest line-up, but as events quickly transpired the game proved an easy canter for Blues.

Vinny Samways was forced to drop out with an injury, but it accorded Fry the opportunity to give Welsh international John Cornforth another outing.

Birmingham gave an early indication of their determination to hit Port Vale on the break and Paul Devlin produced a good effort which forced Paul Musselwhite to make the first of several smart saves.

The start obviously made Birmingham "feel good" and this sparked off some promising moves which kept Neil Aspin under a great deal

John Cornforth holds up a Port Vale attack.

of pressure in the heart of Valiant's defence.

At this stage it appeared as if Birmingham were the team with the long unbeaten run as Port Vale were very ragged and uninspiring.

It was, therefore, of little surprise when Paul Barnes produced a powerful header from Jonathan Hunt's cross which rattled the underside of the crossbar before going into the net after 16 minutes.

A minute before the break Paul Peschisolido obtained his first goal since his return from Stoke when he was involved in a neat one-two with Hunt before slotting home a 15-yard shot.

Birmingham were now coasting and Port Vale were on the verge of being taken to the cleaners.

Paul Tait became the third goalscorer in the 59th minute following a free-kick which was headed on to Tait to force home his close range effort.

There was only a temporary hiccup when Andy Porter headed in a simple goal after 68 minutes following a right wing cross. But Vale lacked the ammunition to really make a fight of it and the game was a foregone conclusion well before the end of the game.

Jonathan Hunt produced some neat work but failed to really hit the high spots.

Newcomers Martin Grainger and Cornforth had reasonable matches in what was a relatively untried Birmingham team. It was really asking too much in the circumstances for the team to make a bid for the play-offs.

Fry himself was somewhat reluctant to admit that Birmingham still had an outside chance of the play-offs, but a great deal depended up the subsequent end of season games starting with the problematic visit to Millwall.

Fry amazingly disclosed that Karren Brady and the club had received threatening letters warning them of the consequences of playing at Millwall. In the circumstances the general opinion was that it would have been better not to have made public these unsavoury facts.

Wednesday 10th April 1996 • New Den • 7.45pm

MILLWALL 2 BIRMINGHAM CITY 0

Half time 1-0 • *Attendance* 9,271

Referee Clive WILKES (Gloucester)

Linesmen C.N. BREAKSPEARE and B.P. FISH

Blue Shirts with White Sleeves, Blue Shorts		Goals	Red Shirts with Blue and White Trim, Red Shorts		Goals
1	Kasey KELLER		1	Bart GRIEMINK	
2	Gerrard LAVIN		2	Gary BREEN ❏	
3	Keith STEVENS		3	Martin GRAINGER ❏	
4	Ben THATCHER		4	Andy EDWARDS	
5	Jason VAN BLERK		5	Michael JOHNSON	
6	Micky WEIR		6	John CORNFORTH	
7	Ricky NEWMAN		7	Jonathan HUNT ‡	
8	Bobby BOWRY	11	8	Paul DEVLIN #	
9	Dale GORDON †		9	Steve BARNES ❏	
10	Chris MALKIN	53	10	Paul PESCHISOLIDO †	
11	Sergei YURAN		11	Paul TAIT	
	Substitutes			*Substitutes*	
12	Darren WEBBER †59		12	Kevin FRANCIS †56	
13	Tony DOLBY		13	John FRAIN ‡56	
14	Richard CADETTE		14	Andy LEGG #56	

BEFORE		P	W	D	L	F	A	pts	AFTER		P	W	D	L	F	A	pts
9	Blues	40	14	12	14	55	53	54	10	Blues	41	14	12	15	55	55	54
20	Millwall	41	12	12	17	39	56	48	18	Millwall	42	13	12	17	41	56	51

FACTFILE

Team unchanged from Port Vale game... Andy Legg back on bench after suspension... With only four points from 12 away games Birmingham finally drop out of the play-offs... Paul Barnes fails to score for the first time in four games... Only 298 Birmingham fans make the trip to the New Den.

Away form still poses problems

Pre-match worries about possible trouble took up most of the attention with doubts being expressed that Birmingham officials should, in fact, not have disclosed that the club had received threatening letters from fans supposedly supporting Millwall.

The police certainly were not taking any chances as the team coach had a full escort and like some presidential cavalcade swept through all the traffic lights on the way to the New Den.

Whether or not this kind of treatment got to the players is uncertain, but what cannot be denied is that Blues conspired to produce one of their most inept performances of the season against a club with an indifferent home record.

Ironically, both Birmingham and Millwall could trace both their slumps in the league to the day they played each other at St. Andrew's. Millwall were top of the table that day but they had since only won four matches going into the New Den encounter.

If Fry thought the hype would lift his players he was sadly mistaken because at no time did Blues produce anything like the performance they turned on in the previous game with Port Vale. In no uncertain terms were they made fully aware that nothing short of a win was good enough if they were to make a late charge to the play-offs.

Prospects were not good judging by Birmingham's previous away record as they had collected only four draws from eleven games away from St. Andrew's.

There was the usual hostility from the Millwall crowd, but it was no different from that aimed at any other opposition.

In any case Birmingham failed dismally to show any real heart for the task in hand and found themselves in deep trouble as early as the eleventh minute when Bobby Bowry collected a pass from Sergei Yuran to fire his shot past Bart Griemink.

Gary Breen, Martin Grainger and Paul Barnes picked up bookings as Birmingham fumbled their way through a match which posed a lot of question marks for Fry. The defeat, however, could hardly be viewed as a surprise in view of the club's previous away record.

Birmingham's inability to compete in midfield was a major reason for a lack-lustre performance and Millwall were always the better side.

Dale Gordon blasted one second half effort against the bar and this posted warning notices to Birmingham as two minutes later Jason Van Blerk floated over a cross which Chris Malkin headed home from close range in the 53rd minute. The goal created the usual response from Fry. He sent on all three substitutes, but to no avail as Millwall were coasting and only a goalline clearance by John Cornforth prevented a third goal.

Fry admitted: "We never even got into the game and were not a patch on the side which defeated Port Vale. I've told the players to watch the match video to see how bad they were on the night.

"We've kissed the play-offs good-bye and we have only ourselves to blame."

Gary Breen.

Saturday 13th April 1996 • St. Andrew's • 3.00pm

BIRMINGHAM CITY 4 LUTON TOWN 0

Half time 1-0 • *Attendance* 15,426

Referee Roger GIFFORD (Llanbradach)

Linesmen D.S. BRAMMER and P.V. NORMAN

Blue Shirts, White Shorts		Goals
1	Bart GRIEMINK	
2	Gary POOLE	
3	Martin GRAINGER ❏	
4	John CORNFORTH #	
5	Gary BREEN	
6	Andy EDWARDS	
7	Jonathan HUNT ‡	
8	Paul DEVLIN	16secs
9	Paul BARNES	77,89
10	Paul PESCHISOLIDO	
11	Paul TAIT ❏ †	

Substitutes

12	Andy LEGG †55	
13	Kevin FRANCIS #70	76
14	Michael JOHNSON ‡61	

Amber and Black Striped Shirts, Black Shorts		Goals
1	Ian FEUER	
2	Graham ALEXANDER	
3	Mitchell THOMAS	
4	Gary WADDOCK †	
5	Marvin JOHNSON	
6	Darren PATTERSON	
7	Bontcho GUENTCHEV ‡	
8	Tony THORPE	
9	David OLDFIELD #	
10	Kim GRANT	
11	Scott OAKES	

Substitutes

12	John TAYLOR ‡55	
13	Richard HARVEY †35	
14	Graeme TOMLINSON #66	

BEFORE		P	W	D	L	F	A	pts
10	Blues	41	14	12	15	55	55	54
23	Luton	40	10	11	19	36	53	41

AFTER		P	W	D	L	F	A	pts
9	Blues	42	15	12	15	59	55	57
23	Luton	41	10	11	20	36	57	41

FACTFILE

Gary Poole returns to the side after an eleven game absence... First time this season that Birmingham score four goals at home... The 60th anniversary of the day Joe Payne scored ten goals in a game for Luton against Bristol Rovers... Luton fail for the fifth time in six games to win at St. Andrew's.

Quick fire Devlin Sparks goal glut

Optimistic talk of still making the play-offs comes from some quarters, but the hard core of Birmingham fans recognised that the Blues have shot their bolt and that the team are going to miss out on even giving themselves a chance of promotion.

In the circumstances it is hardly surprising because the team that is finishing the season is unrecognisable from that which began the campaign on the opening day.

There must be some notice taken of this fact because the club may have made a good profit on the season, but in the process they effectively killed off any real chance of honours.

Luton Town were not the best opposition to attract a bumper gate. They possessed the worst goalscoring record in the division and arrived at St. Andrew's on the back of a shock 2-1 home defeat at the hands of Stoke City after leading with only four minutes left to play.

They were still obviously shell-shocked at the thought of this demoralising experience and found themselves a goal in arrears after just 16 seconds. Martin Grainger collected a ball midway in his own half and sent a long ball forward to Paul Devlin who darted through Luton's defence and suddenly found himself with only goalkeeper Ian Feuer to beat with a low cross shot.

If Paul Peschisolido had not been so selfish and attempted to score himself instead of passing to the unmarked Paul Tait, Birmingham could have been in the driving seat after twenty minutes.

Luton hung on, battling hard but running out of ideas once they hit the 30-yard mark from Birmingham's goal.

There were several good chances created particularly in the early stages of the second period

when Paul Barnes just missed a cross from Andy Legg, who had replaced Tait.

As events transpired the game turned on a 70th minute incident when Kim Grant had to be assisted from the field following a tackle by Grainger. It appeared insignificant at the time but Kevin Francis, who took over from John Cornforth after the former Swansea player broke his nose, began a three goals in 13 minutes spell which consigned Luton to the Second Division for the first time since 1968.

Gary Poole made space with a run to the bye-line before launching a tailor-made high cross to the far post for Francis to head home.

Luton were effectively destroyed and in the following minute Legg put Peschisolido in possesion and his accurate pass to Barnes was finished off in fine style.

Peschisolido, who suddenly made a late impact, created another powerful strike which ended with the little Canadian hitting in a powerful low shot which rebounded back off Feuer into the path of Barnes to notch his second goal of the game.

The scoreline, as Fry later admitted, flattered Birmingham as there was never a four goals difference between the two teams and explains why Birmingham could not seriously consider themselves as play-off candidates with the prospect of three away games at Sunderland, Derby County and Leicester just around the corner. A couple of points from the three games would be considered a bonus on their previous away form, which had produced three successive defeats.

**Andy Edwards –
against all odds.**

Tuesday 16th April 1996 • Roker Park • 7.45pm

SUNDERLAND 3 BIRMINGHAM CITY 0

Half time 2-0 • *Attendance* 19,831

Referee Trevor WEST (Hull)

Linesmen B. LOWE and P. OXLEY

Red and White Striped Shirts, Black Shorts	Goals	Blue Shirts, White Shorts	Goals
1 Alec CHAMBERLAIN		1 Bart GRIEMINK	
2 Dariusz KUBICKI		2 Gary POOLE ❑	
3 Martin SCOTT		3 Martin GRAINGER	
4 Paul BRACEWELL		4 John CORNFORTH	
5 Kevin BALL		5 Gary BREEN	
6 Andy MELVILLE		6 Andy EDWARDS	
7 Michael GRAY	17	7 Michael JOHNSON ‡	
8 Richard ORD		8 Paul DEVLIN #	
9 Craig RUSSELL	20	9 Paul BARNES	
10 Paul STEWART	62	10 Andy LEGG †	
11 Steve AGNEW		11 Paul TAIT	
Substitutes		*Substitutes*	
12 Gareth HALL		12 Jonathan HUNT †45	
13 Micky BRIDGES		13 Paul PESCHISOLIDO ‡45	
14 Lee HOWE		14 Kevin FRANCIS #45	

BEFORE		P	W	D	L	F	A	pts	AFTER		P	W	D	L	F	A	pts
1	Sunderland	42	21	15	6	56	31	78	1	Sunderland	43	22	15	6	59	31	81
9	Blues	42	15	12	15	59	55	57	9	Blues	43	15	12	16	59	58	57

FACTFILE

Sunderland complete an easy double over Birmingham and demonstrate the difference in ability and class between the two teams... It's Sunderland's 16th game without defeat... John Cornforth, son of the Sunderland Echo sports editor, made his first appearance at Roker Park in Birmingham's colours.

Lessons can be learned in defeat

Champions-elect Sunderland were in a destructive mood and confirmed their superiority in a positive fashion.

Simply, Birmingham were not even in contention and were playing above their station on current form.

Sunderland took another step towards clinching the title – but whether they are strong enough or good enough to compete in the Premier League is open to considerable debate.

What was clear cut was the fact that Birmingham were no where near a side that could be considered for the top flight.

Following the 2-0 defeat at the hands of Sunderland in March when they were outclassed, Birmingham attempted a defensive operation but without any real success.

If there was anything to be gleaned from the game it was the fact that you do not have to spend huge amounts of money on new players every other week. Sunderland's side was virtually what Peter Reid inherited when he took over as manager.

His criterion for success is sheer hard graft on the training ground, working the squad into a match winning line-up.

Manager Barry Fry's response to the situation which faced him at Roker Park was to drop both Jonathan Hunt and Paul Peschisolido and to play Michael Johnson as an extra central defender.

The ploy didn't work as Sunderland hit Birmingham with a series of raids which destroyed the Midlanders with two goals in a three minute spell to put into perspective the 4-0 success over Luton three days previously.

Michael Gray opened the scoring in the 17th minute with a terrific swerving shot which again left Bart Griemink seemingly transfixed proving once again just how much Blues have missed Ian Bennett.

So far as Birmingham were concerned the game and a season of mixed fortunes was over three minutes later when Paul Stewart headed in a free-kick.

Fry responded by sending on his three substitutes for the second half but the damage had been done a long time previously and the disjointed appearance of the side only seemed to make the situation worse.

There was no authority in midfield where the industry and tenacity of Mark Ward has been sadly missed. His failure to appear after the home defeat against Derby was a vital turning point in Birmimgham's over-all fortunes.

Another disturbing feature of the game was the fact that Jonathan Hunt was unable to start the game as he appears to be at loggerheads with Barry Fry.

Birmingham's manager makes no secret of the fact that he is unhappy with Hunt's contribution with the player expressing his concern that he is unable to please Fry.

Sunderland, meanwhile, coasted home with Craig Russell adding what amounted to the inevitable third goal after 62 minutes when he broke clear to seal a comfortable win.

Fry admitted afterwards: "Sunderland were in a different class, a different gear compared to my outfit. They all wanted to play and be winners and that was the big difference on the night."

No way through for Paul Devlin.

Saturday 20th April 1996 • Baseball Ground • 3.00pm

DERBY COUNTY 1 BIRMINGHAM CITY 1

Half time 0-0 • *Attendance* 16,757

Referee Terry HEILBRON (Newton Aycliffe)

Linesmen M. SWIFT and P.B. WING

White Shirts, Black Shorts		Goals	Blue Shirts, White Shorts		Goals
1	Russell HOULT		1	Bart GRIEMINK	
2	Gary ROWETT		2	Gary POOLE	
3	Daryl POWELL		3	Martin GRAINGER	
4	Paul TROLLOPE		4	John CORNFORTH	
5	Dean YATES		5	Gary BREEN	74
6	Igor STIMAC ❑		6	Andy EDWARDS	
7	Robin Van Der LAAN #		7	Jonathan HUNT	
8	Ashley WARD		8	Paul DEVLIN	
9	Paul SIMPSON	55	9	Paul BARNES ‡	
10	Ronnie WILLEMS †		10	Paul PESCHISOLIDO †	
11	Lee CARSLEY ‡		11	Paul TAIT	
	Substitutes			*Substitutes*	
12	Marco GABBIADINI †71		12	Andy LEGG ‡61	
13	Steve HODGES #87		13	Kevin FRANCIS †19	
14	Matt CARBON ‡83		14	Michael JOHNSON	

BEFORE		P	W	D	L	F	A	pts	AFTER		P	W	D	L	F	A	pts
2	Derby	43	20	15	8	66	46	75	2	Derby	44	20	16	8	67	47	76
9	Blues	43	15	12	16	59	58	57	9	Blues	44	15	13	16	60	59	58

FACTFILE

Birmingham have still not won away since their 1-0 victory at Reading on November 11... Kevin Francis plays against his old club... Former Blues manager Jim Smith on the verge of guiding Derby to promotion... Gary Cooper has his contract paid up... Vinny Samways unlikely to get a permanent contract.

Breen on target to bag a point

Nervous Derby County displayed all the problems of a team with promotion within their grasp, but knowing that fate could still deal them a bad hand.

It was a situation which Birmingham could exploit, although very few people gave them much chance on their previous form.

Derby had won 4-1 at St. Andrew's and many people had stated that it was this game which proved to be the vital turning point in Birmingham's fortunes.

There was little to predict an upset as Birmingham's failure to find a dominant midfield had proved to be their nadir and not even the fast talking Barry Fry could deny this fact.

The prospects at the Baseball Ground were not very bright before the starting whistle and appeared to take a nose-dive when Paul Peschisolido suffered concussion after only 19 minutes play following a collision with Dean Yates.

But this enabled Fry to send on Kevin Francis against his old club – a situation which was certainly relished by the giant striker who then conspired to upset the opposition at every turn.

Previously Derby had threatened to over-run the Blues, but once Francis was back in familiar territory the game took a dramatic turn and Paul Barnes should have scored for the fifth successive game when Jonathan Hunt created a fine opening.

Derby survived and moved into the second half still looking for the win which would give them promotion and it appeared as if Birmingham had handed them the points on a plate when Paul Trollope gained possession without too much trouble or opposition to enable Paul Simpson to race through and toe-punt the ball past Bart Griemink.

Andy Legg, who was later to hear of his selection for the Welsh national team, was then drafted into the side to the exclusion of Barnes and the former Notts County player was to figure in the equaliser.

He used one of his long throws to the near post where Francis was able to head back towards the far post where skipper Gary Breen was on hand to head home.

Derby then had a severe attack of the jitters and everyone couldn't wait for the final whistle as Birmingham twice went close to sealing the game. Only a great save by Russell Hoult kept the Rams in the game when he pushed an effort from Hunt against the bar.

Francis, who tried desperately hard to get a goal against his old club, failed to make contact only a few yards away from the opposition's goalline as he roared into the thick of the action.

But the last moment of drama occurred when Marco Gabbiadini slammed a header against the bar and Matt Carbon failed to convert the rebound which would have solved all of Derby's problems.

Derby, out of the top flight for five years, ironically put themselves back into the spotlight after selling their star players. Could there be a moral in this for Birmingham City?

Manager Barry Fry later said: "Derby were very nervous and we might well have won in the closing stages. But I hope they go up because Jim Smith deserves the success."

Paul Barnes' determination wins him a 50/50 ball.

Saturday 27th April 1996 • Filbert Street • 3.00pm

LEICESTER CITY 3 BIRMINGHAM CITY 0

Half time 2-0 • Attendance 19,702

Referee Jim RUSHTON (Stoke)

Linesmen A. BLACK and R.E. BODEN

Blue Shirts, Blue Shorts	Goals	Red Shirts with Blue and White Trim, Red Shorts	Goals
1 Kevin POOLE		1 Bart GRIEMINK	
2 Simon GRAYSON		2 Gary POOLE	
3 Mike WHITLOW		3 John FRAIN	
4 Julian WATTS		4 John CORNFORTH ‡	
5 Steve WALSH		5 Andy EDWARDS #	
6 Mustafa IZZETT		6 Michael JOHNSON	
7 Neil LENNON	89	7 Jonathan HUNT †	
8 Scott TAYLOR †		8 Paul DEVLIN	
9 Steve CLARIDGE	33	9 Paul BARNES	
10 Mark ROBINS		10 Paul PESCHISOLIDO	
11 Emile HESKEY	39	11 Paul TAIT	
Substitutes		*Substitutes*	
12 Garry PARKER †76		12 Simon REA #63	
13 Brian CAREY		13 Steve BARNES †45	
14 Colin HILL		14 Richard FORYSTH ‡45	

BEFORE	P	W	D	L	F	A	pts	AFTER	P	W	D	L	F	A	pts
6 Leicester	44	17	14	13	62	60	65	6 Leicester	45	18	14	13	65	60	68
9 Blues	44	15	13	16	60	59	58	12 Blues	45	15	13	17	60	62	58

FACTFILE

Birmingham complete a miserable away season with a record of only five points from their final 15 away games... Steve Claridge made his first appearance against Birmingham since his move to Leicester and marked it with the opening goal... Gary Breen and Martin Grainger were absent because of suspension.

Old boy Steve takes control

With Steve Claridge in the opposition there was a major pre-match topical talking point and it was clearly obvious that the former Blues striker was out to make a point.

He again stressed that he had not wanted to leave Birmingham, but thought he deserved more recognition than he was getting, particularly as on-loan players were earning considerably more than he was on a weekly basis.

That was water under the bridge so far as Birmingham were concerned, but it was clearly an opportunity for Claridge to demonstrate that they had lost an asset when they sold him to Leicester for £1.4m.

He was fired up to do well and as early as the second minute he was in a goalscoring position but found himself blocked out by Andy Edwards.

Birmingham were never in the hunt as they failed to get control of the midfield and their abysmal away form continued to dog them with the predictable outcome.

The disturbing feature of the performance was the lack of a real commitment and this must have been very worrying for Barry Fry.

Claridge badly wanted a goal and was only thwarted by Bart Griemink after ten minutes, but the tenacious striker could not be denied indefinitely as he highlighted in the 33rd minute by grabbing his fourth goal in three games.

He was on hand to head in a cross from Emile Heskey, one of Leicester's up and coming young players.

Despite his pre-match claim that he had no desire to gloat over his old club, Claridge immediately pointed towards the touchline benches and appeared to aim some words towards the tight-lipped Birmingham officials.

With Birmingham losing their grip things went from bad to worse as Leicester deservedly increased their lead with a second goal from Heskey six minutes after the Claridge strike.

As expected, Birmingham made a couple of half time substitutions with Richard Forsyth appearing for the first time in five weeks following an ankle injury.

But there was no real improvement as promotion chasing Leicester held all the aces on this particular occasion with Birmingham badly disjointed.

The third goal finally arrived from Lennon in the last minute of the game with a 20-yard effort which really summed up a hapless Birmingham performance.

Coach Kevan Broadhurst was not very enamoured with the performance and made it plain that unless there was a dramatic improvement any talk of promotion next season could also be forgotten.

He said: "They are not disciplined or organised enough to be a top side. Everything has got to change before the start of next season."

Fry summed up the attitude of the club when he said: "I can't wait to get away. We've had over 70 games this season and we've all had enough."

It summed up the general attitude which also sadly prevailed on the pitch.

Paul Barnes finds a gap in Leicester's ranks.

Sunday 5th May 1996 • St. Andrew's • 3.00pm

BIRMINGHAM CITY 1 READING 2

Half time 1-2 • Attendance 16,233

Referee David ORR (Iver, Bucks)

Linesmen B. RICE and D. RICHARDS

READING F.C
1871

Blue Shirts, White Shorts	Goals		Red Shirts, Red Shorts	Goals
1 Bart GRIEMINK		1	Simon SHEPPARD	
2 Gary POOLE		2	Tom JONES	
3 Martin GRAINGER		3	Mick GOODING	
4 John CORNFORTH †		4	Darren CASKEY †	
5 Gary BREEN		5	Steve SWALES	
6 Andy EDWARDS ‡		6	Darius WDOWCZYK	
7 Jonathan HUNT		7	Michael GILKES	
8 Paul DEVLIN		8	Lee NOGAN	10
9 Paul BARNES	4	9	Jimmy QUINN	23
10 Paul PESCHISOLIDO #		10	Martin WILLIAMS	
11 John FRAIN ❑		11	Paul HOLSGROVE	

Substitutes

Substitutes

12 Steve BARNES #68	12	Andy FREEMAN
13 Richard FORSYTH †45	13	Phil PARKINSON †75
14 Michael JOHNSON ‡45	14	James LAMBERT

BEFORE		P	W	D	L	F	A	pts	AFTER		P	W	D	L	F	A	pts
13	Blues	45	15	13	17	60	62	58	15	Blues	46	15	13	18	61	64	58
19	Reading	45	12	17	16	52	62	53	19	Reading	46	13	17	16	54	63	56

Birmingham end the season on a depressing note with only one point from their last four games... It was only Reading's second win in six visits to St. Andrew's and it was the first time that they had won two successive league games in the season... Barry Fry's last game in charge of Birmingham City.

Bright start soon fades out

A feeling of complete anti-climax surrounded St. Andrew's. Six months previously everyone had hoped the visit of Reading would have been an occasion to celebrate.

Instead it was a low key Sunday afternoon when everyone in the club was silently pleased that it was the final game of the season, a lull before the explosive news of manager Barry Fry's departure.

Obviously it was important to the players to give a good account of themselves because their futures were on the line, but it turned out to be a limp display after a promising start.

Reading arrived only a few days after finally securing their place in the First Division for another season. But they provided opposition that Birmingham would have devoured earlier in the season.

It appeared as if this would be the case on this occasion following a very bright opening when the Birmingham side attacked with pace, vision and purpose.

The highlight of the game occurred as early as the fourth minute when Birmingham produced their best worked goal of the season, involving a seven man passing movement before Paul Barnes finished with a low shot past stand-in goalkeeper Simon Sheppard.

Barnes had another opportunity a minute before Lee Nogan grabbed Reading's equaliser in the tenth minute. Mick Gooding, Reading's joint player-manager, who was always in the thick of the action moved forward in determined style to whack a shot against Birmingham's post.

Griemink could only watch transfixed as the ball whistled past him in both directions for Nogan to score his eleventh goal of the season from the rebound.

Barnes hit Reading's crossbar a few minutes later, but the rebound did not occur so kindly as at the other end. Reading survived and were seemingly boosted by the let-off to hit back with a strong raid down the right.

Darren Caskey, Reading's record £700,000 buy from Spurs, created the cross from which the talented Martin Williams produced a shot which was blocked. The ball ran to veteran Jimmy Quinn who slotted home his 17th goal of the season as if from memory.

That was virtually the end of Birmingham – and Barry Fry. He made his customary half-time substitutions, sending on Richard Forsyth and Michael Johnson, but all the urgency and passion had long since been drained out of the side to make any real difference.

What was painful to watch was a makeshift Reading side, lacking six regulars, pushing Birmingham back onto the defensive and the Blues looking very lightweight.

There were a couple of half chances, but nothing of real significance and Birmingham lost their third game in four matches – a depressing finale to a season which had promised so much up to the start of the new year.

As a result the campaign, which had started so well and appeared to be on course until the Ian Bennett injury and the amazing transfers of their two key players, Liam Daish and Steve Claridge, finished like a glass of flat champagne – completely tasteless and best forgotten.

Paul Barnes wins the race for possession.

Wednesday 26th July 1995 • St Andrew's • 7.45pm

BIRMINGHAM CITY 0 LIVERPOOL 1

Half time 0-0 • *Attendance* 13,178

Referee Vic CALLOW (Solihull)

Linesmen W. BENTON and A. HALL

Blue Shirts, White Shorts	Goals	Red Shirts, Red Shorts	Goals
1 Ian BENNETT		1 David JAMES	
2 Gary POOLE †		2 Michael THOMAS	
3 Gary COOPER †		3 Steve HARKNESS	
4 Mark WARD ‡		4 Dominic MATTEO	
5 Andy EDWARDS †		5 Mark WRIGHT	
6 Liam DAISH §		6 Neil RUDDOCK	
7 Jason BOWEN †		7 Steve McMANAMAN ‡	
8 Steve CLARIDGE †		8 Jamie REDKNAPP	
9 Paul TAIT †		9 Ian RUSH #	73
10 Ken CHARLERY †		10 Nigel CLOUGH	
11 Steve CASTLE †		11 Robbie FOWLER †	

Substitutes	*Substitutes*
2 Scott HILEY †45	12 Stan COLLYMORE †56
3 John FRAIN †45	13 Michael STENSGAARD (Gk)
5 Chris WHYTE †45	14 Mark WALTERS ‡81
7 Jonathan HUNT †45	15 Lee JONES #88
8 Ian MUIR †45	16 Phil CHARNOCK
9 Jae MARTIN †45 #	17 Craig ARMSTRONG
10 Ricky OTTO †45	18 Lee STRATFORD
11 Kenny LOWE †45	
12 Richard FORSYTH ‡65	
13 Ryan PRICE (Gk)	
14 Paul HARDING #68	
15 Jon BASS §82	

FACTFILE

Blues introduce seven of their new signings against a Liverpool side which includes Stan Collymore, the most expensive player in Britain... He creates the winner for his veteran strike partner, Ian Rush.

Saturday 29th July 1995 • St. Andrew's • 3.00pm

BIRMINGHAM CITY 1 GLASGOW CELTIC 0

Half time 0-0 • Attendance 11,381

Referee Vic CALLOW (Solihull)

Linesmen P. ROBERTS and R. OLIVER

Blue Shirts, White Shorts		Goals
1	Ian BENNETT	
2	Gary POOLE	
3	John FRAIN	
4	Mark WARD ††	
5	Andy EDWARDS	
6	Liam DAISH	
7	Paul TAIT §	
8	Steve CLARIDGE †	
9	Jason BOWEN ‡	
10	Ricky OTTO	
11	Steve CASTLE # §62	
	Substitutes	
12	Ian MUIR ‡45	54
13	Ryan PRICE (Gk)	
14	Ken CHARLERY †45	
15	Jon BASS ††71	
16	Richard FORSYTH #45	

Green & White Hooped Shirts, White Shorts		Goals
1	Gordon MARSHALL	
2	Rudi VATA	
3	Tom McKINLAY	
4	Tom BOYD	
5	Tony MOWBRAY §	
6	Peter GRANT #	
7	Simon DONNELLY ††	
8	Stuart GRAY ‡	
9	Andy WALKER	
10	Willie FALCONER †	
11	John COLLINS	
	Substitutes	
12	Phil O'CONNELL #62	
13	Pat BONNER (Gk)	
14	Pierre VAN HOOIJDONK ‡45	
15	Mark McNALLY ††77	
16	Malcolm MACKAY §73	
17	Brian MacLAUGHLIN †45	

FACTFILE — *Celtic's third visit to St. Andrew's and their third defeat... In stifling heat the game is decided by a second half goal from Ian Muir, who cost a bargain £125,000 from Tranmere Rovers... Over 5,000 Celtic fans made the trip from Glasgow.*

Tuesday 1st August • St. Andrew's • 7.45pm

BIRMINGHAM CITY 1 SHEFFIELD WEDNESDAY 3

Half time 0-1 • *Attendance* 5,302

Referee Vic CALLOW (SOLIHULL)

Linesmen R. OLIVER and B. BENTON

Blue Shirts, White Shorts		Goals	Green Shirts, Green Shorts		Goals
1	Ian BENNETT		1	Chris WOODS	
2	Scott HILEY §§		24	Julian WATTS	
3	John FRAIN †		17	Des WALKER ‡	
4	Mark WARD ‡		5	Dan PETRESCU	58
5	Andy EDWARDS		2	Peter ATHERTON	
6	Liam DAISH		15	Andy SINTON #	
7	Jonathan HUNT #		11	John SHERIDAN †	
8	Ian MUIR ††		4	Mark PEMBRIDGE	
9	Ken CHARLERY ‡‡		3	Ian NOLAN	
10	Ricky OTTO §		14	Marc DEGRYSE	
11	Richard FORSYTH ##		10	Mark BRIGHT	2,78

Substitutes			*Substitutes*		
12	Steve CLARIDGE §45	74	16	Graham HYDE #67	
14	Steve CASTLE ‡45		25	Michael WILLIAMS †45	
15	Kenny LOWE ††58		29	Lee BRISCOE ‡48	
16	Simon BLACK ‡‡58				
17	Neil DOHERTY ##58				
18	Gary COOPER †45				
19	Chris WHYTE §§62				
20	Paul TAIT #45				

FACTFILE

Birmingham got away to a poor start in their third pre-season friendly game and never recovered... The feature of the match in humid conditions was Mark Bright's sharp finishing... Manager Barry Fry continued to ring the changes to find his best line-up.

Wednesday 2nd August 1995 • Aggborough • 7.45pm

KIDDERMINSTER HARRIERS 1 BIRMINGHAM CITY 4

Half time 0-3 • *Attendance* 1,245

KIDDERMINSTER HARRIERS FOOTBALL CLUB

Referee Gurnam SINGH (Wolverhampton)
Linesmen K. INGRAM and N. CHRISTOPHER

Red and White Halved Shirts, Red Shorts		Goals	Blue Shirts, White Shorts		Goals
1	Kevin ROSE †		1	Ryan PRICE	
2	Simeon HODGSON		2	Scott HILEY †	
3	Paul BANCROFT §		3	John FRAIN ‡	11
4	Duncan BROWN ‡		4	Richard FORSYTH ##	
5	Martin YATES		5	Chris WHYTE	
6	Jay POWELL		6	Andy EDWARDS #	29
7	John DEAKIN		7	Steve CASTLE	
8	Neil CARTWRIGHT #		8	Ian MUIR	14
9	Kim CASEY	67	9	Simon BLACK §	
10	Paul DAVIES		10	Ricky OTTO ††	
11	Jon PURDIE		11	Paul TAIT ‡‡	
	Substitutes			*Substitutes*	
12	Lee HUGHES §50		12	Jon BASS	
13	Darren STEADMAN †45		13	Ben SEDGEMORE ‡‡45 §§	
14	Martin DEARLOVE ‡45		14	Jonathan HUNT †45	
15	Delwyn HUMPHREYS #45		15	Gary COOPER ‡45	
			16	Ken CHARLERY §45	
			17	Robert CODNER ††45	62
			18	Jae MARTIN §§73	
			19	Liam DAISH #45	
			20	Mark WARD ##56	

FACTFILE

A testimonial game for Richard Forsyth which was part of the transfer fee arrangement made by Barry Fry when he signed the mid-field player from the Aggborough club... Ian Muir grabs his second goal in successive matches.

Saturday 5th August 1995 • St Andrew's • 3.00pm

BIRMINGHAM CITY 0 WEST BROMWICH ALBION 0

Half time 0-0 • Attendance 7,219

Referee Kieran BARRETT (Coventry)

Linesmen M. CAIRNS and T. KEADY

Blue Shirts, White Shorts	Goals	Yellow Shirts with Blue Trim, Blue Shorts	Goals
1 Ian BENNETT		1 Gary GERMAINE	
2 Gary POOLE		2 Daryl BURGESS	
3 John FRAIN		3 Paul EDWARDS	
4 Mark WARD		4 Mike PHELAN	
5 Andy EDWARDS		5 Paul MARDON	
6 Liam DAISH		6 Paul RAVEN	
7 Jonathan HUNT		7 Kevin DONOVAN †	
8 Steve CLARIDGE		8 David SMITH	
9 Ian MUIR		9 Bob TAYLOR ‡	
10 Ricky OTTO		10 Andy HUNT #	
11 Steve CASTLE		11 Tony BRIEN	
Substitutes		*Substitutes*	
12 Ken CHARLERY		12 Stuart CLARKE †29 §	
13 Ryan PRICE (gk)		13 Tony REES ‡45	
14 Paul TAIT		14 Chris HARGREAVES #66	
15 Chris WHYTE		15 Robert HAYTER	
16 Richard FORSYTH		16 James McCUE §72	
17 Neil DOHERTY			

FACTFILE

First time in any game since his appointment that Barry Fry did not make a substitution... Rookie Albion 'keeper Gary Germaine makes some fine early saves to deny Jonathan Hunt and Steve Claridge, who also hit a post in the first half... But then both teams struggle as an attacking unit on a another very hot afternoon... Baggies' Kevin Donovan limps off with a groin strain.

Sunday 6th August 1995 • Highfield Road • 3.00pm

COVENTRY CITY 1 BIRMINGHAM CITY 1

Half time 1-0 • *Attendance* 6,036

Referee Dermot GALLAGHER (Banbury)

Linesmen J. BISHOP and A. WRIGHT

Sky Blue Shirts, Sky Blue Shorts		Goals	Blue Shirts, White Shorts		Goals
1	John FILAN		1	Ryan PRICE	
2	Ally PICKERING		2	Scott HILEY	
3	David BURROWS		3	Gary COOPER	
4	Brian BORROWS		4	Jon BASS §	
5	David RENNIE †		5	Chris WHYTE	
6	Kevin RICHARDSON		6	Richard FORSYTH †	
7	Paul TELFER		7	Steve FINNAN ††	
8	Marques Soares ISAIAS ‡		8	Paul TAIT ‡	
9	Iyseden CHRISTIE #		9	Jae MARTIN	75
10	Dion DUBLIN		10	Ken CHARLERY #	
11	John SALAKO	44	11	Neil DOHERTY	
	Substitutes			*Substitutes*	
12	Julian DARBY †45		12	Robert CODNER †45	
14	Jonathan GOULD		13	Steve ROBINSON ‡45	
15	Gordon STRACHAN ‡75		14	Simon BLACK #55	
16	Carlos Alberto CARLITA #75		15	Simon REA §65	
			16	Ben SEDGEMORE ††68	

Simon Black.

Barry Fry had an entirely different team in action from that which appeared against the Albion the day previously... Youngsters like Simon Black, Simon Rea, Ben Sedgemore and Steve Robinson were given an outing on a big stage.

Monday 7th August 1995 • St Andrew's • 7.45pm

BIRMINGHAM CITY 1 MANCHESTER UNITED 0

Half time 1-0 • Attendance 13,330
Referee Vic CALLOW (Solihull)
Linesmen A. HALL and B. BENTON

Blue Shirts, White Shorts		Goals	Red Shirts, White Shorts		Goals
1	Ian BENNETT		1	Peter SCHMEICHEL	
2	Gary POOLE		2	Paul PARKER †	
3	John FRAIN		3	Denis IRWIN	
4	Mark WARD		4	Steve BRUCE	
5	Andy EDWARDS		20	Gary NEVILLE	
6	Liam DAISH †		6	Gary PALLISTER	
7	Jonathan HUNT §		19	Nicky BUTT	
8	Steve CLARIDGE ††		22	Paul SCHOLES	
9	Ian MUIR #		9	Brian McCLAIR	
10	Richard FORSYTH ‡		16	Roy KEANE	
11	Paul TAIT		5	Lee SHARPE	
	Substitutes			*Substitutes*	
12	Ricky OTTO ‡45		15	Graham TOMLINSON	
13	Ryan PRICE		24	David BECKHAM	
14	Jae MARTIN #56		25	Kevin PILKINGTON (Gk)	
15	Chris WHYTE †38	44	27	Terry COOKE	
16	Steve CASTLE ††83		29	BEN THORNLEY †62	
17	Gary COOPER §79				

FACTFILE

*A fine win for Blues but it was achieved at a heavy price... Skipper Liam Daish
limped out of the game with a leg injury after being accidentally trodden on by
Steve Bruce and could miss the start of the season... Chris Whyte came on to
replace Daish and six minutes later headed in the winner from a Jonathan Hunt
free-kick... Blues were in command throughout and could have won by more as
United were made to look ordinary... Bennett weighed in with two superb saves.*

Wednesday 9th August 1995 • St. Andrew's • 7.45pm

BIRMINGHAM CITY 0 CHELSEA 4

Half time 0-1 • *Attendance* 6,541

Referee Kieran BARRETT (Coventry)

Linesmen B. MILLERSHIP and B. RICE

Blue Shirts, White Short		Goals	Grey and Orange Shirts, Orange Shorts		Goals
1	Ryan PRICE ††		1	Dmitri KHARINE	
2	Scott HILEY		2	Steve CLARKE	84
3	Gary COOPER		3	Andy MYERS	81
4	Jon BASS		4	Ruud GULLIT	
5	Chris WHYTE ‡		5	Erland JOHNSON †	
6	Steve CASTLE		6	Frank SINCLAIR	
7	Neil DOHERTY §		7	Nigel SPACKMAN ‡	
8	Jae MARTIN		8	Mark HUGHES	
9	Steve FINNAN #		9	Mark STEIN	55
10	Ricky OTTO †		10	Gavin PEACOCK	7
11	Kenny LOWE		11	Dennis WISE	
	Substitutes			*Substitutes*	
13	Simon REA ‡45		12	Eddie NEWTON ‡72	
14	Jani VIANDER ††80		13	Kevin HITCHCOCK	
14	Louie DONOWA †45		14	David LEE	
15	Richard FORSYTH		15	Scott MINTO	
16	Simon BLACK §77		16	Jakob KJELDBJERG †45	
17	Ben SEDGEMORE #68				

FACTFILE

Last warm-up match before the serious business starts on Saturday against Ipswich... Barry Fry took no risks of sustaining any more injuries to his possible first team players, with only four possibles in the squad... The second string were no match for the Gullit inspired Chelsea and were fortunate to escape with only four goals conceded... Gary Cooper had an excellent game and the highlight of the second half was an inspired performance from Louie Donowa.

Wednesday 1st May 1996 • St. Andrew's • 7.45pm

BIRMINGHAM CITY 0 ASTON VILLA 6

Half time 0-2 • *Attendance* 7,980

Referee Vic CALLOW (Solihull)

Linesmen B. BENTON and E. CROUCH

Blue Shirts, White Shorts		Goals	Claret and Blue Shirts, Blue Shorts		Goals
1	Bart GRIEMINK		1	Mark BOSNICH ‡	
2	Gary POOLE ‡		2	Scott MURRAY	
3	John FRAIN		3	Alan WRIGHT	
4	Vinny SAMWAYS §		4	Allan EVANS §	
5	Gary BREEN		5	Ugo EHIOGU	
6	Andy EDWARDS		6	Gareth SOUTHGATE	
7	Jonathan HUNT		7	Mark DRAPER ††	15,38
8	Richard FORSYTH		8	Brian LITTLE †	
9	Paul BARNES		9	Savo MILOSEVIC	53,89
10	Paul DEVLIN #		10	Dwight YORKE #	
11	Martin GRAINGER †		11	Andy TOWNSEND	
	Substitutes			*Substitutes*	
12	Steve BARNES †45		12	Julian JOACHIM #45	
13	Michael JOHNSON ‡45		13	Michael OAKES (Gk) ‡45	
14	Ian JONES §50		14	John GREGORY	
15	Neil DOHERTY #45		15	Aaron LESCOTT §53	
			16	Lee HENDRIE †31	59,68
			17	Darren MIDDLETON ††65	

FACTFILE

John Frain, who joined Birmingham City in June 1984, collected an estimated £45,000 from his testimonial game which attracted a crowd of just under 8,000, a good turn-out on such a miserable evening weatherwise... John has been associated with the club since he was a 13-year-old... An embarrassing defeat for Birmingham... Brian Little made his first appearance in Villa's colours for a decade and he layed on the first goal for Mark Draper.

THE MANAGEMENT TEAM

There has never been a manager in the history of Birmingham City such as **Barry Fry**, who has been so controversial and outspoken.

But even Fry, an inveterate gambler on the transfer market, admitted that he never expected the sack which came a couple of days after the final game of the season.

The record of one point from the last four games turned out to be the final straw, although the events of the previous couple of months must have indicated to Fry that he was living on borrowed time at St. Andrew's.

Fry had been put under pressure to part with his two friends, assistant manager, **Edwin Stein** and coach **David Howell**. The writing was on the wall and the end of season results only made the task easier to dispence with Fry's services.

Fry, as chronicled in these pages, made 61 signings in his two and half years at the club and this is a record in itself.

He had been disappointed with the end of season performances but stated: "Unfortunately we have been governed by long term injuries which dictated what side I could select.

"They were mitigating circumstances over which I had no control. The turning point was when Ian Bennett broke his finger in the F.A. Cup tie against Wolves."

Typically, he was not downhearted for long after his departure from St. Andrews and claimed: "You can be sure of one thing, I will be back. I'm not bitter because one thing that is certain in football is that you will get the sack.

"It does hurt that I won't be around to try and steer the club to promotion, but I like to think that I have woken up a sleeping giant. I don't believe for one moment that I had taken the club as far as I could.

"Attendances were triple what they had been when I arrived. The club also made their first operating profit last season and I was in the black on my transfer dealings. Not many managers can make that claim."

Fry appeared to have an insatiable urge to keep signing players and when Birmingham played at Leicester City in the penultimate game of the season he marked the match by using his 46th different player during the season to chalk up a new club record.

It was a recipe that would prove not to be successful at the end of the day, as was proved when such key players as Liam Daish and Steve Claridge were allowed to leave the club for Coventry City and Leicester City respectively.

But no one can question his desire to be successful. Following the previous season, when the club enjoyed the double, there was a massive anti-climax around St. Andrew's and it could be compared to the two faces of the ground itself. The modern, progressive new stand was sadly overshadowed by the dated old main stand.

Of course there was a price to pay for the lack of success and it was the coaching duo of Stein and Howell, who preceded Fry out of St. Andrew's under a cloud and surrounded by innocuous reasons.

The bottom line was that Fry's back-room staff had not produced the goods at a time when Birmingham City desperately wanted to be a high profile outfit.

As outlined twelve months previously, Fry did not hide the fact that it was Stein who was chiefly responsible for first team affairs on the training ground.

What transpired was that **Lil Fuchillo**, the club's chief scout, was promoted as Fry's assistant. Fuchillo was delighted to be back involved in the day to day affairs following a spell as Peterborough United's manager.

Kevan Broadhurst also took on more responsibility at a higher level. A club stalwart, who unfortunately sustained injuries which cut short his very promising playing career, he is a true Blue and welcomed the opportunity to have a bigger say in the running of the club.

He relished working with the senior players and often doubled up his involvement with the two reserve teams.

As the season ended it was re-organisation time again and a completely new back-room staff was on the cards. Out with the old and in with the new...

JONATHAN BASS

Born Weston-super-Mare
1st January 1976
Joined Blues YTS 1992,
professional 30/6/94
Blues debut v
Blackburn Rovers
CCC (h) 4/10/94

A young star of the future. He impressed with his maturity when drafted into the side for the vital games against Norwich and Leeds.

Later he had a four match run against Wolves, Tranmere, Huddersfield and Sunderland to boost his confidence for the future before making way for Richard Forsyth and Gary Poole.

Career Record:

		League		Cups	
Season	Club	Apps	Gls	Apps	Gls
94-95	Blues	-	-	1	-
95-96	Blues	5	-	1	-
TOTAL		5	-	2	-

TREVOR FRANCIS

Trevor Francis returned to St. Andrew's on 9th May 1996 after signing a three-year managerial contract.

His appointment was made official on 13th May and he immediately started his plans for the climb into the Premiership.

Within a matter of days he had appointed a new backroom team. Mick Mills and Frank Barlow were introduced as Joint Assistant Managers, with Arvel Lowe coming in as a Health and Fitness Coach. All three have come from Sheffield Wednesday and worked with Trevor Francis when he was there.

Mr Francis' first move into the transfer market staggered the football world when he persuaded Manchester United's Steve Bruce to join the Club on a free transfer and immediately made him Club Captain. The manager described Bruce as "the best centre half never to play for England."

FRED BARBER

Born Ferryhill
26th August 1963
Joined Blues 22nd
February 1996 from
Luton Town, free transfer
Blues debut v Tranmere
Rovers Lge (a) 9/3/96

Made only one full apperance following his stop-gap move from Luton Town to fill the void left by Ian Bennett's hand injury sustained against Wolves in January.

Played for a host of clubs, including Walsall and Notts County. While at Fellows Park he wore a mask for the first time as a dare. Given free transfer at end of season.

Career Record:

		League		Cups	
Season	Club	Apps	Gls	Apps	Gls
80-81	Darlington	-	-	-	-
81-82	Darlington	-	-	-	-
82-83	Darlington	12	-	-	-
83-84	Darlington	46	-	9	-
84-85	Darlington	45	-	9	-
85-86	Darlington	32	-	6	-
85-86	Everton	-	-	-	-
86-87	Everton	-	-	-	-
86-87	Walsall	36	-	9	-
87-88	Walsall	46	-	15	-
88-89	Walsall	44	-	7	-
89-90	Walsall	25	-	5	-
loan	Peterborough	6	-	-	-
90-91	Walsall	2	-	-	-
loan	Chester C	8	-	-	-
loan	Blackpool	2	-	-	-
91-92	Peterborough	39	-	19	-
92-93	Peterborough	-	-	-	-
loan	Chesterfield	-	-	2	-
loan	Colchester	10	-	-	-
93-94	Peterborough	24	-	4	-
94-95	Luton Town	-	-	-	-
loan	Peterborough	5	-	-	-
95-96	Luton Town	-	-	-	-
loan	Blackpool	2	-	-	-
loan	Ipswich Town	1	-	-	-
95-96	Blues	1	-	-	-
TOTAL		386	-	85	-

PAUL BARNES

Born Leicester
16th November 1967
Joined Blues 3rd March
1996 from York City,
£350,000
Blues debut v Wolves
Lge (h) 5/3/96

Arrived from York City where he had been the Northern club's leading marksman. Took some time to adjust, but then proved himself to be a smart goal poacher and in one spell scored in three successive games.

Looking to show better form next season once he has settled into the West Midlands. Like other strikers he has not had a settled attacking partner during his brief stay at St. Andrew's.

Career Record:

Season	Club	League Apps	Gls	Cups Apps	Gls
84-85	Notts County	-	-	-	-
85-86	Notts County	10(3)	4	-	-
86-87	Notts County	-	-	-(1)	-
87-88	Notts County	4(7)	2	2(3)	3
88-89	Notts County	11(4)	7	-(2)	-
89-90	Notts County	10(3)	2	1(1)	1
89-90	Stoke City	4(1)	-	-	-
90-91	Stoke City	3(3)	-	1	1
loan	Chesterfield	1	-	1	1
91-92	Stoke City	3(10)	3	2(3)	1
92-93	York City	40	21	7	-
93-94	York City	42	24	7	1
94-95	York City	35(1)	16	6	1
95-96	York City	30	15	11	7
95-96	Blues	15	7	-	-
TOTAL		208(32)	101	38(10)	16

STEVE BARNES

Born Harrow
5th January 1976
Joined Blues 6th
September 1995 from
Welling United
Blues debut as sub v
Middlesbrough CCC (h)
20/12/96

Signed from GM Vauxhall Conference side Welling United last summer for a nominal fee. Notts County wanted him on loan but they then moved for West Bromwich Albion's Lee Ashcroft.

Only made a handful of appearances and had his first taste of senior soccer with a substitute appearance against Middlesbrough at St. Andrew's in the Coca-Cola Cup.

Career Record:

Season	Club	League Apps	Gls	Cups Apps	Gls
95-96	Blues	-(3)	-	-(2)	-

LEADING ENDSLEIGH LEAGUE FIRST DIVISION GOALSCORERS

John ALDRIDGE	Tranmere Rovers	27
Bob TAYLOR	West Bromwich Albion	22
Andy BOOTH	Huddersfield Town	21
Dougie FREEDMAN	Crystal Palace	20
Don GOODMAN	Wolverhampton W.	20
Andy PAYTON	Barnsley	20
Iwan ROBERTS	Leicester City	20
Dean STURRIDGE	Derby County	20
Ian MARSHALL	Ipswich Town	19
Alex MATHIE	Ipswich Town	19
Steve BULL	Wolverhampton W.	17
Andy HUNT	West Bromwich Albion	17
Jimmy QUINN	Reading	17
Tony NAYLOR	Port Vale	16
Alex RAE	Millwall	16
Jonathan HUNT	**Birmingham City**	**15**
Craig RAMMAGE	Watford	15
Neil REDFEARN	Barnsley	15
Mike SHERON	Stoke City	15

Includes League and Cup goals.

IAN BENNETT

Born Worksop
10th October 1970
Joined Blues 23rd Dec 1993
from Peterborough for
£325,000
Blues debut v Albion
Lge (h) 28/12/93

Suffered a broken finger in the F.A. Cup tie against Wolves on January 3rd. He later had to have it reset and this was a major blow to both the player and the club.

Manager Fry was convinced that the continued absence of Bennett, rated as one of the best young 'keepers in the country, was the reason why Birmingham did not make the play-offs. His name has been linked with Liverpool.

Career Record:

Season	Club	League Apps	Gls	Cups Apps	Gls
89-90	Newcastle U	-	-	-	-
90-91	Newcastle U	-	-	-	-
90-91	Peterborough U	-	-	-	-
91-92	Peterborough U	7	-	-	-
92-93	Peterborough U	46	-	11	-
93-94	Peterborough U	19	-	6	-
93-94	Blues	22	-	1	-
94-95	Blues	46	-	16	-
95-96	Blues	24	-	13	-
Blues record		92	-	30	-
TOTAL		164	-	47	-

★ *Began his career with Queens Park Rangers and joined Newcastle United on a free transfer. Then he linked up with Peterborough and made 74 appearances for the London Road club.*

JASON BOWEN

Born Merthyr Tydfil
24th August 1972
Joined Blues 4th August
1995 from Swansea City
for £275,000
Blues debut as sub v
Ipswich T Lge (h) 12/8/95

The nippy, little Welsh international missed a long spell after a knee injury sustained against Portsmouth on October 14th.

In and out of the side following his recovery he completed the season in familiar surroundings – in the treatment room after having to have a cyst removed from the back of his knee.

Career Record:

Season	Club	League Apps	Gls	Cups Apps	Gls
89-90	Swansea C	-	-	-	-
90-91	Swansea C	1 (2)	-	-	-
91-92	Swansea C	5 (6)	-	3 (1)	-
92-93	Swansea C	23 (15)	10	4 (2)	2
93-94	Swansea C	39 (2)	11	12	5
94-95	Swansea C	25 (6)	5	11 (3)	4
95-96	Blues	16 (7)	4	5 (7)	4
TOTAL		109 (38)	(30)	35 (13)	15

★ *Welsh International at Youth, Under-21 and Senior levels.*

★ *Scored on his Blues debut after coming on as a second half substitute on the opening day of the season.*

DID YOU KNOW?

Blues have twice recorded 12-0 wins in the Football League.

The first occasion was against Walsall Swifts in December 1892.

The second time it was Doncaster Rovers on the receiving end in April 1903.

GARY BREEN

Born Hendon
12th December 1973
Joined Blues 10th February
1996 from Peterborough
U, straight swap for Charlery
Blues debut as sub v Stoke
City Lge (a) 17/2/96

Joined the club in part exchange for Ken Charlery and proved to be an immediate success as he appeared to relish the challenge.

The young Republic of Ireland international quickly settled into the side and had several games as skipper of the side. Scored a good equaliser in the 1-1 draw at Derby when he bravely headed home at the far post.

Career Record:

Season	Club	League Apps	Gls	Cups Apps	Gls
90-91	Charlton A	-	-	-	-
90-91	Maidstone U	-	-	-	-
91-92	Maidstone U	19	-	-	-
92-93	Gillingham	25 (4)	-	8	-
93-94	Gillingham	20 (2)	-	2	-
94-95	Peterborough	43 (1)	1	7	1
95-96	Peterborough	25	-	11	-
95-96	Blues	17 (1)	1	-	-
TOTAL		149 (8)	2	28	1

★ *Republic of Ireland International – debut v Croatia on 2.6.96 in a 2-2 draw at Lansdowne Road.*

DID YOU KNOW?

Dennis Jennings is the oldest player ever to appear for Blues at first team level.

He was 40 years and 190 days old when he played against Wolverhampton Wanderers at Molineux in May 1950.

GARY BULL

Born Tipton
12th June 1966
Joined Blues 29th
December 1995 from
Nottingham F, free transfer
Blues debut v Rotherham
Lge (a) 13/9/94

Returned to St. Andrew's on a permanent basis from Nottingham Forest, but in a transitional spell early in the new year failed to recapture his form of last term.

He only had a handful of games and made a quick departure to York City in an exchange deal involving Paul Barnes.

Career Record:

Season	Club	League Apps	Gls	Cups Apps	Gls
83-86	Paget Rangers	-	-	2	-
86-88	Southampton	-	-	-	-
87-88	Cambridge U	9	3	-	-
88-89	Cambridge U	4 (6)	1	- (3)	-
88-90	Barnet	-	-	2	-
89-90	Barnet	-	-	3	1
90-91	Barnet	-	-	2	1
91-92	Barnet	42	21	11	6
92-93	Barnet	41	17	6	2
93-94	N. Forest	3 (8)	-	2 (2)	-
94-95	N. Forest	1	1	-	-
loan	Blues	10	6	2	1
95-96	N. Forest	1 (4)	-	- (1)	-
95-96	Blues	3 (3)	-	1 (3)	1
Blues record		13 (3)	6	3 (3)	2
TOTAL		114 (21)	49	31 (9)	12

★ *Returned to Blues this season on a free transfer after having spent a loan spell with the club last term.*

STEVE CASTLE

Born Barking, Essex
17th May 1966
Joined Blues 5th August
1995 from Plymouth
Argyle for £275,000
Blues debut v Plymouth
Argyle CCC (a) 22/8/95

Began the season in the first team following a £150,000 move from Plymouth Argyle but then drifted out of contention.

Had a spell on loan at Gillingham and following his return he regained his senior team place only to drop out with a foot injury which forced him to have surgery.

Career Record:

Season	Club	League Apps	Gls	Cups Apps	Gls
83-84	Leyton Orient	-	-	-	-
84-85	Leyton Orient	20 (1)	1	8	-
85-86	Leyton Orient	19 (4)	4	2 (2)	1
86-87	Leyton Orient	22 (2)	5	6 (1)	1
87-88	Leyton Orient	42	10	6	-
88-89	Leyton Orient	22 (2)	6	4 (1)	-
89-90	Leyton Orient	27	7	6	2
90-91	Leyton Orient	45	12	13	6
91-92	Leyton Orient	35 (2)	10	10	1
92-93	Plymouth A	31	12	7	2
93-94	Plymouth A	44	21	11	1
94-95	Plymouth A	23 (3)	3	1	1
95-96	Blues	11 (3)	1	11	1
loan	Gillingham	5	1	-	-
TOTAL		346 (17)	93	85 (4)	16

KEN CHARLERY

Born Stepney, London
28th November 1964
Joined Blues 5th August
1995 from Peterborough
United for £350,000
Blues debut v Barnsley
Lge (a) 2/9/95

Arrived in the close season from Peterborough United in a deal which was worth £350,000 to the London Road outfit. He struggled to find his prolific goalscoring form as a replacement for the injured Kevin Francis.

He only made 13 appearances and scored six goals before he surprisingly returned to Peterborough as their player-coach in exchange for the young central defender, Gary Breen.

Career Record:

Season	Club	League Apps	Gls	Cups Apps	Gls
88-89	Maidstone U	-	-	-	-
89-90	Maidstone U	19 (11)	1	3 (6)	-
90-91	Maidstone U	22 (7)	9	3 (1)	1
90-91	Peterborough	2 (2)	-	-	-
91-92	Peterborough	33 (4)	16	19	10
92-93	Peterborough	10	3	5	3
92-93	Watford	30 (2)	11	1	-
93-94	Watford	15 (1)	2	3 (1)	-
93-94	Peterborough	26	8	1 (1)	1
94-95	Peterborough	44	16	5	3
95-96	Blues	8 (9)	4	5 (2)	2
TOTAL		209 (36)	70	45 (11)	20

★ *Scored on his Blues debut at Oakwell when he hit the third goal in a fine 5-0 win over Barnsley.*

DID YOU KNOW?

Geoff Vowden netted a hat-trick for Blues against Huddersfield Town in a Second Division match on 7th September 1968 after coming on as a substitute.

STEVE CLARIDGE

Born Portsmouth
10th April 1966
Joined Blues 7th January
1994 from Cambridge
United for £350,000
Blues debut v Notts County
Lge (a) 11/1/94

A major surprise when he moved to Leicester City in a £1.2m deal. The news broke of his apparent unrest after the Coca-Cola Cup semi-final first leg against Leeds United at St. Andrew's.

He had been one of the most consistent players at St. Andrew's, but prior to his departure had gone through a 13 match spell without scoring.

But at the time of his move to Filbert Street no player had appeared in more games than the striker and his transfer was a big shock. His value was seen after he left the club as the attack struggled to find their form.

Career Record:

Season	Club	League Apps	Gls	Cups Apps	Gls
82-83	Portsmouth	-	-	-	-
loan	Fareham Town	-	-	-	-
84-85	Bournemouth	3 (4)	-	-	-
loan	Weymouth	-	-	1	-
88-89	Crystal Palace	-	-	-	-
88-89	Aldershot	37	9	7	1
89-90	Aldershot	20 (4)	10	6 (1)	2
89-90	Cambridge U	-	-	-	-
90-91	Cambridge U	16 (14)	12	4 (3)	1
91-92	Cambridge U	25 (4)	12	4 (3)	2
92-93	Luton Town	15 (1)	2	4	4
92-93	Cambridge U	29	7	1	-
93-94	Cambridge U	24	11	10	3
93-94	Blues	17 (1)	7	-	-
94-95	Blues	41 (1)	20	15	5
95-96	Blues	28	8	15 (2)	2
Blues record		86 (2)	35	30 (2)	7
TOTAL		255 (29)	98	67 (9)	20

GARY COOPER

Born Hammersmith
20th November 1965
Joined Blues 17th December 1993 from Peterborough on free transfer
Blues debut v Charlton Ath
Lge (h) 18/12/93

After an early season sending off in a Coca-Cola Cup game with Tranmere he never re-established himself in the side.

Veteran John Frain was recalled and played for a long spell before he himself gave way to new signing Martin Grainger from Brentford.

Given a free-transfer by Fry before the end of the season to enable him to find another club.

Career Record:

Season	Club	League Apps	Gls	Cups Apps	Gls
83-84	QPR	-	-	-	-
84-85	QPR	1	-	1 (2)	-
loan	Brentford	-	-	-	-
loan	Fisher Athletic	-	-	- (1)	-
89-90	Maidstone	31 (2)	4	10	-
90-91	Maidstone	22 (5)	3	5	1
90-91	Peterborough U	2 (4)	1	-	-
91-92	Peterborough U	33	4	16	2
92-93	Peterborough U	35	3	6	1
93-94	Peterborough U	13 (1)	2	4	1
93-94	Blues	16 (2)	1	1	-
94-95	Blues	26	1	8 (2)	1
95-96	Blues	16 (2)	-	8 (2)	1
Blues record		58 (4)	2	17 (4)	2
TOTAL		195 (16)	19	59 (7)	7

★ *England Youth international (with QPR), (11 caps) also schoolboy honours.*

★ *Won Southern Premiership title in 1986-87 with Fisher Athletic.*

★ *Helped Blues win Auto Windscreens Shield 1995.*

JOHN CORNFORTH

Born Whitley Bay
7th October 1967
Joined Blues 26th March
1996 from Swansea City
for £350,000
Blues debut v Grimsby
Town Lge (a) 30/3/96

Arrived from Swansea City at the back end of the season for another fee of £350,000.

A Welsh international midfielder, he is the son of the Sunderland Echo sports editor and took great delight in playing at Roker Park in April.

Career Record:

Season	Club	League Apps	League Gls	Cups Apps	Cups Gls
84-85	Sunderland	1	-	-	-
85-86	Sunderland	-	-	-	-
86-87	Sunderland	-	-	-	-
loan	Doncaster R	6 (1)	3	2	-
87-88	Sunderland	8 (4)	2	1	-
88-89	Sunderland	10 (5)	-	- (1)	-
89-90	Sunderland	1 (1)	-	1	-
loan	Shrewsbury T	3	-	2	-
loan	Lincoln City	9	1	-	-
90-91	Sunderland	1 (1)	-	- (2)	-
91-92	Swansea City	17	-	2	-
92-93	Swansea City	44	5	12	1
93-94	Swansea City	37 (1)	6	12	-
94-95	Swansea City	32 (1)	3	13	-
95-96	Swansea City	17	2	2	-
95-96	Blues	8	-	-	-
TOTAL		194 (14)	22	47 (3)	1

★ *Welsh International (2 caps).*

LIAM DAISH

Born Portsmouth
23rd September 1968
Joined Blues 10th January
1994 from Cambridge
United for £50,000
Blues debut v Notts Co
Lge (a) 11/1/94

Often described as "Captain Marvel" by Barry Fry, but it still didn't prevent him being transferred to Coventry City in another £1.5m deal.

A strong personality, he was critical of the club's heavy pre-season programme and later fell foul with Fry at Portsmouth when he refused to go on the substitute's bench.

The Republic of Ireland international was often an inspirational player and Fry later struggled to find a replacement. His transfer again enabled Fry to make a handsome profit.

Career Record:

Season	Club	League Apps	League Gls	Cups Apps	Cups Gls
84-85	Portsmouth	-	-	-	-
85-86	Portsmouth	-	-	-	-
86-87	Portsmouth	1	-	-	-
87-88	Portsmouth	1	-	1 (1)	-
88-89	Cambridge U	28	-	5	-
89-90	Cambridge U	42	1	15	1
90-91	Cambridge U	13	1	2	1
91-92	Cambridge U	22	-	5	-
92-93	Cambridge U	15 (1)	1	4	-
93-94	Cambridge U	18	2	10	1
93-94	Blues	19	-	-	-
94-95	Blues	37	3	15	1
95-96	Blues	16 (1)	-	10	2
Blues record		*72 (1)*	*3*	*25*	*3*
TOTAL		212 (2)	8	67 (1)	6

★ *Republic of Ireland International.*

★ *Sold to Coventry City for £1.5m on 20th February 1996.*

PAUL DEVLIN

Born Birmingham
14th April 1972
Joined Blues 28th February
1996 from Notts County
for £250,000 (with Legg)
Blues debut v Sheffield
United Lge (h) 2/3/96

A surprise arrival along with Andy Legg from Notts County. Quickly established himself as a keen competitor capable of scoring vital goals.

Keeps a snake as a pet and displays the same characteristics of being able to slide through the opposition defence as demonstrated with a 16 seconds goal against the luckless Luton Town.

Career Record:

Season	Club	League Apps	Gls	Cups Apps	Gls
91-92	Notts County	1 (1)	-	-	-
92-93	Notts County	28 (4)	3	2	-
93-94	Notts County	40 (1)	7	15 (1)	3
94-95	Notts County	37 (3)	9	11	3
95-96	Notts County	26	6	9	1
95-96	Blues	16	7	-	-
TOTAL		148 (9)	32	37 (1)	7

★ *Bought from Notts County along with Andy Legg for a combined fee of £250,000.*

NEIL DOHERTY

Born Barrow-in-Furness
21st February 1969
Joined Blues 2nd February
1994 from Barrow for
£40,000
Blues debut v Peterborough
United Lge (h) 5/1/94

Only started one first team game against Norwich City in the Coca-Cola Cup at St. Andrew's.

He became frustrated by his lack of opportunities and turned his back on professional football in May 1996 to pursue a career in accountancy.

Career Record:

Season	Club	League Apps	Gls	Cups Apps	Gls
88-89 - 93-94	Barrow	-	-	4	-
93-94	Blues	12 (1)	1	-	-
94-95	Blues	3 (5)	-	1 (2)	-
95-96	Blues	- (2)	1	1 (2)	-
Blues record		*15 (8)*	*2*	*2 (4)*	*-*
TOTAL		15 (8)	2	6 (4)	-

BIRMINGHAM SENIOR CUP FINAL
Monday 6th May 1996,
St. Andrew's, 7.45pm

BIRMINGHAM CITY 2 ASTON VILLA 0
Half time 2-0 Attendance: 1,773
Referee: Simon FRENCH (Wolverhampton)
Linesmen: K. Ingram and A. Horton

Blues: Bart Griemink, Paul Hiles, Martin Grainger, John Cornforth, Paul Challinor, James Bunch, Jason Bowen, Jae Martin (Wayne Dyer 78), Paul Peschisolido, Ricky Otto (Christy McKenzie 81), Ian Jones.
Unused sub: Delroy Francis.

Villa: Michael Oakes, Ben Petty, Les Hines, Andy Mitchell, Paul Browne, David Moore, Lee Burchell, Gareth Farrelly (Scott Murray 71), Neil Davis (Aaron Lescott 47), Julian Joachim, Lee Hendrie.
Unused sub: Stuart Brock.

Blues won the game in the first half, when Jason Bowen took the ball round Oakes to score in the 32nd minute and three minutes before the break, Otto ran 60 yards before setting up Peschisolido for the second.

In the last 15 minutes Jones, Cornforth and Peschisolido and Villa's Petty were all sent off.

LOUIE DONOWA

Born Ipswich
24th September 1964
Joined Blues 30th August
1991 from Bristol City for
£50,000
Blues debut v Darlington
Lge (h) 31/8/91

Talented winger who could not show any consistency. On several occasions the former Bristol City winger was on the verge of joining a new club.

Agreed to sign for struggling Swansea City, but the deal fell through at the last minute because of a medical condition. One of several players to suffer because of Birmingham's extra large playing staff.

Career Record:

Season	Club	League Apps	Gls	Cups Apps	Gls
80-81	Norwich C	-	-	-	-
81-82	Norwich C	-	-	-	-
82-83	Norwich C	- (1)	-	- (1)	-
83-84	Norwich C	23 (2)	4	5 (2)	-
84-85	Norwich C	33 (1)	7	9 (1)	4
85-86	Norwich C	- (2)	-	-	-
85-86	Stoke (loan)	4	1	- (1)	-
86-89	Deportivo La Coruña and Sk Willem II				
89-90	Ipswich T	-	-	-	-
90-91	Ipswich T	17 (6)	1	4 (3)	1
90-91	Bristol City	11 (13)	3	1 (1)	-
91-92	Blues	20 (6)	2	6	-
92-93	Blues	18 (3)	2	4 (2)	-
92-93	Burnley (loan)	4	-	2	-
92-93	Crystal P (loan)	-	-	-	-
93-94	Blues	14 (7)	5	4 (1)	-
93-94	Shr'sbury T (loan)	4	-	-	-
94-95	Blues	26	1	8 (2)	1
95-96	Blues	5 (8)	-	5 (5)	-
Blues record		83 (24)	10	27 (10)	1
TOTAL		179 (49)	26	48 (19)	6

ANDY EDWARDS

Born Epping
17th September 1971
Joined Blues 6th August
1995 from Southend
United for £400,000
Blues debut v Ipswich Town
Lge (h) 12/8/95

Another recruit from Southend United. He had a long unbroken spell in the first team until the surprise arrival of Gary Breen from Peterborough United.

He battled back into the side for the last few matches of the season when he had one particularly good game in the match against promotion chasing Derby County.

Career Record:

Season	Club	League Apps	Gls	Cups Apps	Gls
88-89	Southend U	-	-	- -	-
89-90	Southend U	7 (1)	-	- (1)	-
90-91	Southend U	2	1	3	1
91-92	Southend U	7 (2)	-	1	-
92-93	Southend U	41	-	6	-
93-94	Southend U	41 (1)	1	7	1
94-95	Southend U	42 (2)	3	1	-
95-96	Blues	36 (1)	1	18	2
TOTAL		176 (7)	6	36 (1)	4

DID YOU KNOW?

Joe Bradford scored for Blues in each of the fifteen seasons he was with the club – 1920-21 to 1934-35.

He totalled 267 goals in League and Cup competitions, with his best seasonal haul being 32 in the 1927-28 season.

Joe was a big favourite during his time at St. Andrew's and many remember him as their all-time-great Blues hero and no wonder with such a phenomenal scoring record to his name.

STEVE FINNAN

Born Kent
20th April 1976
Joined Blues 4th August
1995 from Woking for
£100,000
Blues debut v Grimsby
Town CCC (h) 20/9/95

Had a couple of short spells in the first team. Impressed with his ability to cross the ball.

The former Welling player was then loaned out to Notts County, who attempted to sign him before the transfer deadline but Barry Fry turned down their offer.

Career Record:

Season	Club	League Apps	Gls	Cups Apps	Gls
94-95	Woking	-	-	2	-
95-96	Blues	6 (6)	1	4 (3)	-
loan	Notts County	20	3	-	-
TOTAL		26 (6)	4	6 (3)	-

RICHARD FORSYTH

Born Dudley
3rd October 1970
Joined Blues 2nd August
1995 from Kidderminster
Harriers for £50,000
Blues debut v Ipswich
Town Lge (h) 12/8/95

One of the few success stories in a disappointing season. He cost only £50,000 from Kidderminster and proved himself to be a sound investment.

Played with a maturity not expected of a player without league experience. Suffered an ankle injury in the closing weeks and was out of the side. Was mentioned in connection with moves to West Bromwich Albion and Leicester City for a fee in the region of £500,000.

Career Record:

Season	Club	League Apps	Gls	Cups Apps	Gls
91-92	Kidderminster				
92-93	Kidderminster	17	2	-	-
93-94	Kidderminster				
94-95	Kidderminster*				
95-96	Blues	12 (14)	2	12 (3)	-
TOTAL		29 (14)	4	12 (3)	-

* *GM Vauxhall Conference.*

ANGLO-ITALIAN CUP

GROUP A

Birmingham City	4	3	0	1	8	5	9
Port Vale	4	2	2	0	9	5	8
Oldham Athletic	4	1	2	1	2	1	5
Luton Town	4	1	0	3	7	10	3
Genoa	4	2	2	0	7	2	8
Cesena	4	1	2	1	5	6	5
Perugia	4	1	0	3	7	9	3
Ancona	4	1	0	3	2	8	3

GROUP B

Ipswich Town	4	3	1	0	7	3	10
West Bromwich Albion	4	2	1	1	4	3	7
Stoke City*	3	0	3	0	4	4	3
Southend United	4	0	2	2	3	5	2
Foggia	4	2	1	1	5	4	7
Salernitana	4	1	2	1	4	5	5
Brescia	4	0	3	1	3	4	3
Reggiana*	3	0	1	2	3	5	1

SEMI-FINALS
Foggia 0 Cesena 0 – aet
(Cesena win 2-1 on penalties)
Genoa 0 Salernitana 0 – aet
(Genoa win 6-5 on penalties)
Ipswich Town 2 Port Vale 4
Blues 2 West Bromwich Albion 2 – aet
(West Bromwich Albion win 4-1 on penalties)

ITALIAN FINAL

	1st Leg	2nd Leg
Cesena v Genoa	0-4	0-1

ENGLISH FINAL

West Bromwich Albion v Port Vale	0-0	1-3

ANGLO-ITALIAN CUP FINAL (Wembley)
Genoa 5 Port Vale 2

* *Last game postponed and not re-arranged.*

JOHN FRAIN

Born Birmingham
8th October 1968
Joined Blues June 1984
(apprentice) 9th October
1986 (professional)
Blues debut as sub v Newcastle U Lge (h) 9/11/85

In his testimonial year the long serving Birmingham defender enjoyed mixed fortunes.

He collected an estimated £45,000 from his testimonial game against Aston Villa at St. Andrew's on 1st may 1996.

He lost his place following the second league game at Charlton and appeared surplus to requirements, but Gary Cooper's suspension and lack of form opened the door for a return.

Career Record:

Season	Club	League Apps	League Gls	Cups Apps	Cups Gls
85-86	Blues	1 (2)	-	-	-
86-87	Blues	2 (1)	1	-	-
87-88	Blues	12 (2)	2	2	-
88-89	Blues	28	3	4	-
89-90	Blues	36 (2)	1	8	-
90-91	Blues	42	3	12	-
91-92	Blues	44	5	10	-
92-93	Blues	45	6	8	2
93-94	Blues	26	2	4	1
94-95	Blues	6 (1)	-	4	-
95-96	Blues	22 (1)	-	10	-
TOTAL		264 (9)	23	62	3

★ *Won Leyland DAF Cup with Blues in 1991.*

DID YOU KNOW?

Blues went 32 away League matches without registering a single victory between 1980 and 1982.

KEVIN FRANCIS

Born Birmingham
6th October 1967
Joined Blues 28th January
1995 from Stockport
County for £800,000
Blues debut v Swansea City
A.W.S. 31/1/95

Did not play this season until the home game with Leicester City on November 26th because of a knee operation at the end of the previous season.

Subsequently struggled to reach peak fitness and was in and out of the side. Highly rated by manager Fry for his ability to upset opposing defences, but contends he still has to show his best form at St. Andrew's.

Career Record:

Season	Club	League Apps	League Gls	Cups Apps	Cups Gls
88-89	Derby Co	-	-	-	-
89-90	Derby Co	- (8)	1	1 (5)	1
90-91	Derby Co	- (2)	-	-	-
90-91	Stockport Co	11 (2)	5	-	-
91-92	Stockport Co	34 (1)	15	15	11
92-93	Stockport Co	41 (1)	28	14	11
93-94	Stockport Co	45	28	13	6
94-95	Stockport Co	16 (1)	11	4	1
94-95	Blues	15	8	3	1
95-96	Blues	11 (8)	3	9	4
Blues record		*26 (8)*	*11*	*12*	*5*
TOTAL		173 (23)	99	59 (5)	35

★ *Helped Blues win Auto Windscreens Shield, 1995.*

★ *Played for Redditch United and Mile Oak Rovers before Derby.*

★ *Scored on his Blues debut against Swansea City.*

MARTIN GRAINGER

Born Enfield, Middlesex
23rd August 1972
Joined Blues 26th March
1995 from Brentford for
£350,000
Blues debut v Grimsby
Town Lge (a) 30/3/96

A £400,000 signing from Brentford and he was an ever present until the penultimate game of the season at Leicester City when he was forced to drop out because of a suspension.

A tough tackling defender, he added extra bite to the side. Fry was very pleased with his early form in what was often a make-shift line-up.

Career Record:

Season	Club	League Apps	Gls	Cups Apps	Gls
91-92	Colchester U	4 (3)	2	2 (2)	-
92-93	Colchester U	28 (3)	3	4	1
93-94	Colchester U	5 (3)	2	3	-
93-94	Brentford	31	2	2	-
94-95	Brentford	36 (1)	7	9	3
95-96	Brentford	33	3	8	1
95-96	Blues	8	-	-	-
TOTAL		145 (10)	19	28 (2)	5

DID YOU KNOW?

It was previously thought that the word 'City' was added to the name of Birmingham in 1945. It is now known that it was, in fact, in 1943 when the name was changed.

Blues home wartime programmes for the season 1943-44 clearly show the words:
'Birmingham City F.C.'
on the front cover.

BART GRIEMINK

Born Holland
29th March 1972
Joined Blues 5th November
1995 from Emmen FC
(Holland) free transfer
Blues debut as sub v
Cesena AIT (h) 13/12/95

The young Dutch goalkeeper was given an extended run in the first team due to the injury sustained by Ian Bennett early in the New Year.

A little raw in his early games he later gained a great deal of experience and maintained his place despite some indifferent team performances.

Career Record:

Season	Club	League Apps	Gls	Cups Apps	Gls
	Willem II	-	-	-	-
	Emmen FC	-	-	-	-
95-96	Blues	20	-	5 (1)	-

BARRY FRY

Barry Fry parted company with Blues on 7th May 1996 when the Board decided it was time for new blood to come in with fresh ideas in a renewed bid to take the Club into the Premiership.

Everyone at St. Andrew's wishes Barry the best of luck in his new venture; as less than a month after leaving Blues he took over as manager of Peterborough United and also bought a controlling interest in the Posh.

SCOTT HILEY

Born Plymouth
27th September 1968
Joined Blues 12th March
1993 from Exeter City for
£100,000
Blues debut v Bristol City
Lge (h) 13/3/93

Injured last season and out of the running in the early games, the former Exeter City player found himself third or fourth in the pecking order.

Gary Poole, Richard Forsyth and Jon Bass were preferred and eventually he moved to Manchester City following a short spell on loan for £250,000 a few days before the transfer deadline to link up with his former manager, Alan Ball.

Career Record:

Season	Club	League Apps	Gls	Cups Apps	Gls
85-86	Exeter City	-	-	-	-
86-87	Exeter City	-	-	-	-
87-88	Exeter City	12 (3)	2	- (1)	-
88-89	Exeter City	36 (1)	5	5	-
89-90	Exeter City	45 (1)	-	16	-
90-91	Exeter City	46	2	7	-
91-92	Exeter City	33	1	8	-
92-93	Exeter City	33	3	11	-
92-93	Blues	8	-	-	-
93-94	Blues	28	-	6	-
94-95	Blues	9	-	2	-
95-96	Blues	5	-	2	-
Blues record		*50*	*-*	*10*	*-*
TOTAL		255 (5)	13	57 (1)	-

JONATHAN HUNT

Born Camden Town
2nd November 1971
Joined Blues 12th September 1994 from Southend U
Blues debut v
Peterborough United
Lge (h) 18/9/94

Had an exasperating season, during which he was often at cross purposes with manager Barry Fry. He was substituted several times and was far from happy with the situation that developed into a battle of words with the manager.

Undoubtedly has a lot of talent and picks up vital goals from midfield. Fry, however, claims he is not competitive enough in the middle of the field.

Career Record:

Season	Club	League Apps	Gls	Cups Apps	Gls
91-92	Barnet	2 (12)	-	1 (2)	-
92-93	Barnet	10 (9)	-	4 (1)	1
93-94	Southend U	36 (6)	6	7 (3)	-
94-95	Southend U	5 (2)	-	1 (1)	-
94-95	Blues	18 (2)	5	3	3
95-96	Blues	43 (2)	11	14 (4)	4
Blues record		*61 (4)*	*16*	*17 (4)*	*7*
TOTAL		114 (33)	22	30 (11)	8

★ *Played for Woking before Barnet.*

★ *Helped Blues win Auto Windscreens Shield, 1995.*

DID YOU KNOW?

The record crowd for a game at St. Andrew's is: 66,844 against Everton in an F.A. Cup 5th Round tie on 11th February, 1939.

The lowest is: 1,490 v Chesterfield in the Second Division on 17th April, 1909.

MICHAEL JOHNSON

Born Nottingham
4th July 1973
Joined Blues 7th August
1995 from Notts County
for £300,000
Blues debut v Barnsley
Lge (a) 2/9/95

The former Notts County defender fell out of favour in some of the closing games of the season after having lost his place originally through injury.

A good, solid type of defender, but found himself involved in a series of changes with Fry attempting to find a settled defensive formation and was the 'fall guy' on occasions.

Career Record:

Season	Club	League Apps	Gls	Cups Apps	Gls
90-91	Notts County	-	-	-	-
91-92	Notts County	5	-	1	-
92-93	Notts County	37	-	4	-
93-94	Notts County	33 (1)	-	13	-
94-95	Notts County	35 (1)	-	4	-
95-96	Blues	31 (2)	-	10	-
TOTAL		141 (4)	-	32	-

DID YOU KNOW?

A complete 'team' of Birmingham City players has won full England caps whilst with the club:

Merrick, Hibbs, Charsley, Tremelling; Hall, Barton, Corbett, Grosvenor, Smith, Stoker, Hellawell, Francis, Bradford, Astall.

The first four names on the list are all goalkeepers, reflecting the long tradition of excellent 'keepers to have exhibited their talents at St. Andrew's.

Which one is your choice as Number One?

ANDY LEGG

Born Neath
28th May 1966
Joined Blues 28th February
1996 from Notts County
for £250,000 (with Devlin)
Blues debut v Sheffield
United Lge (h) 2/3/96

Arrived with Paul Devlin from Notts County and immediately created a favourable impression with his ability to throw the ball long distances.

Played on the left wing and at left back and did not regret his move to St. Andrew's as he was subsequently selected to play for Wales at the age of 29.

Career Record:

Season	Club	League Apps	Gls	Cups Apps	Gls
88-89	Swansea City	6	-	-	-
89-90	Swansea City	20 (6)	3	7 (2)	-
90-91	Swansea City	37 (2)	5	10 (1)	4
91-92	Swansea City	46	9	11	1
92-93	Swansea City	46	12	12	3
93-94	Notts County	29 (1)	2	11 (1)	3
94-95	Notts County	37 (2)	3	8	1
95-96	Notts County	25	4	11	2
95-96	Blues	9 (3)	1	-	-
TOTAL		255 (14)	39	70 (4)	14

★ *Bought from Notts County along with Paul Devlin for a combined fee of £250,000.*

★ *Welsh International – made his debut in an away fixture against Switzerland, a match which Wales lost 2-0 on 24th April 1996.*

KENNY LOWE

Born Sedgefield
6th November 1961
Joined Blues 17th
December 1993 from
Stoke City for £75,000
Blues debut v Charlton
Lge (h) 18/12/93

Never really figured in manager Fry's team plans. In view of the number of players at the club he went out on loan and was eventually transferred to Gateshead in December 1995.

His only appearances for Blues in the season were two substitute call-ups. He didn't settle at Gateshead and was transfer listed before the end of the season.

Career Record:

Season	Club	League Apps	Gls	Cups Apps	Gls
80-81	Hartlepool U	-	-	-	-
81-82	Hartlepool U	3 (1)	-	-	-
82-83	Hartlepool U	20 (2)	1	-	-
83-84	Hartlepool U	27 (1)	2	4 (1)	-
84-88	Gateshead, Barrow, Morecambe				
87-88	Scarborough	4	-	-	-
88-90	Barrow	-	-	2	-
90-91	Barnet	18	2	-	-
91-92	Barnet	26 (10)	3	7	-
92-93	Barnet	29 (7)	2	4 (1)	-
93-94	Stoke City	3 (6)	-	4	-
93-94	Blues	10 (2)	1	1	-
94-95	Blues	4 (3)	2	4 (3)	-
94-95	Carlisle U (loan)	2	-	-	-
95-96	Blues	- (2)	-	-	-
Blues record		*14 (7)*	*3*	*5 (3)*	*-*
TOTAL		146 (34)	13	26 (5)	-

JAE MARTIN

Born London
5th February 1976
Joined Blues 1st September
1995 from Southend
United on free transfer
Blues debut as sub v Genoa
AIT (h) 5/9/95

A free transfer capture from Southend United last summer. He impressed in his early outings, mainly as a substitute, but then faded from the scene.

The only game he started was against Port Vale at Vale Park in a 2-1 win.

Career Record:

Season	Club	League Apps	Gls	Cups Apps	Gls
92-93	Southend U	-	-	-	-
93-94	Southend U	1 (3)	-	- (1)	-
94-95	Southend U	- (4)	-	1 (1)	-
loan	Leyton Orient	1 (3)	-	1	-
95-96	Blues	1 (6)	-	- (2)	-
TOTAL		3 (16)	-	2 (4)	-

PRODIGAL SONS

Prior to the appointment of Trevor Francis as manager of Birmingham City Football Club on 9th May 1996, seven former Blues players have subsequently taken over as team manager at St. Andrew's, they are:

> BOB McROBERTS
>
> BILLY BEER
>
> BILL HARVEY
>
> GEORGE LIDDELL
>
> ARTHUR TURNER
>
> GIL MERRICK
>
> GARY PENDREY

IAN MUIR

Born Coventry
5th May 1963
Joined Blues 2nd August
1995 from Tranmere
Rovers for £125,000
Blues debut v Ipswich Town
Lge (h) 12/8/95

Cost £125,000 from Tranmere Rovers last summer when he joined Birmingham for a second time. He made his debut in the opening game of the season and never started another match.

Went on loan to Darlington and was later linked with Shrewsbury Town before being transfer listed.

Career Record:

Season	Club	League Apps	Gls	Cups Apps	Gls
79-80	QPR	-	-	-	-
80-81	QPR	-	-	-	-
81-82	QPR	-	-	-	-
82-83	QPR	2	-	-	-
loan	Burnley	1 (1)	1	-	-
83-84	Blues	1	-	1	-
83-84	Brighton	2	-	-	-
84-85	Brighton	1 (1)	-	-	-
loan	Swindon T	2	-	1	-
85-86	Tranmere R	28 (4)	14	6	1
86-87	Tranmere R	45 (1)	20	5 (1)	5
87-88	Tranmere R	43	27	6	2
88-89	Tranmere R	46	21	14	8
89-90	Tranmere R	46	23	19	12
90-91	Tranmere R	33 (2)	13	10	8
91-92	Tranmere R	13 (7)	5	-	-
92-93	Tranmere R	7 (4)	2	3 (4)	-
93-94	Tranmere R	10 (6)	9	2 (4)	-
94-95	Tranmere R	12 (7)	7	3 (2)	3
95-96	Blues	1	-	- (1)	-
loan	Darlington	4	1	-	-
Blues record		2	-	1 (1)	1
TOTAL		297 (33)	143	70 (12)	39

RICKY OTTO

Born Hackney
9th November 1967
Joined Blues 17th
December 1994 from
Southend U for £800,000
Blues debut v Cambridge
United Lge (h) 26/12/94

Plagued by injuries throughout the season. As a result, he could not show any consistent form and was one of the casualties of Barry Fry's frequent changes.

He failed to live up to the £800,000 fee that Birmingham paid Southend to acquire his services in January 1995.

Was linked with Sheffield United but the transfer never materialised and his season came to a premature end when he damaged his thigh against Crystal Palace in February.

Career Record:

Season	Club	League Apps	Gls	Cups Apps	Gls
90-91	Leyton O	- (1)	-	-	-
91-92	Leyton O	23 (9)	5	8	2
92-93	Leyton O	18 (5)	8	2 (2)	-
93-94	Southend U	44 (1)	13	11	2
94-95	Southend U	19	4	1	-
94-95	Blues	18 (6)	4	7	2
95-96	Blues	6 (12)	2	6 (3)	-
Blues record		24 (18)	6	13 (3)	2
TOTAL		128 (34)	36	35 (5)	6

★ *Played for Haringey Borough before Orient.*

★ *Helped Blues win Auto Windscreens Shield 1995, setting up winning goal for Paul Tait.*

IAN MUIR *(continued)*

★ *Ian Muir was Tranmere Rovers' record goal-scorer with 180 goals between 1985 and 1995*

★ *Ian Muir's debut against Ipswich was his second for the club as he also spent a brief period at St. Andrew's during the 83-84 season.*

PAUL PESCHISOLIDO

Born Scarborough, Canada
25th May 1971
Joined Blues 28th March
1996 from Stoke City for
£400,000
Blues debut as sub v
Grimsby T Lge (a) 30/3/96

Husband of the club's Managing Director. Returned to St. Andrew's following a spell at Stoke City.

The small, tenacious striker cost Blues £400,000 when manager Barry Fry completed the deal with the Potteries club. Struggled to show his best form in the early games on his return and was later absent with concussion.

Career Record:

Season	Club	League Apps Gls		Cups Apps Gls	
92-93	Blues	16 (3)	7	1 (2)	-
93-94	Blues	21 (3)	9	2	1
94-95	Stoke City	39 (1)	13	8 (1)	2
95-96	Stoke City	20 (6)	6	6	3
95-96	Blues	7 (2)	1	-	-
Blues record		*44 (8)*	*17*	*3 (2)*	*1*
TOTAL		103 (15)	36	17 (3)	6

★ *Canadian International.*

★ *Joined Blues from Toronto Blizzard in 1992 for his first spell at St. Andrew's.*

★ *Returned to Blues for a second spell two years after leaving St. Andrew's for Stoke City.*

DID YOU KNOW?

Birmingham City's first-ever game in a major European competition was against Internationale (Milan) in Italy on 15th May 1956 in the Inter Cities Fairs Cup.

A crowd of 8,000 saw Blues come away with a very creditable 0-0 draw.

GARY POOLE

Born Stratford, London
11th September 1967
Joined Blues 12th
September 1994 from
Plymouth Argyle
Blues debut v Peterborough
United Lge (h) 18/9/94

Took over as skipper following the surprise departure of Liam Daish to Coventry City. Was first choice for most of the season, but collected a thigh injury in February at Crystal Palace which restricted his appearances.

The former Southend United player returned to the side for the closing matches and helped to stabilise the defence in some difficult games.

Career Record:

Season	Club	League Apps Gls		Cups Apps Gls	
85-86	Tottenham H	-	-	-	-
86-87	Tottenham H	-	-	-	-
87-88	Cambridge U	41 (1)	-	6	-
88-89	Cambridge U	1	-	1	-
88-89	Barnet*	-	-	2	-
89-90	Barnet*	-	-	2	-
90-91	Barnet*	-	-	1	-
91-92	Barnet	39 (1)	2	9	1
92-93	Plymouth A	39	5	8 (1)	2
93-94	Southend U	38	2	7	-
94-95	Southend U	5 (1)	-	2	-
94-95	Blues	34	1	12	1
95-96	Blues	27 (1)	-	15	2
Blues record		*61 (1)*	*1*	*27*	*3*
TOTAL		224 (4)	10	65 (1)	6

* *GM Vauxhall Conference.*

★ *GM Vauxhall Conference winner with Barnet in 1991.*

★ *Helped Blues win Auto Windscreens Shield, 1995.*

SIMON REA

Born Coventry
20th September 1976
Joined Blues as a trainee in 1994, as a
professional on 21st September 1994
Blues debut v Perugia in the Anglo-Italian Cup
(a) 11/10/95

One of the few players to break through
into the first team from Birmingham's
youth programme.

He can operate in either central defence
or attack. Made his first team debut against
Perugia in the Anglo-Italian Cup in Italy.

Career Record:

Season	Club	League Apps	Gls	Cups Apps	Gls
94-95	Blues	-	-	-	-
95-96	Blues	- (1)	-	1 (1)	-
TOTAL		- (1)	-	1 (1)	-

IAN RICHARDSON

Born London
22nd October 1970
Joined Blues August 1995
from Dagenham &
Redbridge
Blues debut v Perugia
AIT (a) 11/10/95

Another recruit from non-league soccer
joining Birmingham from Dagenham.
Made a favourable impression at St.
Andrew's and Barry Fry's decision to sell
him to Notts County following a loan spell
came as a big surprise.

Career Record:

Season	Club	League Apps	Gls	Cups Apps	Gls
95-96	Blues	3 (4)	-	6 (3)	-
loan	Notts County	18	-	-	-
TOTAL		21 (4)	-	6 (3)	-

FANS ROLL CALL FOR 1997

If you wish to have your name, or that of a family member or
friend, recorded in the next edition of The Blues Review
(1997), then simply write to Sports Projects Ltd. at the address
below, with your name, address, telephone number and name
to be included in the Fans' Roll Call.

Closing date for the 1997 edition is Friday 30th May 1997.

**Sports Projects Ltd, 188 Lightwoods Hill, Smethwick, Warley,
West Midlands B67 5EH
Telephone: 0121 632 5518   Fax: 0121 633 4628**

PAUL TAIT

Born Sutton Coldfield
31st July 1971
Joined Blues June 1987
(YTS), 2nd August 1988
(professional)
Blues debut v Barnsley
Lge (h) 1/10/88

Had a mid-season trial at Coventry City but rejoined Blues to give the team some badly needed flair.

A determined player with a great deal of ability he is one of the few home-grown players in the side.

He can always be relied upon to give 100% effort and was a big asset to the club in their mid-season slump when relegation was a possibility.

Career Record:

Season	Club	League Apps	Gls	Cups Apps	Gls
88-89	Blues	6 (4)	-	1	-
89-90	Blues	7 (7)	2	1 (3)	-
90-91	Blues	17	3	4	-
91-92	Blues	10 (2)	-	3	1
92-93	Blues	28	2	9	-
93-94	Blues	9 (1)	-	3	-
94-95	Bolton (loan)	-	-	-	-
94-95	Millwall (loan)	-	-	-	-
94-95	Blues	18 (6)	4	5 (4)	3
95-96	Blues	24 (4)	3	5 (3)	-
TOTAL		119 (24)	14	31 (10)	4

★ *Helped Blues to win the Auto Windscreens Shield in 1994-95 season when he hit the only goal of the game in sudden-death extra-time against Carlisle United at Wembley.*

DID YOU KNOW?

During World War Two Cyril Trigg scored 88 goals in 95 games for Blues. He claimed eight hat-tricks – four in season 1944-45.

MARK WARD

Born Huyton
10th October 1962
Joined Blues 19/3/94
(on loan), 12/8/94
(permanently) from
Everton £500,000
Blues debut v Middlesbro'
Lge (h) 20/3/94

Player-coach at St. Andrew's where he was the highest paid player. Suffered back problems and his last appearance for the club was in the 4-1 home defeat against Derby County in November.

A tenacious player, Ward was unable to regain his fitness to enable him to play in the first team and it was therefore a big surprise when he joined Huddersfield Town on a free transfer.

Career Record:

Season	Club	League Apps	Gls	Cups Apps	Gls
80-81	Everton	-	-	-	-
81-83	(Northwich Victoria)	-	-	3	2
83-84	Oldham A	42	6	4	-
84-85	Oldham A	42	6	4	-
85-86	West Ham U	42	3	10	-
86-87	West Ham U	37	1	12	-
87-88	West Ham U	37	1	5	-
88-89	West Ham U	30	2	10 (1)	-
89-90	West Ham U	17 (2)	5	6	-
89-90	Man City	19	3	3	-
90-91	Man City	36	11	9	2
91-92	Everton	37	4	5	-
92-93	Everton	19	1	-	-
93-94	Everton	26 (1)	1	6	1
93-94	Blues	9	-	-	-
94-95	Blues	41	3	14	1
95-96	Blues	13	3	4 (1)	-
Blues Total		*63*	*6*	*18 (1)*	*1*
TOTAL		447 (3)	50	95 (2)	6

★ *Won England semi-professional cap with Northwich Victoria.*

★ *Was transferred to Manchester City for £1m and then to Everton for £1.1m.*

★ *Helped Blues win Auto Windscreens Shield, 1995.*

CHRIS WHYTE

Born Islington
2nd September 1961
Joined Blues 12th August
1993 from Leeds United for
£250,000
Blues debut v Plymouth A
CCC (h) 17/8/93

The much travelled defender was a casualty of the many signings made by manager Fry.

He had loan spells at both West Ham United and Coventry City before finally moving to Charlton.

A versatile player, he never let the club down even when called up as a stop-gap measure.

Career Record:

Season	Club	League Apps	Gls	Cups Apps	Gls
78-79	Arsenal	-	-	-	-
79-80	Arsenal	-	-	-	-
80-81	Arsenal	-	-	-	-
81-82	Arsenal	32	2	5 (1)	-
82-83	Arsenal	36	3	12	-
83-84	Arsenal	14 (1)	2	4	-
84-85	Arsenal	-	-	-	-
84-85	Crystal P (loan)	13	-	4	-
85-86	Arsenal	4 (3)	1	1	-
88-89	West Brom	40	3	4	-
89-90	West Brom	43 (1)	4	8	2
90-91	Leeds U	38	3	15	1
91-92	Leeds U	41	1	7	-
92-93	Leeds U	34	1	11 (1)	-
93-94	Blues	33	-	6	-
94-95	Blues	31	1	9 (1)	-
95-96	Blues	4	-	5	-
loan	West Ham U	-	-	-	-
loan	Coventry C	1	-	-	-
Blues Total		68	1	20 (1)	-
TOTAL		364 (5)	21	91 (3)	3

★ *Won 4 England Under-21 caps when at Arsenal.*
★ *Played for Los Angeles Lazers before West Brom (1985-88).*
★ *Won First Division Championship medal with Leeds United in 1992.*

DANNY HILL

Born Enfield
1st October 1974
Joined Blues 24th
November 1995 on loan
from Tottenham Hotspur
Blues debut v Leicester City
Lge (h) 26/11/95

Came on loan from Spurs but he was forced to return to White Hart Lane just before his two month spell was completed because Blues found themselves with a goalkeeping problem. Manager Fry snapped up goalkeeper Paul Sansome on loan from Southend, so Hill had to go back to Spurs.

95-96 Record:

Season	Club	League Apps	Gls	Cups Apps	Gls
95-96	Tottenham H	- (1)	-	-	-
loan	Blues	5	1	2	-

★ *England Schoolboy International.*

DAVID PREECE

Born Bridgenorth
28th May 1963
Joined Blues 24th
November 1995 on loan
from Derby County
Blues debut v Leicester City
Lge (h) 26/11/95

Preece, a tiny, busy midfield player came from Derby County. The best spell of his career was undoubtedly with Luton Town where he was a stalwart before his move back to the Midlands.

95-96 Record:

Season	Club	League Apps	Gls	Cups Apps	Gls
95-96	Derby County	10 (3)	1	2	-
loan	Blues	6	-	1	-

SIGURD RUSHFELDT

Born Norway 11th December 1972
Joined Blues 29th October 1995 on three
month loan from Tromsø IL
Blues debut as sub v Port Vale Lge (a) 29/10/95

95-96 Record:

Season	Club	League Apps	Gls	Cups Apps	Gls
95-96	Blues	3 (4)	-	2	1

★ *Norwegian International.*

DAN SAHLIN

Born Sweden 18th April 1967
Joined Blues 16th November 1995 on one
month loan from Hammarby IF
Blues debut as sub v Leicester Lge (h) 26/11/95

95-96 Record:

Season	Club	League Apps	Gls	Cups Apps	Gls
95-96	Blues	- (1)	-	-	-

VINNY SAMWAYS

Born Bethnal Green
27th October 1968
Joined Blues 15th February
1996 on loan from Everton
Blues debut v Stoke City
Lge (a) 17/2/96

95-96 Record:

Season	Club	League Apps	Gls	Cups Apps	Gls
95-96	Everton	5 (1)	1	1	1
loan	Wolves	3	-	-	-
loan	Blues	12	-	-	-

★ *England Youth and Under-21 (5 caps)
international.*

PAUL SANSOME

Born New Addington
6th October 1961
Joined Blues 8th January
1996 on loan from
Southend United
Blues debut v Norwich City
CCC (a) 10/1/96

A late inclusion in the Coca-Cola Cup tie at
Norwich after Ian Bennett was injured
playing against Wolves in the F.A. Cup.

He came on loan from Southend and was
given another outing in the 4-3 home
defeat at the hands of Charlton and then
returned to Roots Hall.

95-96 Record:

Season	Club	League Apps	Gls	Cups Apps	Gls
95-96	Southend U	-	-	-	-
loan	Blues	1	-	1	-

JOHN SHERIDAN

Born Stretford
1st October 1964
Joined Blues 8th February
1996 on loan from
Sheffield Wednesday
Blues debut v Leeds United
CCC SF1 (h) 11/2/96

He played in three games, but made no
impact before he returned to Sheffield
Wednesday where he won a Premier League
recall and was promptly named man of the
match in his first game!

95-96 Record:

Season	Club	League Apps	Gls	Cups Apps	Gls
95-96	Sheff Wed	13 (4)	-	-	-
loan	Blues	1 (1)	-	2	-

★ *Republic of Ireland Youth and full International.*

FIRST TEAM APPEARANCES & GOALSCORERS

	LEAGUE		FA CUP		LGE CUP		AIT		TOTAL	
	Apps	Gls	Apps	Gls	Apps	Gls	Apps	Gls	Apps	Gls
Jonathan BASS	5	-	-	-	1	-	-	-	6	-
Fred BARBER	1	-	-	-	-	-	-	-	1	-
Paul BARNES	15	7	-	-	-	-	-	-	15	7
Steve BARNES	-(3)	-	-	-	-(1)	-	-(1)	-	-(5)	-
Ian BENNETT	24	-	1	-	8	-	4	-	37	-
Jason BOWEN	16(7)	4	-(2)	-	3(5)	2	2	2	21(14)	8
Gary BREEN	17(1)	1	-	-	-	-	-	-	17(1)	1
Gary BULL	3(3)	-	-(2)	-	-(1)	-	1	1	4(6)	1
Steve CASTLE	11(3)	1	1	-	7	-	3	1	22(3)	2
Ken CHARLERY	8(9)	4	-	-	3(2)	2	2	-	13(11)	6
Steve CLARIDGE	28	8	2	-	11(1)	1	2(1)	1	43(2)	10
Gary COOPER	16(2)	-	-	-	6(1)	1	2(1)	-	24(4)	1
John CORNFORTH	8	-	-	-	-	-	-	-	8	-
Liam DAISH	16(1)	-	2	-	7	2	1	-	26	2
Paul DEVLIN	16	7	-	-	-	-	-	-	16	7
Neil DOHERTY	-(2)	1	-	-	1(1)	-	-(1)	-	1(4)	1
Louie DONOWA	5(8)	-	1	-	3(5)	-	1	-	10(13)	-
Andy EDWARDS	36(1)	1	2	-	11	1	5	1	54(1)	3
Steve FINNAN	6(6)	1	-	-	2(2)	-	2(1)	-	10(9)	1
Richard FORSYTH	12(14)	2	2	-	7(2)	-	3(1)	-	24(17)	2
John FRAIN	22(1)	-	2	-	6	-	2	-	32(1)	-
Kevin FRANCIS	11(8)	3	2	-	6	4	1	-	20(8)	7
Martin GRAINGER	8	-	-	-	-	-	-	-	8	-
Bart GRIEMINK	20	-	1	-	3	-	1(1)	-	25(1)	-
Scott HILEY	5	-	-	-	1	-	1	-	7	-
Danny HILL	5	-	-	-	2	-	-	-	7	-
Jonathan HUNT	43(2)	11	1(1)	1	8(3)	2	5	1	57(6)	15
Michael JOHNSON	31(2)	-	1	-	5	-	4	-	41(2)	-
Andy LEGG	9(3)	1	-	-	-	-	-	-	9(3)	1
Kenny LOWE	-(2)	-	-	-	-	-	-	-	-(2)	-
Jae MARTIN	1(6)	-	-	-	-	-	-(2)	-	1(8)	-
Ian MUIR	1	-	-	-	-(1)	-	-	-	1(1)	-
Ricky OTTO	6(12)	2	-	-	3(3)	-	3	-	12(15)	2
Paul PESCHISOLIDO	7(2)	1	-	-	-	-	-	-	7(2)	1
Gary POOLE	27(1)	-	2	1	10	-	3	1	42(1)	2
David PREECE	6	-	-	-	-	-	1	-	7	-
Simon REA	-(1)	-	-	-	-	-	1(1)	-	1(2)	-
Ian RICHARDSON	3(4)	-	2	-	3(1)	-	1(2)	-	9(7)	-
Sigurd RUSHFELDT	3(4)	-	-	-	1	1	-	-	5(4)	1
Dan SAHLIN	-(1)	-	-	-	-	-	-	-	-(1)	-
Vinny SAMWAYS	12	-	-	-	-	-	-	-	12	-
Paul SANSOME	1	-	-	-	1	-	-	-	2	-
John SHERIDAN	1(1)	-	-	-	2	-	-	-	3(1)	-
Paul TAIT	24(4)	3	-	-	4(1)	-	1(2)	-	29(7)	3
Mark WARD	13	3	-	-	3(1)	-	1	-	17(1)	3
Chris WHYTE	4	-	-	-	4	-	1	-	9	-
Own Goals	-	-	-	-	-	1	-	2	-	3

BLUES FACTS & FIGURES 1995-96

HIGHEST AND LOWEST

Highest home attendance:
24,781 v Leeds United (CCC SF1) 11.2.96
Lowest home attendance:
7,446 v Grimsby Town (CCC 2/1) 20.9.96
Biggest win:
5-0 v Barnsley (a) 2.9.95
Heaviest defeat:
0-4 v Oldham Athletic (a) 16.12.95

DEBUTANTS

Andy Edwards
v Ipswich Town Lge (h) 12.8.95
Richard Forsyth
v Ipswich Town Lge (h) 12.8.95
Jason Bowen
v Ipswich Town (sub) Lge (h) 12.8.95
Steve Castle
v Plymouth Argyle CCC (a) 22.8.95
Ken Charlery
v Barnsley Lge (a) 2.9.95
Michael Johnson
v Barnsley Lge (a) 2.9.95
Jae Martin
v Genoa (sub) AIT (h) 5.9.95
Steve Finnan
v Grimsby Town CCC (h) 20.9.95
Simon Rea
v Perugia AIT (a) 11.10.95
Ian Richardson
v Perugia (sub) AIT (a) 11.10.95
Sigurd Rushfeldt
v Port Vale (sub) Lge (a) 29.10.95
Danny Hill
v Leicester City Lge (h) 26.11.95
Dave Preece
v Leicester City Lge (h) 26.11.95
Dan Sahlin
v Leicester City (sub) Lge (h) 26.11.95
Bart Griemink
v Cesena (sub) AIT (h) 13.12.95
Steve Barnes
v Middlesbrough (sub) CCC (h) 20.12.95
Paul Sansome
v Norwich City CCC (a) 10.1.96
John Sheridan
v Leeds United CCC SF1 (h) 11.2.96

Vinny Samways
v Stoke City Lge (a) 17.2.96
Gary Breen
v Stoke City (sub) Lge (a) 17.2.96
Paul Devlin
v Sheffield United Lge (h) 2.3.96
Andy Legg
v Sheffield United Lge (h) 2.3.96
Fred Barber
v Tranmere Rovers Lge (a) 9.3.96
John Cornforth
v Grimsby Town Lge (a) 30.3.96
Martin Grainger
v Grimsby Town Lge (a) 30.3.96

RED CARDS

Two Blues players got their marching orders
during the season; they were:
Gary Cooper v Tranmere Rovers, 24.10.95
and Gary Poole v Norwich City, 24.1.96,
both at St. Andrew's.
Opposition players to see Red whilst playing
against Blues were:
Tom Cowan (Huddersfield) 30.8.95; David
Watson (Gk) and Charlie Bishop (both
Barnsley) 2.9.95 and Brian Law (Wolves)
17.1.96. All sent off on their own grounds.

PENALTIES

Blues:
Jonathan Hunt v Norwich City Lge (h)
26.8.95; v Barnsley Lge (a) 2.9.95; v Leicester
City Lge (h) 26.11.95; v Charlton Athletic
Lge (h) 14.1.96
Mark Ward v Derby County Lge (h) 21.11.95
Paul Devlin v Wolves Lge (h) 5.3.96; v
Wolves Lge (a) 23.3.96 v Portsmouth Lge (h)
2.4.96.

Opponents:
Andy Porter (Port Vale) Lge (a) 29.10.95;
Andy Thompson (Wolves) Lge (a) 23.3.96.

HAT TRICKS

Jonathan Hunt scored Blue's only hat-trick
of the season in a League match against
Norwich City at St. Andrew's on 26th August
1995 in a game which Blues won 3-1.

FINAL TABLE

			Home				Away				Total				
	Pl	W	D	L	F	A	W	D	L	F	A	W	D	L	F	A	Pts
1 Sunderland	46	13	8	2	32	10	9	9	5	27	23	22	17	7	59	33	83
2 Derby County	46	14	8	1	48	22	7	8	8	23	29	21	16	9	71	51	79
3 Crystal Palace	46	9	9	5	34	22	11	6	6	33	26	20	15	11	67	48	75
4 Stoke City	46	13	6	4	32	15	7	7	9	28	34	20	13	13	60	49	73
5 Leicester City	46	9	7	7	32	29	10	7	6	34	31	19	14	13	66	60	71
6 Charlton Athletic	46	8	11	4	28	23	9	9	5	29	22	17	20	9	57	45	71
7 Ipswich Town	46	13	5	5	45	30	6	7	10	34	39	19	12	15	79	69	69
8 Huddersfield Town	46	14	4	5	42	23	3	8	12	19	35	17	12	17	61	58	63
9 Sheffield United	46	9	7	7	29	25	7	7	9	28	29	16	14	16	57	54	62
10 Barnsley	46	9	10	4	34	28	5	8	10	26	38	14	18	14	60	66	60
11 West Bromwich A.	46	11	5	7	34	29	5	7	11	26	39	16	12	18	60	68	60
12 Port Vale	46	10	5	8	30	29	5	10	8	29	37	15	15	16	59	66	60
13 Tranmere Rovers	46	9	9	5	42	29	5	8	10	22	31	14	17	15	64	60	59
14 Southend United	46	11	8	4	30	22	4	6	13	22	39	15	14	17	52	61	59
15 **Birmingham City**	46	11	7	5	37	23	4	6	13	24	41	15	13	18	61	64	58
16 Norwich City	46	7	9	7	26	24	7	6	10	33	31	14	15	17	59	55	57
17 Grimsby Town	46	8	10	5	27	25	6	4	13	28	44	14	14	18	55	69	56
18 Oldham Athletic	46	10	7	6	33	20	4	7	12	21	30	14	14	18	54	50	56
19 Reading	46	8	7	8	28	30	5	10	8	26	33	13	17	16	54	63	56
20 Wolverhampton W.	46	8	9	6	34	28	5	7	11	22	34	13	16	17	56	62	55
21 Portsmouth	46	8	6	9	34	32	5	7	11	27	37	13	13	20	61	69	52
22 Millwall	46	7	6	10	23	28	6	7	10	20	35	13	13	20	43	63	52
23 Watford	46	7	8	8	40	33	3	10	10	22	37	10	18	18	62	70	48
24 Luton Town	46	7	6	10	30	34	4	6	13	10	30	11	12	23	40	64	45

PLAY-OFFS

SEMI FINALS

Charlton Athletic 1 Crystal Palace 2
Crystal Palace 1 Charlton Athletic 0
Crystal Palace win 3-1 on aggregate

Leicester City 0 Stoke City 0
Stoke City 0 Leicester City 1
Leicester City win 1-0 on aggregate

FINAL (at Wembley)

Crystal Palace 1 Leicester City 2 *(aet)*
Roberts   Parker (pen), Claridge

ROLL OF HONOUR

Division One Champions: Sunderland
Runners-up: Derby County
Promoted through play-offs: Leicester City
FA Cup winners: Manchester United
Coca-Cola Cup winners: Aston Villa

FACTS AND FIGURES

Most goals: 79, Ipswich Town
Most home goals: 48, Derby County
Most away goals: 34, Leicester & Ipswich
Least goals: 40, Luton Town
Least home goals: 23, Millwall
Least away goals: 10, Luton Town
Least goals conceded: 33, Sunderland
Least home goals conceded: 10, Sunderland
Least away goals conceded: 22, Charlton A.
Most goals conceded: 70, Watford
Most home goals conceded: 34, Luton Town
Most away goals conceded: 44, Grimsby T.
Best home record: 50 pts, Derby County
Best away record: 39 pts, Crystal Palace
Worst home record: 27 pts, Luton & Millwall
Worst away record: 17 pts, Huddersfield T.

BLUE'S LEADING SCORERS

(Including League and Cup games)

15	Jonathan Hunt
10	Steve Claridge
8	Jason Bowen
7	Paul Barnes
7	Paul Devlin
7	Kevin Francis

Strength in depth pays off as reserves put silverware on shelf

Birmingham City's huge playing staff warranted playing in both the Pontins and the Avon League – with mixed success.

The highlights of the season, ironically, came in the closing weeks of the season when they won the Avon Insurance League Cup, beat Aston Villa in the final of Birmingham Senior Cup and also had the distinction of beating Manchester United's powerful second team 1-0 at St. Andrew's in the Pontins League.

But it was significant that in all three games Blues fielded teams that would not have been out of place in the Football League.

Paul Devlin scored the only goal of the game in the 44th minute to earn a win over Plymouth at Home Park. A look at the Birmingham team of: Griemink, Poole, Grainger, Tait, Rae, Challinor, Hunt, Devlin, Donowa, Bowan, Barnes. Subs: Cornforth, Forsyth, Martin; gives an indication of Birmingham's intention to win the final.

Devlin was again the match winner in the 1-0 home success over Manchester United in front of a 5,000 crowd. The result was the highlight of the season, but yet again it was a very strong Birmingham side which also saw Dave Barnett have one of his few games of the season after being sidelined for several months.

The welcome success over Aston Villa in the Birmingham Senior Cup Final at St. Andrew's was an unhappy match with four players, three from Birmingham and one from Villa, being sent off.

Board room decisions to reduce the size of the playing staff and also prune the youth policy will be instrumental in a considerable cash saving in future although it has to be pointed

out that this stop-go-stop policy has been witnessed on several occasions in the past with conflicting results.

A number of Birmingham's youngsters have therefore been released, indicating the harsh world of professional sport.

In the Pontins League the Blues finished in mid-table with the club having the doubtful distinction of possessing the second worst defensive record in the division. Only bottom of the table West Bromich Albion had a worse record.

Steve Finnan, earlier in the season, and Jae Martin were a couple of youngsters who gained considerable benefit from playing in the reserves as did Steve Barnes.

Whether they can prosper from the experience remains to be seen but one player who did as a youngster several years ago was a certain Trevor Francis when Birmingham struck gold with his goalscoring bonanza.

PONTIN'S LEAGUE DIVISION ONE TABLE

	P	W	D	L	F	A	Pts
Manchester United	34	22	5	7	71	35	71
Derby County	34	17	10	7	59	43	61
Stoke City	34	17	8	9	57	42	59
Leeds United	34	17	8	9	40	32	59
Liverpool	34	16	8	10	57	42	56
Tranmere Rovers	34	17	4	13	70	62	55
Everton	34	14	10	10	50	41	52
Oldham Athletic	34	12	11	11	55	54	47
Newcastle United	34	13	6	15	55	59	45
Bolton Wanderers	34	12	9	13	51	52	45
Birmingham City	34	13	5	16	57	64	44
Nottingham Forest	34	12	8	14	46	55	44
Sheffield Wednesday	34	11	8	15	66	63	41
Blackburn Rovers	34	9	13	12	48	44	40
Sheffield United	34	8	13	13	40	61	37
Wolverhampton W.	34	10	5	19	42	48	35
Notts County	34	9	7	18	48	64	34
West Bromwich Albion	34	5	6	23	33	84	21

FA YOUTH CUP

Nov 15	A	Wolverhampton W. (Rd 1)	6-5
Dec 7	**H**	**Basildon** (Rd 2)	5-0
Dec 14	A	Millwall (Rd 3)	2-5

RESERVE TEAM RESULTS & SCORERS 1995-96

PONTIN'S CENTRAL LEAGUE

Aug	14	H	**Newcastle United**	3-1	Codner, Black, Finnan
Aug	28	H	**Oldham Athletic**	0-2	
Sept	4	A	Wolverhampton W.	2-1	Martin, Forsyth
Sept	11	A	Everton	2-3	Short (og), Doherty
Sept	18	H	**Tranmere Rovers**	2-1	Forsyth, Doherty
Sept	26	A	Sheffield Wednesday	3-8	Rea 2, Richardson
Oct	3	A	Sheffield United	2-1	Rea 2
Oct	9	H	**Derby County**	0-2	
Oct	18	A	Manchester United	0-3	
Oct	23	H	**Notts County**	3-1	Forsyth, Black, Challoner
Oct	31	A	West Bromwich Albion	2-1	S. Barnes 2
Nov	13	H	**Stoke City**	1-3	Hunt
Nov	20	A	Leeds United	0-1	
Dec	4	A	Tranmere Rovers	2-3	Frain (pen), Martin
Dec	11	H	**Sheffield Wednesday**	1-1	Charlery
Dec	18	A	Liverpool	2-4	Castle, Muir
Jan	2	A	Nottingham Forest	2-2	Rushfeldt, Ward
Jan	10	A	Blackburn Rovers	0-3	
Jan	15	H	**Everton**	5-1	Bowen, Martin, Castle, Doherty 2
Jan	22	A	Newcastle United	5-2	Finnan 2, Otto, Bull 2
Feb	12	H	**Blackburn Rovers**	3-2	Bowen 3
Feb	22	A	Stoke City	0-4	
Mar	4	H	**West Bromwich Albion**	3-0	Robinson, Muir, S. Barnes
Mar	14	H	**Nottingham Forest**	3-0	Challinor, Fleming, Donowa
Mar	18	H	**Liverpool**	0-1	
Mar	25	H	**Sheffield United**	5-1	Donowa 2, S. Barnes, Otto 2
Mar	28	H	**Wolverhampton W.**	0-1	
Apr	4	A	Oldham Athletic	1-1	Francis
Apr	9	A	Derby County	1-3	S. Barnes
Apr	15	H	**Bolton Wanderers**	1-3	Martin
Apr	17	A	Notts County	0-1	
Apr	22	H	**Manchester United**	1-0	Devlin
May	1	A	Bolton Wanderers	0-2	
May	6	H	**Leeds United**	1-1	Samways

BIRMINGHAM COUNTY FA SENIOR CUP

Dec	5	A	Sandwell Borough (Rd 2)	2-1	Black, Jones
Jan	8	A	Dudley Town (Rd 3)	3-0	Tait, Rushfeldt, Charlery
Feb	29	A	Wolverhampton W. (Rd 4)	3-2	Rae, Martin, Barnes
Apr	11	A	Walsall (SF)	1-0	Legg
May	6	H	**Aston Villa**	2-0	Bowen, Peschisolido *(see p.153 for details)*

YOUTH TEAM RESULTS

MIDLAND PURITY YOUTH LEAGUE

5th Aug	Aston Villa	A	0-3
12th Aug	**Wolves**	H	3-3
19th Aug	**Coventry City**	H	3-4
26th Aug	Derby County	A	1-1
2nd Sept	**Grimsby Town**	H	3-2
9th Sept	Leicester City	A	2-7
23rd Sept	**Mansfield Town**	H	3-0
30th Sept	**Northampton T.**	H	3-0
7th Oct	Notts County	A	2-1
28th Oct	Grimsby Town	A	2-1
4th Nov	**Port Vale**	H	2-1
11th Nov	Shrewsbury Town	A	2-0
25th Nov	Walsall	A	1-4
16th Dec	West Bromwich A.	A	2-1
13th Jan	Wolves	A	1-3
20th Jan	**West Bromwich A.**	H	4-0
17th Feb	**Lincoln City**	H	4-0
24th Feb	Mansfield Town	A	1-0
2nd Mar	Northampton T.	A	1-0
5th Mar	**Aston Villa**	H	1-2
9th Mar	**Stoke City**	H	0-2
19th Mar	**Notts County**	H	1-1
23rd Mar	Nottingham Forest	A	2-4
30th Mar	**Peterborough U.**	H	3-3
3rd Apr	**Notts County**	H	2-1
6th Apr	Port Vale	A	0-2
8th Apr	Lincoln City	A	3-0
10th Apr	**Shrewsbury Town**	H	4-0
16th Apr	**Leicester City**	H	1-1
20th Apr	Stoke City	A	0-3
24th Apr	Coventry City	A	1-0
27th Apr	**Walsall**	H	2-1
30th Apr	Peterborough U.	A	1-1
4th May	**Nottingham Forest**	H	0-1

ATTENDANCES

THE GATE LEAGUE

	Best	Average
Wolverhampton W.	27,381	24,785
Birmingham City	23,251	18,097
Sunderland	22,027	17,503
Leicester City	20,911	16,197
Crystal Palace	19,354	15,190
West Bromwich Albion	23,858	15,123
Norwich City	18,435	14,580
Derby County	17,460	14,327
Huddersfield Town	18,495	13,150
Sheffield United	20,050	12,894
Ipswich Town	20,355	12,596
Stoke City	18,897	12,279
Charlton Athletic	14,643	11,201
Millwall	14,220	9,538
Watford	20,089	9,456
Portsmouth	14,434	9,407
Reading	12,828	8,917
Port Vale	16,737	8,217
Barnsley	13,669	8,118
Tranmere Rovers	16,193	7,861
Luton Town	9,454	7,223
Oldham Athletic	10,271	6,626
Southend United	8,363	5,915
Grimsby Town	8,155	5,865

★ *Endsleigh League Division One games only*

MIDLAND MELVILLE YOUTH LEAGUE TABLE

	P	W	D	L	F	A	Pts
Aston Villa	34	23	6	5	88	30	75
Leicester City	34	20	8	6	90	50	68
Coventry City	34	20	6	8	83	52	66
Wolverhampton W.	34	17	9	8	58	43	60
Notts County	34	17	7	10	67	47	57
Birmingham City	34	17	6	11	62	54	57
Stoke City	34	16	5	13	59	57	53
Walsall	34	14	8	12	50	43	50
Nottingham Forest	34	14	4	16	49	52	46
Northampton Town	34	13	7	14	39	44	46
Derby County	34	12	9	13	54	45	45
Port Vale	34	12	8	14	47	54	44
Grimsby Town	34	11	10	13	49	43	43
Peterborough United	34	7	12	15	36	61	33
Lincoln City	34	9	6	19	39	68	33
Mansfield Town	34	9	4	21	45	65	31
West Bromwich Albion	34	8	6	20	28	67	30
Shrewsbury Town	34	5	4	25	39	99	19

Back row, left to right: Lil Fuccillo, Kenny Lowe, Ken Charlery, Peter Shearer, Dave Barnett, Simon Black, Ryan Price, Liam Daish, Andy Edwards, Chris Whyte, Steve Castle, John Frain (Club Captain), Neil McDairmid (Physio). Middle row: David Howell (Assistant Manager), Ian Muir, Jon Bass, Paul Challinor, Steve Claridge, Paul Harding, Ian Bennett, Gary Poole, Ben Sedgemore, Neil Doherty, Steve Finnan, Paul Tait, Edwin Stein (Assistant Manager). Front row: Richard Forsyth, Ricky Otto, Jason Bowen, Steve Robinson, Jae Martin, Barry Fry (Manager), Jonathan Hunt, Louie Donowa, Mark Ward (Player/Coach), Scott Hiley, Gary Cooper.

The Birmingham City 1995-96 Youth Team Squad.

001 Robin Phillips	049 John Evans	097 A. J. Garbett
002 Keith Short	050 John R. W. Hamblett	098 Paul Coltman
003 Louis Short	051 Carl Smith	099 Duffy
004 Kirstyn Short	052 Frank J. Benson	100 Craig Sykes
005 Lloyd Short	053 Gareth Burton	101 Malcolm Chambers
006 Scott Short	054 Steve Shirley	102 Steven Bartholomew
007 Colin Cook	055 Reg Love	103 Debra Prigg
008 Sammy Orr	056 Ian Parker	104 Gary Birch
009 Gary Taylor	057 Samantha Parker	105 David Knibb
010 Adam Taylor	058 Melissa Parker	106 Paul Lauder
011 Jane Taylor	059 Neil Philpott	107 Steve Crathorn
012 Rachael Taylor	060 Paul Aldridge	108 Cob Webb
013 Sarah Carney	061 Peter Ricketts	109 Sam Joseph
014 Karen Carney	062 Paul Ricketts	110 Ian Stokes
015 Gary Chambers	063 Carla Ricketts	111 Phil Stokes
016 Jo Chambers	064 Sheryl Ricketts	112 Craig Jones
017 Rachael Chambers	065 Stephen Abbots	113 Don Gibson
018 Liam Chambers	066 Barry Abbots	114 John Emsden
019 Athol Dipple	067 Ryan Ainge	115 Roger Harrison
020 Toby Dipple	068 Craig Robinson	116 Margaret and Graham Wood
021 Sam Dipple	069 Michael Boyd	117 Richard P. A. Alonzo
022 David Marklew	070 Kevin Boyd	118 Mike Marie
023 Roy N. Tew	071 Bryony Boyd	119 Gail Taylor
024 Darren R. Tew	072 Richard White	120 William J. Moore
025 Kelly J. Hines	073 Sue White	121 Richard Taggart
026 Kirsty J. Hines	074 Andrew White	122 Ken Turner
027 Graham L. Frost	075 Mark Chapman	123 Darren Scott Newton
028 Hayley M. Tew	076 Roy "Bluenose" Flowers	124 Christopher John Dando
029 Margaret O'Grady	077 Aly Hood	125 E. G. Dawe
030 Kevin O'Grady	078 Susan Fletcher	126 Jean Payne
031 Mike Donohoe	079 Kevin Fletcher	127 James Payne
032 Natalie Woodward	080 Kerry Fletcher	128 Steve Moore
033 John Harrison	081 Stuart Fletcher	129 Bridget Fricker
034 Ann Hastilow	082 Jonathan Sancaster	130 Jason Boliver
035 Gary O'Rourke	083 Mike Purvis	131 Mr Jack Sharrard
036 Carol Mills	084 Sheila Purvis	132 Steven Edwards
037 Paul Hill	085 Chris Purvis	133 David Glynn
038 Kevin Douglas	086 David Purvis	134 Jonathan Sly
039 Maria Douglas	087 Graham Sisam	135 Alan Harrison
040 Rachel Douglas	088 Andrew Reilly	136 Amanda Harrison
041 Kevan J. Robinson	089 Neil Whitehead	137 Tracey Harrison
042 Rick Roddy	090 Richard Paul Evans	138 George and Margaret
043 Michael Richards	091 Frazer Higgins	Greenow
044 Darren Richards	092 Richard Conn	139 Neil Bullock
045 Lee Richards	093 A. W. W. Smith	140 Martin J. Edmonds
046 Matthew McCormack	094 Cliff Ash	141 Andrew W. J. Edmonds
047 James McCormack	095 Andrew Graham Jones	142 Paul M. R. Edmonds
048 Susan Fletcher	096 Carl Sly	143 Adam Edwards

144 Trevor Edwards	191 Mr. S. Peckover	239 Mark Simmonds
145 Mark Raper	192 Mark Kerr	240 Ray Smith
146 Adrian Maund	193 Paul Berry	241 Warren Smith
147 Mike Carlin	194 Keith D. Lawrence	242 Nicci Phillips
148 Iain Carlin	195 David Green	243 Ian George
149 Dave Carlin	196 Gavin Troth	244 Richard Stanley
150 Darren Carlin	197 Paul Crutchley	245 Robert and Maureen Davis
151 Lloyd C. Gray	198 Emma McAnulty	246 Ethel Smith
152 Steve Crabtree	199 Terry Payne	247 Robin Horton
153 Alex "Blue Nose" Patterson	200 P. G. Buckley	248 Geoff Bennett
154 Colin Humber	201 Richard Bell	249 Linda Bennett
155 Anne Cooper	202 Katy and Nicholas Trahearn	250 Stewart Bennett
156 Malcolm Geoffrey Hyde	203 Andrew Rudd	251 Neil Bennett
157 Mr Jeacock	204 Sarah Ingleston	252 Debbie Hartley
158 Mark and Sam Shepherd	205 Ian Davis	253 Jim Tidmarsh
159 R. D. Coleman	206 Paul Davis	254 Dave Nutt
160 M. Heaviside	207 Andreas Ervik	255 Martin Jones
161 Stephen T. Glynn	208 Michael Cowley	256 Steve Doggrell
162 Melvyn and Michael and	209 Gordon Manford	257 Phil Cunnington
Matthew	210 Craig Joy	258 Mark Galloway
163 Jimmy Martin	211 Stuart and Mitchell Joy	259 Matthew Edwards
164 Mark Bowen	212 M. W. Williams	260 Adrian Doyle
165 Christopher Weaver	213 Eddie Lees	261 P. B. Ingram
166 Chris Measey	214 Simon Hopewell	262 Val Baller
167 Anthony John Quinn	215 Baz Bagot Blues	263 Damien Baller
168 Aidan and Sabrina Courts	216 Gary "Zulu" Taylor	264 Carl Baller
169 David Beechey	217 Sarah Redding	265 Matthew McCormack
170 Ian Hodges	218 Gemma Shaw	266 James McCormack
171 Dawn Hodges	219 Simon James Harker	267 Annette Jones
172 Lee Hodges	220 Rick and James Chilton	268 Mark Masters
173 Laura Hodges	221 Stephen Mander	269 Paul Cowen
174 John Hodges	222 Aly Hood	270 Louise Cowen
175 Tom Martin	223 Stephen Brookes	271 Louise Witcomb
176 Graham Martin	224 F. Evans	272 James Witcomb
177 Emily Martin	225 Tim Reed	273 Ron Pearson
178 Raymond William Thomas	226 Peter J. Harding	274 Jane Pearson
179 Lindsay Warren	227 Paul Jude Watts	275 Keith Clarke
180 Garry Aplin	228 Paul Stephen Wilson	276 Brian Darley
181 Don Nash	229 Ian Wall	277 Chris Darley
182 Gary Newsom	230 Simon Cornelius	278 Andrew Payne
183 Raymond A. Nickless	231 Gary O'Rourke	279 Jamie Harper
184 P. Matthews	232 Amanda Jayne Hart	280 Simon Harper
185 L. E. K. Matthews	233 Keith Topham	281 Katie Harper
186 Victoria Olivia Drapier	234 Steve Bodfish	282 John Rogers
187 Angela and Nigel Lunn	235 Gareth Burton	283 Margaret Smith
188 Kevin Paul Mark Barber	236 Steve Jones	284 Dave Smith
189 Megan Reeves	237 Carl S. Smith	285 John Percy
190 Miss K. P. Peckover	238 Paul Richard Darke	286 Rick and Ann Coleman